Guide to Analysis of Language Transcripts

Third Edition

Kristine S. Retherford, Ph.D.

pro-ed
An International Publisher
8700 Shoal Creek Boulevard
Austin, Texas 78757-6897
800/897-3202 Fax 800/397-7633
www.proedinc.com

pro·ed
An International Publisher

8700 Shoal Creek Boulevard
Austin, Texas 78757-6897
800/897-3202 Fax 800/397-7633
www.proedinc.com

ISBN 978-1-4164-0414-9 (previously published by Thinking Publications® University as ISBN 1-888222-41-7)

Cover design by Kris Gausman and Tony Mitchell

Printed in the United States of America

1 2 3 4 5 6 7 8 9 10 17 16 15 14 13 12 11 10 09 08

Dedication

To Emily Katherine

Contents

Guide Practice CD-ROM
installation instructions on p. 334.

Contents

Tables

Completed Analysis Forms

Chapter 2: Semantic Analysis

Chapter 3: Syntactic Analysis

Chapter 4: Pragmatic Analysis

PREFACE

Guide to Analysis of Language Transcripts evolved from the frustration experienced when attempting to teach undergraduate and graduate student clinicians to analyze language production in children. While many procedures are available, most failed to meet my needs as an instructor; they lacked explicit directions and offered limited interpretation of results. The procedures included in *Guide* attempt to improve existing procedures by providing explicit directions, guided practice, and principles for interpretation of results.

Guide takes readers from the data collection stage through the organization and analysis of data to the early stages of treatment planning. The selection of procedures to include for semantic analysis was influenced by my familiarity with an elaborate set of semantic categories for describing children's productions varying from approximately two to five morphemes in length. Procedures for analyzing productions of children in the one-word stage were included, as was a procedure for analyzing vocabulary diversity. Of the many syntactic analysis procedures available, Jon Miller's procedures for assigning structural stage were selected for inclusion in *Guide,* with modifications as deemed appropriate. The selection of procedures for analyzing pragmatic aspects of language production was difficult. Sets of procedures for describing the functions of utterances were included, as were procedures for analyzing turn taking and appropriateness judgments. No attempt has been made to describe procedures for analyzing narrative abilities or phonological aspects of language. Overall, the semantic, syntactic, and pragmatic procedures described in *Guide* provide an organized, systematic approach to the analysis of language production.

The procedures consolidated in *Guide* have been applied to transcripts of the language of preschool children. An understanding of the variability in the productions of children developing normally is essential before accurate diagnosis of children with language delays and/or disorders can occur. The relevance of the procedures must be learned by first applying them to transcripts such as those included in *Guide.* A companion CD-ROM has been developed to give students additional practice making the judgments demonstrated in *Guide.* Students are encouraged to use the CD-ROM, along with the practice items included in each chapter of *Guide,* before attempting the full transcripts included in the book.

To ease readability, masculine pronouns are occasionally used in *Guide* to refer to "the child." In no way does the use of masculine pronouns imply that only boys' language is analyzed; neither does the use of masculine pronouns imply a lessening of importance of the female gender. Masculine pronouns, which are to be interpreted generically in *Guide,* are used whenever confusion might occur from the use of nonsexist plural pronouns.

I am grateful to many individuals for their assistance in the preparation of *Guide to Analysis of Language Transcripts.* My students provided inspiration; for their criticism of and confusion over existing procedures, I offer thanks. Nancy McKinley contributed many hours of careful editing to this and earlier editions; her attention to detail is greatly appreciated. My reviewers of the first edition—Marc Fey, Vicki Lord Larson, Linda Maro, and Susan Schultz—offered insightful suggestions; I am grateful for their input. Vivian Joubert provided expert technical advice; I appreciate her explanations. Florence Clickner endured endless revisions on the first and second editions; I am particularly grateful for her enthusiasm and cheerfulness. Dan provided understanding and encouragement for the first edition; I shall always be grateful. My children have been born and moved on into the hectic pace of upper elementary and middle school years since the first edition was published. They have endured adjustments in schedules and compromises of activities for the most recent edition to be completed. I thank

Emily and David for their patience, understanding, and encouragement. You are the best!

The revisions to *Guide* have been in the works almost from the time the first edition was in print. Some revisions have evolved from class discussions and serve to clarify ambiguity. Other revisions have grown out of suggestions offered by instructors who use *Guide* and add information or additional interpretation. To both of these groups, I extend my gratitude. Marietta Plummer and Michele Roddick contributed many hours of analysis and completed transcript rechecks for *Guide;* I am grateful for their persistence. Sharon Fredericks provided reliability checks and made suggestions for the glossary; I am grateful for her assistance. Florence Clickner again endured the revisions and format modifications with cheerfulness and enthusiasm; I appreciate her endurance. Marie Stadler offered numerous suggestions to clarify recurring confusion by students; several of the new examples were hers, and I appreciate her suggestions. Becca Hubing provided detailed scrutiny of the new transcript; her perseverance is greatly appreciated. Inclusion of adult utterances for analysis in Chapter 4 grew out of discussions with Lucy Hess; I appreciate her insistence that exclusion of the conversational co-participant would make the analysis impossible to interpret. Linda Schreiber contributed endless hours of careful editing and insightful discussion to the first two editions; I appreciate her attention to detail. Kris Gausman devoted many, many hours to designing tables and forms and then redesigning them as each edition brought about changes and revisions; I appreciate her creativity and eye for detail. Sarah Tobalsky served as technical editor for this latest edition of *Guide;* her attention to clarity and correctness has made a significant contribution to this most "user-friendly" edition, and I am enormously grateful. Debbie Olson's eye for "readability" in page set-up is greatly appreciated as well. Lucy Hess and Deb Sewards of Indiana University spent many hours developing the practice sets of utterances and the screen formats for the companion CD-ROM. This edition of *Guide* is greatly enhanced by the addition of Guide Practice, and I am very grateful to Lucy and Deb for their contributions. Ken Ray made the CD-ROM fully functional; his vision is much appreciated.

And Jessica Stickler and Krista Curtis, as 4-year-olds, provided priceless examples of rich sentence elaboration. These utterances were central to my in-class discussions long before the first edition of *Guide.* And now these examples have found their way into the glossary of this edition. I am grateful for their willingness to talk about anything and everything. Although these two are in college now, when I use one of their utterances as an example, I will always remember their fourth summer. My all-time favorite utterances describe the search for "jellies what have holes for your toes." Thanks, Jess and Krista.

Acknowledgments

Table 2.9	Rules for Counting Number of Words to Complete Templin's Type-Token Ratio from "Certain Language Skills in Children: Their Development and Interrelationships," by M.C. Templin, 1957, *Institute of Child Welfare Monograph Series, 26.* © 1957 by the University of Minnesota Press. © renewed 1985 by Mildred C. Templin. Adapted with permission.
Table 2.10	Calculating Vocabulary Diversity Using Type-Token Ratio (N = 480) from "Certain Language Skills in Children: Their Development and Interrelationships," by M.C. Templin, 1957, *Institute of Child Welfare Monograph Series, 26.* © 1957 by the University of Minnesota Press. © renewed 1985 by Mildred C. Templin. Reprinted with permission.
Table 3.2	Predicted MLU Ranges and Linguistic Stages of Children within One Predicted Standard Deviation of Predicted Mean from "The Relation between Age and Mean Length of Utterance in Morphemes," by J.F. Miller and R.S. Chapman, 1981, *Journal of Speech and Hearing Research, 24*(2), p.158. © 1981 by the American Speech-Language-Hearing Association. Reprinted with permission.
Table 3.3	Brown's (1973) Target MLU in Morphemes and Upper Bound Lengths for Each Stage from *A First Language: The Early Stages* (p. 56), by R. Brown, 1973, Cambridge, MA: Harvard University Press. © 1973 by the President and Fellows of Harvard College. Reprinted with permission.
Table 4.1	Pragmatic Characteristics of the Child with Specific Language Impairment from "Pragmatic Characteristics of the Child with Specific Language Impairment: An Interactionist Perspective," by H. Craig, 1991, in T. Gallagher (Ed.), *Pragmatics of Language: Clinical Practice Issues* (pp. 178–179), San Diego, CA: Singular Publishing Group. © 1991 by Holly Craig. Adapted with permission.

About the Author

Kristine S. Retherford, Ph.D., is a professor of communication disorders at the University of Wisconsin—Eau Claire. She was Director of Clinical Programs in Communication Disorders for seven years and currently supervises undergraduate and graduate students working with preschool and school-age children who have language disorders, in the Center for Communication Disorders. She teaches graduate and undergraduate courses in normal communication development, clinical procedures in communication disorders, pediatric organic disorders, and treatment of language delays and disorders in children. Dr. Retherford frequently presents at inservices and workshops on language analysis and on intervention strategies for children with language disorders.

GETTING STARTED WITH *GUIDE*

Chapter 1

OVERVIEW

Guide to Analysis of Language Transcripts provides guidelines for (1) identifying three aspects of language production: semantics, syntax, and pragmatics; (2) analyzing the identified structures' developmental levels; and (3) interpreting these analyses' results. Blank analysis sheets and summary forms are provided, and practice in making crucial judgments is incorporated into the discussion of each procedure. *Guide* differs from other sources in that it includes an integration of procedures for analyzing three components of language (i.e., semantics, syntax, and pragmatics) and includes a framework for gaining experience making judgments before applying the procedures to sample transcripts.

Although phonology is considered to be a primary component of language, no procedures for describing or analyzing spontaneous sound systems of children are included in *Guide.* The experienced clinician may be able to complete some type of phonologic analysis of transcripts obtained and transcribed using conventions described in *Guide,* such as an inventory of sounds used by a child while engaged in conversation or a summary of phonological processes using procedures described by Shriberg and Kwiatkowski (1980), Ingram (1981), and Hodson (1986). However, *Guide* will not demonstrate any type of phonologic analysis. Nor has any attempt been made to describe procedures for analyzing narrative abilities. The analysis procedures described in *Guide* are based on spontaneous conversational interaction. To analyze narration, sampling procedures would differ greatly from those described here.

Guide is intended for use with undergraduate and graduate students in communication disorders clinical education programs. It is a tool for teaching students how to obtain quality language production transcripts and how to analyze the semantic, syntactic, and pragmatic aspects of those transcripts. *Guide* may also be helpful to the practicing speech-language clinician who is looking for a comprehensive set of procedures for analyzing all three conversational components of the language production system. In addition, *Guide* can be used as a tool to enhance appropriate development of intervention goals and objectives based on results of the analysis procedures described in this resource. *Guide* is helpful in developing goals and objectives for intervention even when the analysis procedures described are not used, as would be the case if computer analysis procedures were used.

A companion CD-ROM, Guide Practice, has been developed to give students additional opportunities to make the judgments demonstrated in *Guide.* Students are encouraged to use the CD-ROM, along with the practice examples included in each chapter of the book, before attempting the full transcripts included in *Guide.*

The Glossary in *Guide* serves as a useful tool for students to quickly look up puzzling or unfamiliar terms. Also included in *Guide* are three appendices. Appendix A contains blank, reproducible copies of all the forms used throughout the book; Appendix B contains an analyzed transcript; and Appendix C contains two unanalyzed transcripts for further practice.

TARGET POPULATION

Guide to Analysis of Language Transcripts is designed to provide analysis procedures for use with language transcripts obtained from children at the one-word level through Stage V++ of linguistic production (Miller and Chapman's, 1981, extension of Brown's, 1973, original five stages), or the ages of 12 months through 6 years for children developing normally. Some procedures are appropriate for use with children older than 6 years of age; however, the focus is on analysis of semantic, syntactic, and pragmatic aspects of language production during Brown's stages of linguistic development, and minimally beyond. Within each chapter are procedures appropriate for use within a more limited age range than 1 to 6 years, and guidelines are provided for determining which procedures to use with a particular child.

A word needs to be said about the use of language production measures to identify children with language delays and/or disorders. The procedures described in *Guide,* when combined with other information about a child (i.e., chronological age, cognitive level, comprehension level), can identify a child whose productive language level differs from that expected on the basis of chronological age and/or cognitive level and comprehension level. Whether such children are language delayed or language disordered may not be clinically relevant. Various criteria have been used to determine language delays and language disorders, including performance two standard deviations below the mean (Bloom and Lahey, 1978), performance below the 10th percentile (Lee, 1974; Rizzo and Stephens, 1981), and delays greater than six months (Crystal, Fletcher, and Garman, 1976). For purposes of *Guide,* the child whose productive language is at least one production stage below expectations or one standard deviation below the mean (whenever available) based on either chronological age or cognitive level (whichever is lower) or whose language behaviors are penalizing to him as a conversational participant, will be considered a candidate for language intervention. Language production measures alone cannot be used to determine the existence of a language disorder. It is not this author's intent to resolve the debate regarding the definition of language delay and/or disorder, but rather to make it clear that *Guide* adheres to a developmental perspective in that once a level of language performance has been determined, and the decision has been made that a child is a candidate for intervention, the accomplishments of the next developmental level (whether that be semantic, syntactic, or pragmatic) can be targeted during intervention.

TARGET USERS

Guide to Analysis of Language Transcripts is intended for use in teaching undergraduate and graduate students in communication disorders clinical education programs to obtain quality language production transcripts and to analyze the semantic, syntactic, and pragmatic aspects of those transcripts. The terminology used assumes minimal clinical background, and the extensiveness of the practice sections, both in the book and the CD-ROM, are designed to provide the clinician-in-training with introductory exposure to the types of judgments necessary for successful analysis of language transcripts.

Guide may also be helpful to the practicing speech-language clinician who is looking for a comprehensive set of procedures for analyzing all three components of the language production system. While the *use* of practice examples in the book and in the CD-ROM's worksheets may not be necessary for those familiar with similar analysis procedures, an *examination* of all the practice sections is encouraged since many of the judgments to be made are not clear in the demonstrations of the procedures occurring before the practice sections.

RATIONALE

One of the goals of the speech-language clinician is to identify children with language delays and/or disorders. To identify such children, an evaluation battery must include the two major processes of language performance—language comprehension and language production—plus the interaction of these two processes in ongoing conversation. Numerous formal assessment procedures that have statistically documented validity and reliability measures with diverse sample populations are available for the evaluation of comprehension abilities. Among these are the *Peabody Picture Vocabulary Test–III* (Dunn and Dunn, 1997), the *Boehm Test of Basic Concepts–Revised* (Boehm, 1986), the *Comprehensive Receptive and Expressive Vocabulary Test* (Wallace and Hammill, 1994), the *Test of Auditory Comprehension of Language–3* (Carrow-Woolfolk, 1999), the *Miller-Yoder Language Comprehension Test* (Miller and Yoder, 1984), the *Preschool Language Scale–3* (Zimmerman, Steiner, and Pond, 1992), the *Test of Early Language Development–3* (Hresko, Reid, and Hammill, 1999), and the *Test of Language Development–Primary–3* (Newcomer and Hammill, 1997). While many of these formal procedures also include cursory measures of language production, few result in a thorough description of production abilities. A few standardized tests of spoken language are available, including the *CASL: Comprehensive Assessment of Spoken Language* (Carrow-Woolfolk, 1999), the *Expressive One-Word Picture Vocabulary Test 2000* (Brownell, 2000) and the *WORD Test–Elementary* (Huisingh, Barrett, Zachman, Blagden, and Orman, 1990). Inventories of language are also available, including the *Carrow Elicited Language Inventory* (Carrow-Woolfolk, 1974), the *Sequenced Inventory of Communication Development* (Hendrick, Prather, and Tobin, 1984), the *Expressive Language Test* (Bowers, Huisingh, Orman, and LoGiudice, 1998), and the *Test of Children's Language* (Barenbaum and Newcomer, 1996). The language production information obtained from these measures, however, is contrived and not necessarily a reflection of conversational abilities. In addition, formal procedures for the analysis of communicative interaction are relatively few in number, the exceptions being the *Test of Pragmatic Skills* (Shulman, 1985), the *Let's Talk Inventory for Adolescents* (Wiig, 1982), the *Let's Talk Inventory for Children* (Bray and Wiig, 1985), and the *Test of Pragmatic Language* (Phelps-Terasaki and Phelps-Gunn, 1992).

To analyze language production, one must compare various aspects of production with data obtained from the language of children developing normally. Determining the appropriate linguistic behaviors to compare to normative data may be difficult, and comparison under conditions identical to those under which the data were collected may be impossible. In addition, it may be difficult to efficiently manage data leading to synthesis for the development of intervention goals and objectives.

Guide to Analysis of Language Transcripts provides guidelines for identification of three aspects of language production, for analysis of the identified structures' developmental levels, and for interpretation of these analyses' results. Summaries of the data relevant to each analysis procedure are provided, and methods for comparing analysis data to normative data are described. Once each component of language production is analyzed, strategies for synthesis of data as the foundation for intervention are discussed. In addition, practice in making the necessary judgments is provided for each of the analysis procedures described. With practice, the task of analyzing language transcripts becomes easier and more efficient.

Many sets of procedures are available for the analysis of specific aspects of language production. Commercially available procedures are typically designed to analyze one aspect of language production. For example, the *Developmental Sentence Analysis,* described by Lee (1974), provides a procedure for analyzing subject + verb complete utterances on the basis of the developmental level of eight grammatical categories: indefinite and personal pronouns, primary and secondary verbs, negation, conjunctions, interrogative reversals, and *wh-* questions. Although some of the categories analyzed would be considered semantic, the major intent is to provide a syntactic analysis of language production. The *Language Assessment, Remediation, and Screening Procedure (LARSP),* developed and described by Crystal, Fletcher, and Garman (1976, 1991), provides for analysis of sentences, clauses, phrases, and word types. Again, some semantic information can be gleaned from this analysis procedure, but the primary result is analysis of syntax production. The *Language Sampling, Analysis, and Training (LSAT-3),* by Tyack and Venable (1998), provides guidelines for determining syntactic rules employed by children during spontaneous conversation. The results of the analysis described may help pinpoint oral language problems as well as specific reading comprehension problems. For analyzing semantic production abilities, the *Environmental Language Inventory* (MacDonald, 1978) provides a format for analysis of a child's use of "semantic-grammatical" rules. A variety of semantic relations are identified and scored as used in the language transcript. Although syntactic and pragmatic analyses are suggested, procedures are not specified in the *Environmental Language Inventory.*

In addition to commercially available procedures, procedures described in the literature may make reference to syntactic and semantic aspects of language production, but no guidelines for the integration of these two components are described. For example, the Assigning Structural Stage procedure described within Miller's (1981) *Assessing Language Production in Children* includes identification of the developmental level of a variety of grammatical forms for syntactic analysis. Miller also identifies a variety of semantic analysis procedures, and Chapman (1981) summarizes a variety of pragmatic taxonomies. Application of semantic, syntactic, and pragmatic analyses to the same language transcript is not provided. The procedures described in *Guide,* however, have been developed to be used together to analyze semantic, syntactic, and pragmatic aspects of the same language transcript.

Computer-Based Analysis Procedures

One might ask, "Why should I learn to analyze language transcripts when computers can do the work?" It is true that a variety of software programs have been developed for analysis of language transcripts. However, available programs differ in the types of analyses performed and the ease with which the coding procedures are learned and the analyses are accomplished. For example, Lingquest 1: Language Sample Analysis (Mordecai, Palin, and Palmer, 1982) offers three major types of analyses. First, the grammatical form analysis provides a frequency-of-use to opportunities-for-use comparison of eight major categories of grammatical forms: nouns, verbs, modifiers, prepositions, conjunctions, negations, interjections, and *wh-* words. Error analysis and pattern identification can be accomplished. Second, the lexical analysis results in a frequency-of-use to opportunities-for-use comparison of vocabulary plus a measure of vocabulary diversity (a type-token ratio [TTR] [Templin, 1957]). A mean length of utterance (MLU) in words can be obtained as well as an MLU in morphemes. Third, the structure analysis provides frequency-of-use to opportunities-for-use comparison of a variety of phrase, sentence, and question types. Utterances to be analyzed must be transcribed with coding to identify structures to be analyzed. In addition, an expanded version of the utterance must be transcribed. This process may be difficult and time-consuming. No tutorial is included with Lingquest 1. Resulting summaries are valuable; however, frequency-of-occurrence data and error pattern identification can only be interpreted with a working knowledge of developmental data. No developmental stage information is provided.

Systematic Analysis of Language Transcripts (SALT) (Miller and Chapman, 2000) has evolved since the early 1980s to become one of the most flexible yet complicated software programs available. As with Lingquest 1, three types of analyses can be performed. First, morphologic analysis can be accomplished resulting in MLU, TTR, and omission summaries. Second, structural analysis is possible with verb element, question form, and negative form summaries. Third, utterance analysis can be performed, resulting in, among other things, preceding and following utterance-match summaries. In addition, numerous other options can be selected and/or created by the user. Because of its sophistication, considerable practice is necessary to master the SALT program. However, a tutorial program is included to facilitate coding. Again, interpretation of results is dependent on a comparison of the results to developmental norms and/or the user's knowledge and experience.

A third software program for the analysis of language transcripts is the Computerized Language Sample Analysis (CLSA), developed by Weiner (1984). This program results in summaries of the frequency of occurrence and accuracy of use for 14 grammatical categories. Analysis of nouns, verbs, sentence types, length of utterance, and word usage can be accomplished. In addition, more detailed analyses can be selected. In his review of CLSA, Schwartz (1985) contends that familiarity with language analysis is crucial for the interpretation of these analyses. Weiner provides a tutorial to assist in learning to code utterances and to use the CLSA program. An updated version of this program is available under the title Parrot Easy Language Sample Analysis (PELSA) (Weiner, 1988).

Another language sample analysis program developed by Pye (1987) is the Pye Analysis of Language (PAL). PAL permits morphologic, syntactic, and phonologic analysis using procedures described by Ingram (1981). In addition, it is possible to create other analyses by manually coding the transcript. PAL requires knowledge of DOS commands for coding and analysis.

Computerized Profiling (CP), developed by Long, Fey, and Channell (2000), contains several analysis systems, including many traditional manual analysis procedures. Among these are *LARSP,* found within *The Grammatical Analysis of Language Disability* (Crystal, Fletcher, and Garman, 1976, 1991); *PRISM,* found within *Profiling Linguistic Disability* (Crystal, 1992); and *Developmental Sentence Scoring (DSS),* found within *Developmental Sentence Analysis* (Lee, 1974). Pragmatic and phonological analyses are possible as well. Depending on the type of analysis performed, complex manual coding is necessary and time-consuming. Only the *DSS* and *Conversational Acts Profile* found within CP contain normative data for interpretation.

Although the development of software programs represents a major advance in resources available to the speech-language clinician, without a thorough understanding of what each program accomplishes or does not accomplish, a knowledgeable development of intervention programming is impossible. In his review of existing software, Schwartz (1985) contends that software programs for the analysis of language production "are only as accurate as the coded transcriptions on which they are based" (p. 39). In other words, accurate analysis can be obtained only if the language sample is representative of the child's production abilities, has been transcribed correctly, and has been coded appropriately. Obviously, these same criteria apply to manual procedures as well. The timesaving advantage of computer software comes with the frequency-of-use summaries. Responsibility for interpretation of the results obtained from either software programs or manual procedures continues to be dependent on the knowledge and abilities of the clinician. The procedures described in *Guide* can aid in understanding what computer analyses accomplish and can assist in the interpretation of results of computer analyses.

In addition to being dependent on user skill for coding and interpretation, there are a number of analysis limitations that software programs have. First, software programs currently available are not capable of accomplishing semantic roles analyses that rely on nonlinguistic context for making these judgments. Second, with the exception of the conversational context search provided by SALT (Miller and Chapman, 2000), no existing program can perform analyses of pragmatic aspects of language production, including speech act analysis, topic maintenance analysis, and appropriateness judgments. Third, existing programs are incapable of analyzing nonverbal variables that may influence interpretation of an utterance, such as eye gaze, gestures, and intonation. Finally, software programs available at this time do not provide analysis of stylistic variations in speakers that may influence a listener's judgments of the speaker.

Thus, judicious use of software programs for the analysis of language production can save time in tallying the frequency of occurrence of specific structures. In addition, software programs can permit the clinician to accumulate sufficient data so that, over time, local norms for specific behaviors can be developed. *Guide to Analysis of Language Transcripts* can facilitate use of software programs by familiarizing the beginning speech-language clinician with a set of structures to be identified and coded for computer analysis and summary. The practice provided in *Guide* facilitates more accurate coding of target structures and assists in the interpretation of results of computer analysis. In addition, the procedures delineated in *Guide* can provide analysis of structures and/or aspects of language production currently not available through computer analysis. Finally, development of intervention goals and objectives from computer analysis may be enhanced with *Guide.*

USING *GUIDE* TO LEARN LANGUAGE TRANSCRIPT ANALYSIS

Guide to Analysis of Language Transcripts was developed to provide a comprehensive set of analysis procedures encompassing semantic, syntactic, and pragmatic aspects of language production. *Guide* differs from other sources previously available in that it provides a set of procedures for analyzing all three components of language. Each analysis procedure is demonstrated with a sample transcript. Blank analysis sheets and summary forms are provided, and practice in making crucial judgments is incorporated into the discussion of each procedure. Working through the practice examples for each procedure should increase accuracy in identifying and coding targeted structures and should increase the reliability of the resulting analyses. The accompanying CD-ROM includes in-depth practice for many of the procedures. No other source currently available includes a framework for gaining experience making judgments before applying the analysis procedures to sample transcripts. Four additional transcripts also are provided in Appendices B (one analyzed) and C (three unanalyzed) for continued practice.

In the analysis of a single child's language production, the developmentally appropriate procedures from each chapter should be applied to thoroughly describe the child's production abilities. In some cases, the developmental level of the child precludes the use of syntactic analysis procedures; typically, however, examination should proceed from semantic to syntactic to pragmatic analysis. For example, some form of semantic analysis will be performed for all language transcripts. Depending on the child's age and/or developmental level, that semantic analysis may be an analysis of the meanings expressed in one-word utterances, analysis of semantic roles and relations expressed in multiword utterances up to approximately four words in length, and/or analysis of vocabulary diversity using Templin's (1957) Type-Token Ratio. If a child's MLU is over 1.0 morphemes, analysis of syntactic aspects of the transcript must be performed. Such analysis may be cursory in that very few target structures are present; however, analysis is necessary to document emergence of early structures. The child whose MLU exceeds 6.0 morphemes may be at a level beyond which the structures analyzed with procedures in *Guide* can be documented. However, unless the structures described here are present in the child's production, and the highest level for each is observed, that conclusion cannot be drawn. In all cases, some form of pragmatic analysis must be performed. Again, depending on the child's age and/or developmental level, such analysis may be limited to the function of one-word utterances or may be as extensive as a conversational acts analysis with measures of appropriateness. In nearly every case, thorough analysis of language transcripts involves semantic, syntactic, and pragmatic analyses.

Clinical experience has demonstrated the effectiveness of proceeding with analysis in the order mentioned above. This order is consistent with the ordering of chapters in *Guide.* Rules for deciding which of the three sets of procedures (i.e., semantic, syntactic, or pragmatic) to use with any particular child are discussed in each chapter. An interpretation of each analysis procedure's results is incorporated into the discussion of that procedure and can be used as the foundation for intervention.

Documentation of the clinical validity of analysis procedures is not provided as such documentation does not exist. However, use of these procedures has proven to be helpful in identifying children with language production delays and/or disorders evaluated in university and school settings, and intervention programs have been based on the results of the described procedures. *Guide* should be used as a manual to learn each of the analysis procedures presented. Clinical use of the procedures should be supplemented with the practice exercises on the CD-ROM and with readings on the theoretical foundation of each procedure, for which sources are provided in Chapters 2, 3, and 4.

Obtaining Language Samples

The first step in analyzing language production transcripts is to obtain samples of the child's productive language. When collected appropriately, this language sample may be the best picture of the child's production abilities. In fact, Gallagher (1983) contends that "spontaneous language sampling is the centerpiece of child language assessment" (p. 2). However, the communicative interaction often is contrived to such an extent that the resulting sample is anything but representative of the child's usual productive language.

The term *representative* has been used in various ways in the literature. Miller (1981) supports the notion that a representative sample is one that is reliable and valid. McLean and Snyder-McLean (1978) suggest that a representative sample reflects the child's optimal performance. Gallagher (1983) reports that throughout the years, a sample has been considered to be representative if it portrays the child's usual performance. In *Guide,* the term *representative* is used to describe a child's usual productive language, including language that may be somewhat below or somewhat above his usual language performance.

Factors Affecting Sample Representativeness

Miller (1981) contends that a number of aspects of the communication interaction affect sample representativeness, and that each aspect can be controlled to ensure representativeness. Examining each factor and then taking steps to optimize conditions in each will improve the quality of the sample. High-quality representative samples are the foundation for accurate production analysis.

Nature of the Interaction

The first variable—nature of the interaction—refers to the person with whom the child is interacting and to whether that participant asks questions or engages in conversation during interactive play. Miller supports the notion of obtaining a number of language samples with the child interacting with a variety of people, including the speech-language clinician, a parent, and a sibling or peer. While the general assumption has been that a child will produce language that is most representative when interacting with his mother, studies comparing mother-child and clinician-child interaction have been inconclusive. Olswang and Carpenter (1978) found that the only variable of 21 lexical, grammatical, and semantic measures that was significantly different in the two interactions was the total number of utterances. Children produced significantly more utterances when interacting with their mothers than they did with familiar clinicians, but other length and complexity measures were not significantly different. Other studies comparing mother-child interactions obtained at home and clinician-child interactions obtained in the clinic have found that some children produce longer utterances with the clinician, other children produce longer utterances with the mother, and still other children produce utterances of equal length with both conversational co-participants (Kramer, James, and Saxman, 1979; Scott and Taylor, 1978). Gallagher (1983) suggests that the numerous research design differences between these studies may have contributed to the differences in results.

Studies comparing fathers to mothers as interactive partners also are fraught with inconsistencies in conclusions. Gallagher's (1983) sampling of relevant studies found some that indicated no significant differences between the interactive style of mothers and fathers (Golinkoff and Ames, 1979; Smith and Daglish, 1977; Wilkinson, Hiebert, and Rembold, 1981).

Gallagher also found studies supporting the contention that the language fathers use with children is different from the language mothers use with children. She supports the contention that the "most facilitating communication partner" may be one or the other of the parents, or neither. None of the studies cited by Gallagher compared fathers interacting with children to clinicians interacting with the same children.

Peer and/or sibling interaction may result in some language differences; however, the exact differences are not easy to predict. For example, some studies document length and complexity adjustments when children are interacting with a younger child (Sachs and Devin, 1976; Shatz and Gelman, 1973). Other studies emphasize differences in conversational acts, including more responses to adults' questions (Martlew, Connolly, and McCleod, 1978) and more repetitions, attention holders, and directives with peers than with adults (Wilkinson, Hiebert, and Rembold, 1981). Gallagher (1983) concludes that child-child communicative behavior has not been described sufficiently with regard to a single variable to predict the effects on communicative interaction.

Results of studies comparing children interacting with various conversational partners are mixed. Although it is possible to predict that a range of differences will occur, it is not possible to predict which differences will occur with a particular child and a particular conversational co-participant. Therefore, instead of pairing the child with only one conversational co-participant to obtain a language sample, it is prudent to obtain samples with the child interacting with various partners. Differences in samples add to the picture of the child's overall communicative abilities.

Miller (1981) includes conversational act variables, such as questioning and responding, as aspects of the nature of the interaction. He suggests that in attempting to obtain a representative sample, clinicians should keep question asking to a minimum. The assumption is that children will produce longer and more complex utterances when spontaneously conversing than when responding to questions. However, in a study in which children were asked to retell a story as they acted it out with toys, to tell what they were doing while playing with toys, and to respond to questions about toys as they played with them, Stalnaker and Craighead (1982) found inconclusive results. General group trends followed the order mentioned above for language complexity, but these authors conclude that none of the methods of language sampling was superior to the others.

Overall, it is apparent that a conversation in which one partner asks questions and the other responds is not a natural interaction. As conversational partners, clinicians should try to reduce the number of questions asked and to permit the child to take the lead in the interaction. However, complete absence of questions on the part of the clinician would be impossible to attain and may not result in a representative sampling of the child's production abilities.

Setting

The second variable that Miller (1981) indicates may affect sample representativeness is setting. Miller specifies a number of alternatives to the therapy room and asserts that using more than one setting is optimal. He suggests that samples be obtained in a variety of locations, such as at home, at school, in a residential facility, or at a clinic. Although Miller contends that "representative samples can be collected almost anywhere" (p. 11), differences may arise in the language of the child because of the setting. For example, the differences found in the mother-child versus clinician-child studies previously mentioned (Kramer, James, and Saxman, 1979; Scott and Taylor, 1978) may have been due primarily to the differences in setting. The mother-child samples were obtained in the home, and the clinician-child samples were obtained in the clinic. In two other studies, the effects of two settings on the language use of 3- to 4-year-old children were compared (Dore, 1978; Hall and Cole, 1978). Results indicated that a supermarket setting did not elicit more complex language than the classroom, and that differences, again, were related more to the interactive style of participants than to the setting (Dore, 1978).

While it may not be possible to predict which setting will result in representative language for a particular child, obtaining samples in more than one setting is optimal. The resulting differences, if any, add to the description of the child's communicative abilities.

Materials

The third variable that Miller (1981) believes may affect sample representativeness is the materials that are present. He reports that children with language disorders talk more about new and unique toys than they talk about familiar toys. Accordingly, Nisswandt (1983) reports the opposite for children with normal language. Numerous authors have found that different types of materials result in different language behaviors. Longhurst and File (1977) examined the effect of single-object pictures, multi-object pictures, toys, and no materials present on the language complexity of 4- to 5-year-old children. While group data supported increases in complexity in the order above, individual data indicated that increases in complexity could occur in any ordering of the stimulus conditions. Cook-Gumperz and Corsaro (1977) report differences in the communicative demands placed on 3- and 4-year-old children with three different sets of materials: those for a playhouse, a sandbox, and an adult-directed arts and crafts activity. Results indicated language differences across conditions, with very few initiative turns in the arts and crafts activity, adherence to role-play conventions in the playhouse, and unpredictable fantasy interactions in the sandbox. Cook-Gumperz and Corsaro conclude that the sandbox was the most difficult of the three settings in terms of interactive demands and resulted in an increased use of repetition and expansion, semantic typing, and verbal descriptions of behaviors.

Again, different materials may result in differences in language frequency and complexity. The differences, however, do not appear to be predictable for children. Therefore, it is wise to provide a variety of developmentally appropriate materials and to encourage the child to interact with as many materials as possible. Differences, again, will contribute to the overall picture of the child's communicative abilities.

Sample Size

The fourth variable that Miller (1981) indicates will affect sample representativeness is sample size. He contends that sample size can be determined in two ways. The first is to obtain a specific number of utterances from the child (or transcribe that number from a sample containing a larger number). For example, various authors have suggested numbers of utterances ranging from 50 to 200 for the sample to be representative (Crystal, Fletcher, and Garman, 1976, 1991; Lee, 1974; Miller, 1981; Tyack and Gottsleben, 1974). The alternative is to obtain utterances during a particular period of time—for example, 30 minutes—regardless of how many utterances occur during that period. This 30-minute period is likely to result in 100 to 200 utterances for children functioning at a 2-year level or older (Miller). Longer periods of time will be necessary to obtain 100 utterances from children younger than 2 years of age, and it may be prudent to supplement a sample with diary accounts from parents. The obvious conclusion is, the more utterances, the better; however, in an effort to be realistic, practical, and efficient, 100 utterances gathered under various conditions typically result in a respectably diverse sample.

Method of Recording

A fifth variable that Miller (1981) contends will affect sample representativeness—the method of recording—is really a variable affecting the overall *quality* of the resulting transcription. The optimum method is videotaping, because it permits the clinician either to interact freely with the child or to watch undistracted as others interact with the child. Transcription from videotape recordings is considered to be the most reliable method and permits detailed delineation of changes in nonverbal context.

Another method of recording is audiotaping. The clinician is free to interact with the child, but must make notes about the child's activities during the taping to provide the nonverbal context for transcription. Audiotape recorders are readily available in most clinical settings, and battery-operated recorders can be taken anywhere the sample is being collected. Also, most laptop computers (Macinotsh and Windows) have a sound-recording feature and can be taken anywhere. The quality of all audio recordings can be improved by using an external microphone.

An additional method of recording suggested by Miller (1981) is on-line transcription (i.e., transcribing what the child says, as the child says it). This method is useful in settings where videotaping and/or audiotaping is not practical. On-line transcription is particularly useful to record a child's productions on field trips or other outings away from the clinical setting. The major criticism of on-line transcription is that it results in transcriptions that underrepresent or overrepresent the child's actual productions. The key to obtaining reliable on-line transcriptions may be to use one of the procedures suggested by Miller: time sampling. Using this procedure, the clinician transcribes for a few minutes, then rests for a few minutes before continuing. This method maximizes attention during transcription. The alternative, writing down everything the child says, can be cumbersome and exhausting. As in audiotaping, nonverbal context notes should be made during on-line transcription.

Regardless of the method of recording the interaction, quality transcripts can be obtained. Miller (1981) reports a high reliability for MLU computations based on on-line transcriptions and transcriptions from both videotape and audiotape recordings. Each method has its own problems and advantages, and each relies on accurate representation of the child's productions for valid and reliable transcripts.

Specification of Context

The final variable, which also affects the *quality* of the obtained language transcript, is the specification of context. This includes the conversational co-participant's utterances as well as the nonverbal or situational context. The utterances preceding and following a child's utterances may dramatically affect the interpretation of the child's utterance. In addition, the objects that are present and the events that are taking place as the child produces an utterance greatly influence interpretation of the child's utterance. It will become obvious in the following chapters that semantic and pragmatic analyses require the specification of nonverbal context; such specification is also helpful with syntactic analysis. Overall, a quality transcription must include a detailed account of both the linguistic and nonlinguistic context.

Guidelines for Interaction

The preceding discussion highlighted numerous variables that are important to consider when obtaining representative language samples and producing quality transcripts. The following guidelines for interacting with a child are offered as a synthesis of the preceding discussion. Guidelines 1–3 should be adhered to in sequence to establish the conversational interaction. Guidelines 4–9 are general guidelines to be followed throughout the interaction.

1. Begin with parallel play and parallel talk. With a young child at the one-word stage, imitate his verbalizations and use many animal sounds and vehicle noises. With a child older than 2 years, talk about what you are doing as you play using role-playing dialogue (e.g., "I'm gonna make my guy drive. Here's the tractor for him. 'Wow, what a big tractor. I'm gonna go fast!'").

2. Move into interactive conversation. With the young child, use some routine questions (e.g., "What's a doggie say?") and elicit finger plays (e.g., "Let's play Patty Cake"). With the older child, invite him to participate in play (e.g., "You be the service station guy. I'll bring my car in. It needs fixing"). Continue in role-playing dialogue, unless establishing rules for play. Encourage the child to participate in plans for play, including what toy people/animals will be doing (e.g., "Hey, how about having a picnic?").

3. Continue the child's topic. If he is role-playing, stay in the role. If he shifts out of role, follow his lead. Respond to questions, acknowledge comments, and solicit more information about a topic.

4. Attempt to restrict your use of questions to approximately one question for every four speaking turns. Eliminating use of questions is unnatural, but too many questions may reduce the length of the child's utterances. The often suggested "Tell me about this" can also break down the conversation and result in descriptive strings from the child. Instead, carry on a conversation with the child at the child's level.

5. Give the child options that are presented as alternative questions (e.g., "Should we play gas station or have a picnic?"). While children under 3 years of age may not comprehend the alternate question form (Beilin, 1975), pointing to each option provides contextual support for the choice prior to full comprehension of the question form. By using alternate question forms, the shy or uncooperative child does not have the option of saying no, but can feel in control by choosing one of your options.

6. Use utterances that are, on average, slightly longer than the child's utterances. Keep the number of utterances per speaking turn to approximately the same number as the child's.

7. Learn to be comfortable with pauses in the conversation. If you are too quick to take a speaking turn in order to fill a pause, you deny the child the opportunity to take a turn. In addition, the child may come to expect you to fill pauses and thus feel no obligation toward continuing the conversation. If a pause becomes too long (longer than eight seconds), continue with parallel play and parallel talk until the child moves back into interactive conversation.

8. Have a variety of materials available to keep the child's motivation high, but do not move abruptly from activity to activity. Offer the child the option of changing activities and follow his interests. A diverse combination of materials might include role-playing toys like cars, trucks, people, farm sets, and kitchen sets, as well as manipulative materials like clay, paints, paper, pens, markers, and items for making a snack.

9. Do not be afraid to be silly and have fun. Many a shy child has been brought into the interaction by asking silly, obvious questions (e.g., "Those are great shoes. Can I wear them?") or by making silly comments (e.g., "There's a mouse in your pocket!"). Enjoy the child and the child will enjoy the interaction.

Transcribing Language Samples

The next step in obtaining a language transcript for analysis is to transcribe the interaction recorded. Table 1.1 summarizes a number of conventions that are helpful in transcribing language samples obtained from videotape recordings, audiotape recordings, and on-line interactions. Adult and child utterances can be transcribed in Standard English orthography except when utterances are unintelligible or when the child's approximation deviates substantially from expectations. Conventions for specifying the nonlinguistic or situational context are described, since this information is crucial for each of the analysis procedures delineated in *Guide.* When transcription from videotapes is not possible, audiotape recordings or on-line transcriptions may be used. However, it is important that you have made context notes during the interaction so that the situational context may be specified in the transcript.

For those who find transcription time-consuming, technology is available to shorten the time required to transcribe videotaped or audiotaped language samples. For example, Transcript Builder (Moore, 2000) has a split-screen design that allows digital video or audio files to be played while the user transcribes them onscreen. The play/rewind functions are controlled through the computer keyboard so that the sample can be transcribed quickly and efficiently. Speech can also be slowed to help decipher unintelligible utterances.

A sample transcript for a girl named Bridget has been provided (see pages 19–34) to demonstrate the transcription conventions used in *Guide.* In addition, a blank transcription form is provided in Appendix A.

TABLE 1.1

Transcription Conventions for Child Language Samples

(Adapted from Bloom and Lahey, 1978)

Style Conventions

1. Fully transcribe all speech produced by the child and to the child (or within the child's auditory field) in Standard English orthography. Transcribe words that appear to function as one word for the child as one word (e.g., *lookit, alldone, goodnight).* (Note that in Bridget's transcript, *look it* is written as two words because there is evidence elsewhere in the transcript that she has productive control over *look* and *it.)* For adults, use Standard English segmentation. Whenever possible, transcribe unclear or mispronounced words using the International Phonetic Alphabet (IPA). Common familiar pronunciations such as *ya* for *you, da* for *the,* and *'em* for *them* need not be transcribed phonetically. Transcribe utterances produced by the child in the right-hand column and utterances produced by other speakers in the left-hand column. Place information about the situational context in the middle column and enclose it in parentheses. Identify individuals within the situational context by an initial (e.g., M for Mom, D for Dad, J for Jane).

Continued on next page

TABLE 1.1—Continued

	(M takes toy from boy and offers	
	it to J)	
Look at this/		
	(J takes toy)	
		puppy/

2. Capitalize proper names within utterances. Do not capitalize the initial letter of a child utterance. The initial letter of an adult utterance typically is capitalized.
3. Place an action or event that occurs simultaneously with an adult or a child utterance on the same line as that utterance.

	(J banging cars together)	boom/
A new car/	(M handing car to J)	

4. When an utterance precedes or follows an action or event, transcribe the utterance on the preceding or succeeding line. When in doubt about the situational context, use separate lines for young children.

	(J eats cracker)	
		allgone/
		more cracker/
	(J reaches for bag)	

5. Different verb tenses should be used to describe situational context: Use the present progressive tense for simultaneous action; use the simple present tense for actions or events that precede or follow an utterance.

Punctuation Conventions

6. Use a slash (/) to punctuate an utterance boundary. The boundary is determined by length of pause before the next utterance and apparent terminal contour. Pauses greater than two seconds prior to the next utterance typically mark utterance boundaries, with or without rising or falling terminal contour. Specification of pauses of any length to mark utterance boundaries is viewed as secondary to other criteria.

Continued on next page

***TABLE 1.1**—Continued*

7. When emphasis or exclamation is apparent, follow utterances by an adult with an exclamation mark and no slash. When a child utterance is exclamatory, it should be followed by both an exclamation mark and a slash.

Wow!	(J taking wheel off car)	
		there!/

8. Indicate adult questions with question marks. For child utterances, one of two procedures should be used: (1) For *wh-* questions, use a question mark and a slash.

	(J looking in bag)	where's da cracker?/

(2) When a child utterance seems to be a question because of its rising intonation, use a rising arrow (↑) instead of a question mark and follow it with a slash.

	(J shaking empty bag)	no more in there↑/

Even for a well-formed yes/no question (i.e., one with subject-verb inversion), use the arrow to indicate rising intonation, since it is more informative than a simple question mark.

	(J meeting K at door)	do you have cookies↑/

9. Use a dot (·) to indicate a pause of less than two seconds within an utterance.

	(J trying to fit wheel on car)	put · this one on/

10. Indicate a long pause either between speakers or between utterances of the same speaker by placing three horizontal dots in the context column. Only use this convention if the situational context remains the same.

	(J trying to get wheel on)	wheel go there/
	• • •	
	(J succeeds)	
		there!/

Continued on next page

TABLE 1.1—Continued

If the situational context changes, indicate a long pause by placing three vertical dots in the context column.

	(J playing with blocks)	make a tower/
	•	
	•	
	•	
	(J running to bathroom)	potty/

11. Use a colon to indicate that an utterance or word is drawn out.

	(J trying to fit large peg into	no:/
	small hole)	

12. Use a curving arrow (⤴) when there seems to be an utterance boundary but the utterance is drawn out, such as when the child is counting or listing.

	(J pointing to raisin)	one⤴/
	(J touching next raisin)	two⤴/
	(J touching next raisin)	three⤴/

13. Use stress marks to indicate strongly emphasized words.

Do you want this′ one?	(M giving J a blue crayon)	
		no!/
	(J reaching for red crayon)	that′ one/

Continued on next page

***TABLE 1.1**—Continued*

14. An utterance should be followed by a falling arrow (↓) when it is important to emphasize the fact that the utterance has falling terminal contour.

	(J looking in box)	cow↑/
	(J pulls out cow)	
		cow↓/

15. Use a line (________) to indicate an abrupt stop when the child interrupts himself or when another speaker suddenly interrupts (either verbally or nonverbally) leaving the utterance unfinished.

Do you want some ________ /		
	(J picks up cup and spills milk)	

16. Use a self-correct symbol (s/c) when the child interrupts himself or when another speaker interrupts to change or correct it.

Those are your $_{s/c}$ my cookies/		
		more cookie $_{s/c}$ cracker/

17. Use three *X*s (XXX) to indicate an unintelligible utterance or a portion of an utterance. Whenever possible, use a phonetic transcription instead, and if possible, provide an interpretation in brackets.

	(J reaching for bag)	XXX/
	(J pointing to sky)	/ʌpə/ [airplane]

18. The following abbreviations may be used to indicate the manner in which an utterance was produced:

(lf) = laugh
(cr) = cry
(wn) = whine
(gr) = grunt
(wh) = whisper
(wm) = whimper
(yl) = yell
(sg) = sing

The abbreviation should follow the utterance in parentheses.

	(J holding finger to mouth)	she's sleeping/ (wh)

Numbering Language Transcripts

The final step in preparing language transcripts for analysis is to number the utterances. Each fully intelligible utterance to be analyzed should be assigned an utterance number. If an utterance is repeated with no intervening activity or utterance by the other speaker, the utterance is considered a repetition and does not receive an utterance number. In addition, totally or partially unintelligible utterances should not be assigned an utterance number. Finally, incomplete utterances resulting from self-interruptions or overlapping speakers are not assigned utterance numbers. The alternative would be to number all child utterances and exclude repetitions, unintelligible utterances, and incomplete utterances from analysis. The convention of not numbering these utterances has been selected to aid in managing the process of coding individual utterances and computing percentages.

Obviously, there may be times when a repetition or an incomplete utterance is erroneously assigned a number. If that happens, it should not be included in analysis. Utterances do not have to be renumbered; additional utterances should simply replace repetitions or incomplete utterances if additional sequential utterances are available following the original 100 utterances (i.e., add one or more lines to the transcript form and label the utterances as 101, 102, etc.). If replacement utterances are not available, percentage and mean computations must be adjusted to reflect the number eliminated from 100 utterances.

All analysis procedures described in *Guide to Analysis of Language Transcripts* are based on 100 child utterances. As previously reported, there is considerable variability in the literature regarding the number of utterances recommended for analysis. While it may be difficult to obtain 100 utterances from children less than 2 years of age (Miller, 1981), for the purposes of the analysis procedures described in *Guide,* a minimum of 100 utterances collected under a variety of conditions has been judged necessary to capture the variability in performance present in spontaneous language. Utterance numbers appear handwritten on the sample transcript to demonstrate the conventions for numbering described in *Guide.* The same conventions should be followed in numbering adult utterances for the pragmatic analyses described in Chapter 4. Although you may end up with more than or less than 100 adult utterances, these surrounding adult utterances are important for interpreting the 100 child utterances.

One final word about transcription of samples of children's productive language: Transcription is a time-consuming task that becomes easier and faster with practice. The validity of the analysis procedures applied to language transcripts is contingent upon the quality of the transcriptions. Therefore, an investment of time and energy in transcribing and numbering the utterances is necessary to ensure that quality transcripts are being used for analysis. The remaining three chapters present how to apply semantic, syntactic, and pragmatic analysis procedures following accurate transcription.

A sample transcript of a 28-month-old child (Bridget) appears on pages 19–34. Review the transcript to study the transcription conventions described in Table 1.1. Bridget's transcript will be analyzed throughout Chapters 2, 3, and 4, so it may be helpful to photocopy the transcript at this time.

Name of Child: Bridget — Chronological Age: 28 months

Type of Situation: free play in living room — Date: 3-12

Length of Tape: 1 hr, 20 min — Length of Transcript: 100 utterances — Time of Day: 1:30 pm

Materials Present: circus set, dolls, doll buggy, tea set, kitchen set, toy telephone

People Present: M = Mom; B = Bridget (Bill, camera operator, & Kay, context transcriber)

ADULT	CONTEXT	CHILD
	(B trying to put lion on bar by tail)	/wʊp/ [whoops] 1
1 What happened to the lion?		
		fall down/ 2
2 Did he get hurt?		
		no/ 3
	(B looks at M)	
		yes/ 4
3 He did?		
4 What happened to him?		
What happened to him?		
	(B reaches to lion)	
	(B pointing to tail of lion)	hurt his tail there/ 5
		see↑/ 6
5 Uh-huh/		
	(B looking back)	XXX/ (lf)
		what else?/ 7
6 What else?		
How about _______ /		
7 Yes/		
	(B taking giraffe from box)	giraffe/ 8
8 What is that?		

ADULT	CONTEXT	CHILD
		giraffe/ 9
9 That's right/		
	(B giving giraffe to M)	here/ 10
10 What's that?		
		put upside down/ 11
11 Put him upside down too?		
		yeah/ 12
12 Okay/		
	(B taking back giraffe and	bar/ 13
	pointing to bar)	
		here/ 14
13 Up there/		
14 You do it/		
	(B tossing giraffe to M)	Mommy you do it/ 15
15 Don't you want to do it honey?	(M holding out giraffe)	
	(B looks in box)	
16 You make him stand up here/		
17 You wanna see if he can go like	(M placing giraffe; B watching	
this maybe/	M hold box)	
18 Oh/		
	(B looking in box)	what else?/ 16
19 What else?		
20 Find something/		
	(B reaching in box)	lookie in the box/ 17
	(B pulls out two toys)	
21 The monkey's right here/		
		XXX/
22 The monkey's right here/		

ADULT	CONTEXT	CHILD
	(B looks where M points)	
		that's not enough/ 18
	(B looks back in box)	
		what else?/ 19
23 Find something/		
24 Where did you put the	(B pulling toys out of the box and	
elephant this morning?	setting them on the floor)	
Where did you put the		
elephant this morning?		
25 You were playing with him/		
		he's not here/ 20
26 Where is he?		
	(B scans the floor with her eyes)	
27 Where did you put him?		
		I don't know/ 21
28 What?		
	(B pushes toys on the floor)	
29 Where did you put him?		
		find him/ 22
30 Find him?		
		where it is?/ 23
		where that elephant go?/ 24
31 I don't know/		
Did you put him in with _______ /		
32 Oh what's that?		
	(M points to a toy on other side of	
	room; B looks)	
33 What's that over there?		

ADULT	CONTEXT	CHILD
		the elephant/ 25
34 Will you get it?		
	(B stands up)	
	(B walks over and gets the elephant,	
	brings it back to M)	
		stand up/ 26
	(B holding legs of elephant)	legs/ 27
		stand up/ 28
35 Oh I think he might be too heavy/		
	(B stoops, stands up, stoops again	
	to stand up elephant)	
36 Let's put another one of these	(M pulling box around B and	
up here/	over to her)	
Let's put another one of these		
up here/		
	(B stands; M pulls ladder	
	from box)	
37 How does this work?		
		huh↑/ 29
38 Do you know how this works?		
	(M attaches ladder)	
39 Like this?		
		yeah/ 30
40 Oh okay/		
41 Put him up on top/	(B stooping)	
42 Is he too big?		
43 Up here/		
44 Put him up there/		

ADULT	CONTEXT	CHILD
	(B sitting on floor holding toy)	you do it upside down/ 31
45 Oh:/	(B putting elephant on ladder)	
	(B pointing)	there's a elephant/ (lf) 32
46 There's another one/		
47 Do you want to put him up there too?		
		no it's heavy/ 33
	(B wipes nose on shirt sleeve)	
48 Oh it's heavy/		
49 Okay/		
50 Is he too heavy?	(M pointing to toy on floor)	
		yeah/ 34
51 He's just a baby one/		
	(B looking around floor)	where's another one?/ 35
52 How about the circus man?		
	(B turns and kicks toy structure)	
53 Woo: what happened here?	(M catching toy structure)	
54 What happened?		
		I kick 'im/ (lf) 36
55 You kicked him?		
		yeah/ 37
56 You know what you need?		
	(M turns and brings back tissue)	
57 You need a Kleenex/		
	(B reaching for tissue)	gimme/ 38
58 Can I help you?		
	(B wipes nose and gives tissue to M)	
	(M wipes B's nose)	
59 Look/		

ADULT	CONTEXT	CHILD
	(B turns head away)	
		ick/ 39
60 Let me see that/		
	(B looking at hand)	owie/ 40
61 Okay/		
		owie/ 41
62 What happened?		
63 Did you fall down?		
	(B looks at M)	
	(B holding her own hand)	yeah/ 42
64 Oh:/		
65 How does it feel?		
		pretty better/ 43
66 It feels better/		
	(B kisses finger)	
67 Okay/		
68 Can I kiss it too?		
	(B extends finger so M can kiss it)	
	(M kisses finger)	
69 Okay/		
	(B extends arms and pulls toy	
	structure back into lap)	
	(M rebuilds structure)	
70 You wanna put 'em back up again?		
71 Let's put 'em back up again/		
72 You gonna make them fall		
down again?		
	(B watching M)	he fall/ (lf) 44

ADULT	CONTEXT	CHILD
73 Why did you kick him?		
	(B elevates body and returns to sit)	
		I kick him/ 45
74 Aw:/		
	(B leans forward and with a wave	
	of her hands, knocks the toy over)	
		fall down · boom/ 46
75 Is that funny?		
		yeah/ (lf) 47
76 You think so?		
		yeah/ 48
77 Are you done playing with this?		
78 Should we do something else?		
		yeah/ 49
79 You want to take this man for a		
ride in the buggy?		
	(M pulls buggy over)	
80 You want to take him for a ride		
in the stroller?		
81 Hmm?		
	(B pulling buggy)	/sokə/ [stroller] 50
	(M stands bed up and moves other	
	toys away, then points to bed)	
82 Can you bring him over here and		
put him in bed?		
		yeah/ 51
83 Okay/		
	(B places man in bed)	

	ADULT	CONTEXT	CHILD	
			go to sleep/	52
			shh/	53
84	Shh/			
85	Did you give him a kiss and tell			
	him good night?			
		(B bending over bed)	goodnight/	54
86	There he is/			
		(B points to bed and whispers to M)		
87	Is he tired? (wh)			
			yeah/ (wh)	55
		(B squeals as she turns man over)		
		(B lifts man out of bed)		
88	Oh you woke him up/			
		(B puts man in bed and touches		
		nose with finger; M puts finger		
		to her lips)		
89	Shh/			
90	What else should we do?			
	What else should we do?			
		(B picks man up; M leans over her)		
			I wake him up/ (yl)	56
91	How about having some coffee?			
		(B puts man in bed)		
92	Should we go get some coffee?			
93	Will you go get me a cup of coffee	(M pushing aside toys)		
	please in your kitchen?			
94	Can you go get me a cup of coffee			
	in your kitchen?			

ADULT	CONTEXT	CHILD
95 I want some coffee/		
96 Can I have some coffee?		
	(B stands up and walks to kitchen)	
		all right/ 57
97 Oh I'll have some milk too/		
98 What's that?		
		cow/ 58
99 Who makes the milk?		
		huh↑/ 59
100 Who makes the milk?		
101 Woo:/		
102 The dishes are dirty/		
	(B picking up a ball and turning	there's a ball↑/ 60
	toward camera)	
103 Yeah but I want to have		
some coffee/		
	(B walking with ball and milk	d · d · d · dere's a ball/ 61
	carton in hand)	
		dere's a ball/
104 Okay come on/		
105 Let's have some coffee/		
106 Come on/		
107 Come on Bridget/		
108 Can I have a cup of coffee please?		
109 Here's the milk/		
110 Get me a cup of coffee/		
	(B moves hands in air and walks	
	back to cabinet)	

ADULT	CONTEXT	CHILD	
111 You have one too/			
112 Okay?			
	(B stooping at cabinet and pulling	this yours/	62
	out a cup)		
113 Okay here's mine/			
	(M extends arm)		
114 Thank you/			
115 Can I get a plate too?			
	(B holds teapot in position to pour		
	into cup and hands cup to M)		
116 Thank you very much/			
		welcome/	63
117 Can I have a plate please?			
	(B reaching for a plate)	okay/	64
118 I want to eat something too/			
		here's yours/	65
119 This is mine?			
120 What about yours?			
121 Do you want some too?			
	(B puts pot down on cabinet and		
	moves dishes around)		
		/wʌzət/ else?/ [what else?]	66
		else/	67
		else/	
		else/	
122 Bridget?			
123 You mean those?			
124 The other ones are over there/			

ADULT	CONTEXT	CHILD
	(B walking, banging pot and cup	huh↑/ 68
	together)	
125 Huh · uh-oh/		
126 You're going to give some coffee		
to Bill and Kay?		
127 Is that what you're going to do?		
	(B walking back to M)	yeah/ 69
128 Let's sit down and have some		
first okay?		
129 You sit down okay?		
130 Sit down/		
	(B sits down)	
131 Tastes good/		
132 How does yours taste?		
		more↑/ 70
133 How does yours $_{s/c}$ yes please/		
	(B pours from pot into M's cup)	
134 Thank you/		
135 You want some more?		
	(B standing up, extending arm	Bill/ 71
	toward camera, but Bill just winks	
	and continues filming)	
		take 'em Bill/ 72
136 I think Bill's full/		
		take 'em Bill/ 73
137 I don't think he's hungry/		
	(B sitting down)	huh↑/ 74
138 I don't think he's hungry/		

ADULT	CONTEXT	CHILD	
139 But I'd like some more please/			
	(M places her cup on floor in front of B,		
	then B pours from her cup to M's cup)		
140 How does yours taste?			
		taste good/	75
141 Does it taste good?			
	(B hitting her cup against her foot)	yeah/	76
142 What else?			
143 Does it taste delicious too?			
		yeah/	77
144 Could I have some cookies please?			
Could I have some cookies please?			
	(B shaking head back and forth)	no cookies/	78
145 Hmm?			
		allgone/	79
146 Are they?			
		yeah/	80
147 Who ate them?			
Who ate them?			
148 Who ate the cookies?			
		somebody ate the cookies/	81
149 Who ate them?			
	(B claps pot and cup together, then		
	takes drink from cup)		
150 Can I have a piece of toast please?			
	(B shakes head and drops pot and cup)		
151 There's some in there/			
	(M points to cabinet)		

ADULT	CONTEXT	CHILD
152 See it?		
	(B looks toward cabinet)	
153 Get me some toast please/		
	(B crawls to cabinet)	
		XXX/
	(B takes something from	
	cabinet and looks toward M)	
154 Uh-huh/		
		okay/ 82
	(B stands and walks to M)	
		way up here/ 83
		plate/ 84
155 A plate/		
156 Oh/		
157 Oh you're going to give me		
toast on a plate/		
	(M extends plate)	
158 Can I have one piece please?		
	(B turns her plate over M's plate)	
159 Thank you/		
	(M tastes "toast")	
160 Tastes good/		
		yeah/ 85
161 Could I have some peanut butter		
on it?		
	(B waves her plate near M's "toast")	
162 Will you put some peanut butter		
on it?		

ADULT	CONTEXT	CHILD
	(B drops plate)	
163 Please?		
164 Here put some peanut butter		
on my toast/		
	(B takes "toast" from M, puts hand	
	in mouth, then behind her back)	
165 Oh you ate mine/		
166 You ate mine/		
	(B giggles and then points to mouth)	
167 Oh give me that/		
	(B points to mouth again)	
		ate mine/ 86
168 Oh/		
169 I'm going to eat up your tummy/		
	(B walks toward M, extends	
	her tummy)	
170 A rum rum rum/		
	(B backs off and returns)	
171 A rum rum rum/		
	(B holding M's head to tummy,	look at it/ 87
	talking to camera)	
172 I see it/		
		look at it/ 88
173 A rum rum rum/		
		look it Bill/ 89
174 A rum rum rum/		
		look it Bill/ 90
175 A rum rum rum/		

ADULT	CONTEXT	CHILD
	(B releases M's head and puts	
	hand on tummy)	
176 Want me to eat you all up?		
		huh↑/ 91
177 Would you like me to eat you all up?		
		yeah/ 92
178 Why?		
	(B walks to M's face, tummy	
	extended)	
179 Why?		
Why?		
180 Why would you like me to eat		
you up?		
181 Hmm?		
182 What are you doing now?		
	(B lies on floor and holds toy)	
183 Hmm?		
184 What are you doing now?		
	(B getting up)	telephone/ 93
185 Let's see here/		
		telephone/ 94
		telephone/
186 Want to talk on the telephone?		
		yeah/ 95
187 I think we'll play with the other		
telephone/		
188 You want to talk on the phone?		
189 Here you sit down and I'll get it/		

ADULT	CONTEXT	CHILD
	(B turns around; M stands up)	
190 I'll get it/		
	(B walks over to M)	
191 Uh-oh/		
		what happened?/ 96
192 Where did it go?		
		in that box/ 97
193 Here it is/		
	(M picks up phone)	
194 I found it/		
195 There/		
196 You want to talk?		
	(M puts phone on floor)	
197 Why don't you call up Grandma?		
198 Turn around/		
	(B sits on floor)	
199 Call up Grandma?		
	(B picks up receiver)	
200 Dial first/		
	(B dials phone)	
		hello/ 98
		Grandma here/ 99
	(B holds out phone to M)	
		you talk/ 100

SEMANTIC ANALYSIS

Chapter 2

INTRODUCTION

Semantic analysis of language transcripts provides valuable information for determining the developmental level of children with potential language delays. A variety of procedures are appropriate, including analysis of individual semantic roles (Bloom, 1973; Nelson, 1973; Retherford, Schwartz, and Chapman, 1981), analysis of prevalent semantic relations (Brown, 1973), and analysis of vocabulary diversity (Templin, 1957). Most of these analyses are based on data obtained from transcripts of children who are developing normally, interacting with their mothers. While these procedures have not been standardized, results of semantic analysis can support other judgments regarding the presence of language delays, including syntactic and pragmatic analysis results. In addition, semantic analysis procedures yield data crucial for developing intervention goals and objectives.

The following analysis procedures have been selected on the basis of clinical relevance. The majority of the procedures are appropriate for use with children producing utterances primarily between one and three words in length. The Type-Token Ratio (Templin, 1957), however, is applicable for children up to 8 years of age. The procedures delineated in this chapter have been selected to work together, resulting in a complete analysis of the semantic content of a child's productions. Each procedure may also be used separately to provide an analysis of a single aspect of the semantic content. All procedures will be described in detail with directions and examples, and all procedures will be demonstrated using the transcript of Bridget (pages 19–34).

When analyzing the semantic content of child language transcripts, an important distinction must be made between the referential and the relational aspects of the child's productions, since analysis of these two aspects yields different results. *Referential analysis* describes the child's use of individual words to refer to objects or classes of objects and events in the environment. *Relational analysis* describes the meaning relationships expressed by words in relation to aspects of objects or events in the environment, or by words in relation to other words. This distinction can be seen in the difference between the child's use of a word to label (or refer to) an object in the environment (e.g., "Ball") versus the child's use of a word to describe the relationship between a previous situation and a current situation (e.g., "All gone" after eating a cookie) or two object labels in combination to describe the relationship between the two objects in the environment (e.g., "Daddy ball"). This chapter examines five types of analysis procedures: (1) Bloom's One-Word Utterance Types, (2) Nelson's One-Word Utterance Types, (3) Retherford et al.'s Semantic Roles, (4) Brown's Prevalent Semantic Relations, and (5) Templin's Type-Token Ratio. They are organized by the length of the utterances being analyzed.

ANALYZING SEMANTIC CONTENT OF ONE-WORD UTTERANCES

When children are predominantly using one-word utterances (i.e., more than 50% of their utterances are one-word in length), it is appropriate to analyze the semantic content of the utterances. The first step, then, is to identify the prevalence of one-word utterances in the transcript. To analyze the semantic content, two different procedures can be used: (1) a categorization of one-word utterance types described by Bloom in 1973 and (2) a classification scheme provided by Nelson, also in 1973. While both types of analyses are appropriate for use with productions one word in length, each provides slightly different information. Each will be considered in detail before examining the differences in results.

Bloom's One-Word Utterance Types

Bloom's (1973) categorization scheme describes the three types of words that children use in their one-word utterances. The first type is a SUBSTANTIVE WORD. A SUBSTANTIVE WORD refers to a generic object or event, like *ball* or *cookie* or *chair.* At times, children refer to particular objects or events, and these words are part of the second type: NAMING WORDS. The child might use a NAMING WORD to refer to a family pet, parents, siblings, or other important people in the environment. It is important to be familiar with the names of significant people and animals in the child's environment before attempting to categorize the child's utterances as either of these two types. The third type of word in Bloom's categorization scheme is a FUNCTION WORD. FUNCTION WORDS refer to conditions shared by many objects or events and make reference across classes of objects or events. A word like *up* is not just a direction; it may refer to the desired relationship between a child and a parent, or it may describe the location of an object in relation to another object. A word like *more* does not just refer to an object, but indicates the recurrence, or desired recurrence, of an object. By describing the child's use of these three types of one-word utterances, we can build a picture of how the child uses words to convey meanings.

A few typical one-word utterances are provided below for practice in using Bloom's categorization scheme before attempting to categorize Bridget's utterances. Cover the right side of the page with your hand or a sheet of paper, categorize each example utterance, and then check your answers with those provided in the shaded section. An explanation for each utterance is included to help clear up any discrepancies.

Practice Examples for Bloom's Analysis

(C picks up toy horse) horsie/	SUBSTANTIVE WORD This utterance refers to a real or pretend object.
(C hears door opening) Dada/	NAMING WORD This utterance refers to a particular person, the child's father.
(C reaches for cup on table) cup/	SUBSTANTIVE WORD This utterance labels an object.

Continued on next page

Practice Examples—*Continued*	
(C picks up car with no wheels) broke/	FUNCTION WORD This utterance does not label an object, but refers to its condition.
(dog barking in background) Dee Dee/	NAMING WORD This utterance refers to the family pet and names it. Remember, it is important to be familiar with the names of significant people and animals in the child's environment before attempting to categorize the child's utterances.
(C takes a drink from cup) juice/	SUBSTANTIVE WORD This utterance provides a label for the liquid refreshment.
(M says, "Where is that shoe?"; C points to chest of drawers and says) there/	FUNCTION WORD This utterance refers to the condition (or location) of an object.
(C points to picture of a baby in picture book) baby/	SUBSTANTIVE WORD This utterance provides a generic label for a person.
(C points to self in mirror) Baby/	NAMING WORD Here, the child is referring to himself, not just labeling a baby. The nonlinguistic context is crucial for making judgments like this. If the child had been labeling the object, the utterance would have been categorized SUBSTANTIVE WORD.
(C picks up music box and looks at M) no/	FUNCTION WORD While it is impossible to determine the type of negation being expressed without the additional nonlinguistic context, various types of negation are coded in this way to make reference across classes of objects or events.
(C carries cup to sink while holding it out for more juice) drink/	SUBSTANTIVE WORD Again, the nonlinguistic context is crucial for differentiating the labeling of the liquid refreshment from the description of an activity. In the second case, the utterance would have been categorized FUNCTION WORD.

At this point, the one-word utterances in the sample transcript need to be identified and categorized. Using Bridget's transcript (pages 19–34) and the *Bloom's One-Word Utterance Types* analysis sheet from Appendix A (page 229), put each one-word utterance into the appropriate column on the analysis sheet. If a particular word occurs more than once, tally additional instances of that word next to the original recording (e.g., "ball ~~||||~~ /" means the word *ball* occurred seven times in the transcript). After you finish, check your analysis sheet against the completed sheet on page 39.

Calculating the Results Obtained Using Bloom's One-Word Utterance Types

Following the identification of each one-word utterance and the categorization of each into one of Bloom's (1973) three categories, the frequency of occurrence of each type is calculated. Proceed as follows:

1. Count the number of words in each column, including additional instances of each word, and put the total for each type in the blank provided. (Keep in mind that short phrases such as *good night, all right,* and *all gone* are listed as one word because they typically function as such for children this age.)

2. Add all instances to obtain the total number of one-word utterances, and put that number in the blank provided. Double-check this number by returning to the transcript and counting the one-word utterances.

3. Return to each one-word utterance type and compute the percentage of total one-word utterances accounted for by each type. This is accomplished by dividing the number of instances of the type by the total number of one-word utterances, using the fourth decimal place to round up or down to the nearest thousandth, and multiplying that number by 100.

4. Determine the percentage of total utterances accounted for by one-word utterances. Do this by dividing the total number of one-word utterances by the total number of utterances.

In the sample transcript, there were 11 SUBSTANTIVE WORDS, which when divided by 52 total one-word utterances, yielded .2115. After rounding this off to .212 and multiplying by 100 to convert to a percentage, this means that 21.2% of the one-word utterances were categorized as SUBSTANTIVE WORDS. (See page 39 and note where this number is filled in on the analysis sheet.) One instance of a NAMING WORD divided by 52 yielded 1.9%. There were 40 FUNCTION WORDS, which when divided by 52 total one-word utterances yielded 76.9% of the one-word utterances. Finally, the total number of one-word utterances (52) was divided by the total number of utterances (100), yielding 52%. This means that 52% of the total utterances were one word in length.

But look again at Bloom's FUNCTION WORD category on the completed analysis sheet on page 39. The most striking thing about the words listed is the preponderance of *yeahs*. A look at each FUNCTION WORD listed reveals that there are several variations of yes/no responses and many routine responses (e.g., *hello, good night, welcome).* These responses can be called *conversational devices* and *communication routines* respectively; they will be presented in detail on pages 69–71. If these responses are eliminated, six words are left, one of which occurs twice. Those are checked (✓) on the adjusted analysis sheet on page 40. This changes

Bloom's One-Word Utterance Types

Name of Child: Bridget

Substantive Words	Naming Words	Function Words
giraffe /	Bill	whoops
bar		no
legs		yes
owie /		see
stroller		here /
cow		yeah ~~||||~~ ~~||||~~ ~~||||~~ /
plate		huh ||||
telephone /		gimme
		ick
		shh
		goodnight
		allright
		welcome
		okay /
		else
		more
		allgone
		hello

Although "shh" does not have syllable structure, it clearly carries semantic content. Bloom probably would not have included this as a word, but it now appears in dictionaries and so it is counted here.

11 Substantive Words = 21.2 % of Total One-Word Utterances

1 Naming Words = 1.9 % of Total One-Word Utterances

40 Function Words = 76.9 % of Total One-Word Utterances

TOTAL NUMBER OF ONE-WORD UTTERANCES 52

TOTAL NUMBER OF UTTERANCES 100

52 **% OF TOTAL UTTERANCES**

Bloom's One-Word Utterance Types—Adjusted

Name of Child: Bridget

Substantive Words	Naming Words	Function Words
giraffe /	Bill	~~whoops~~
bar		~~no~~
legs		~~yes~~
owie /		see ✓
stroller		here / ✓
cow		~~yeah //// //// //// /~~
plate		~~huh~~ ////
telephone /		gimme ✓
		~~ick~~
		~~shh~~
		~~goodnight~~
		~~allright~~
		~~welcome~~
		~~okay~~ /
		else ✓
		more ✓
		allgone ✓
		~~hello~~

Although "shh" does not have syllable structure, it clearly carries semantic content. Bloom probably would not have included this as a word, but it now appears in dictionaries and so it is counted here.

11 Substantive Words = ~~21.2~~ 57.9 % of Total One-Word Utterances

1 Naming Words = ~~1.9~~ 5.3 % of Total One-Word Utterances

~~40~~ 7 Function Words = ~~76.9~~ 36.8 % of Total One-Word Utterances

TOTAL NUMBER OF ONE-WORD UTTERANCES ~~52~~ 19

TOTAL NUMBER OF UTTERANCES 100

~~52~~ 19 **% OF TOTAL UTTERANCES**

the total number of one-word utterances to 19 and the individual computations to 57.9% SUBSTANTIVE WORDS (11 SUBSTANTIVE WORDS divided by 19 one-word utterances), 5.3% NAMING WORDS (1 NAMING WORD divided by 19 one-word utterances), and 36.8% FUNCTION WORDS (7 FUNCTION WORDS divided by 19 one-word utterances). Exclusion of certain one-word utterances from the analysis may appear to be an arbitrary decision; however, an examination of Bloom's examples of FUNCTION WORDS will indicate that this is an appropriate decision. Finally, the percentage of total utterances accounted for by one-word utterance types must be calculated. In the sample transcript, there were 19 one-word utterances, which when divided by 100 total utterances revealed that 19% of total utterances were one-word utterance types, allowing for the exclusion of conversational devices and communication routines.

Interpretation of Results Obtained Using Bloom's One-Word Utterance Types

Now the results of the semantic analysis can be interpreted. To begin, note that only 19% of Bridget's total utterances were one word in length. This indicates that more than half of the child's utterances with semantic content in this sample were longer than one word in length. At this cursory level, one might suspect that the child is beyond the one-word stage. Thus, it could be concluded that the child's lexicon exceeds 50 words (Bloom, 1973), because a child's lexicon containing less than 50 words would have a greater percentage of total utterances accounted for by one-word utterances, even after exclusions. Consequently, the analysis of one-word utterance types may not be the most important analysis regarding this particular child's semantic abilities.

However, some conclusions about the types of words used can be drawn. Note that Bridget used more SUBSTANTIVE WORDS than either FUNCTION or NAMING WORDS. Various authors have described the proportion of one-word utterances accounted for by various types of one-word utterances. Some authors contend that the first 50-word lexicon is comprised primarily of nouns, or in this categorization scheme, SUBSTANTIVE or NAMING WORDS (Benedict, 1979; Gleitman, Gleitman, and Shipley, 1972; Huttenlocher, 1974; McNeill, 1970). Only later in the one-word stage do children add FUNCTION WORDS. This would suggest that the child in the sample transcript is in an early stage of language production.

On the other hand, Bloom, Lightbown, and Hood (1975) describe a nominal-pronominal continuum in children at the one-word utterance stage. Children whose one-word utterances refer predominately to nouns are considered to be on the nominal end of the continuum. Children whose one-word utterances refer predominately to nouns, but are in the pronominal form (e.g., *this, it, that),* and to relations between objects and events are considered to be on the pronominal end of the continuum. This apparent tendency is reported to persist into the preschool years (Horgan, 1979). From Bridget's transcript, it may be concluded that in this sample, this child tends to be predominately nominal. In addition, considering that 19% of total utterances were one-word in length, it may be concluded that this child has progressed beyond a simple labeling stage and is cognizant of the functional relations that exist between objects and events.

More data are necessary to substantiate this hypothesis. For example, would this same distribution occur in another transcript of this child obtained under variations in the conditions described in Chapter 1?

This example points out the need for multiple samples of the child's productions. Overall, the results of this analysis indicate that examination of more diverse aspects of the child's productions is necessary to accurately assess the child's semantic abilities.

Nelson's One-Word Utterance Types

The second categorization of one-word utterances that will be used was developed by Nelson (1973) to describe the first 50-word lexicons of children approximately 18 months of age. The five categories that Nelson used to analyze one-word utterances are listed and defined in Table 2.1. Her data were obtained from diary accounts of children's productions that were analyzed to provide a frequency distribution of five categories. In this analysis, one-word utterances produced in 100-utterance language transcripts are used. This analysis procedure may not be appropriate for language transcripts, but it is being completed for the purpose of demonstrating Nelson's analysis. Thus, data from the sample transcripts cannot be compared directly to Nelson's data. Only diary accounts of productions of a child being assessed can be compared directly to Nelson's normative data.

Miller (1981) describes a format for obtaining diary accounts from parents. Miller's description includes directions to parents regarding the format for what to record, what context information to specify,

TABLE 2.1
NELSON'S ONE-WORD UTTERANCE TYPES
(Adapted from Nelson, 1973)

1. **NOMINAL**
   a. **SPECIFIC NOMINAL:** Word used to refer to a particular instance of a person, an animal, or an object (e.g., *Mama, Bill).*
   b. **GENERAL NOMINAL:** Word used to refer to a general instance of an object, a substance (e.g., *snow),* an animal, a person (including pronouns), an abstraction (e.g., *birthday),* a letter, or a number.
2. **ACTION WORD:** Word used to refer to an action through a description (e.g., *bye-bye, go),* an expression of attention (e.g., *look, see),* or a demand for attention (e.g., *up, out).*
3. **MODIFIER:** Word used to refer to a property or quality of a thing or an event, including expressions of recurrence, disappearance, attribution, location, and possession (e.g., *there, little, pretty).*
4. **PERSONAL-SOCIAL WORD:** Word used to express an affective state (e.g., *want, feel)* or a social relationship (e.g., *please, thank you, yes, no).*
5. **FUNCTION WORD:** Word used to fulfill a grammatical function (e.g., *what, where, is, for).*

and when to collect data. Concerns regarding accuracy of recording will always exist, but diary accounts can be very helpful in obtaining samples from children at the one-word stage.

One-word utterances are provided for practice before attempting to categorize the utterances in the sample transcript. As before, cover the right side of the page, categorize each example utterance, and then check your categorizations with those provided in the shaded section. The explanations may help clear up discrepancies. Some of the same practice examples used for Bloom's categories are also used for Nelson's, along with a few new ones.

Practice Examples for Nelson's Analysis

(C picks up toy horse) horsie/	GENERAL NOMINAL This utterance refers to a real or pretend animal.
(C hears door opening) Dada/	SPECIFIC NOMINAL This utterance refers to a particular person.
(C reaches for cup on table) cup/	GENERAL NOMINAL Again, this is an example of a general instance of an object.
(C picks up car with no wheels) broke/	MODIFIER This utterance describes the quality of the car.
(C reaches up to M, who has entered bedroom) up/	ACTION WORD This utterance provides a description of an action or a request for an action. In either event, it is coded ACTION WORD.
(dog barking in background) Dee Dee/	SPECIFIC NOMINAL Since Dee Dee is the family pet, this is an example of a particular instance of an animal.

Continued on next page

Practice Examples—*Continued*

(C takes a drink from cup) juice/	GENERAL NOMINAL This utterance refers to a substance that is general in nature.
(M says, "Where is that shoe?"; C points to chest of drawers and says) there/	MODIFIER This utterance describes the location of something and therefore refers to a property of that object.
(C points to picture of a baby in picture book) baby/	GENERAL NOMINAL This child's utterance provides a general label for a person.
(C points to self in mirror) Baby/	SPECIFIC NOMINAL It is important to know that this other child refers to himself, but no one else, as "baby" to determine that this is an example of a particular baby.
(C picks up music box and looks at M) no/	MODIFIER This particular utterance refers to the previous prohibition of an object; therefore, it is coded MODIFIER. If the context had revealed that the child was responding to a question (e.g., "Do you want to go night-night?"), the utterance would have been coded PERSONAL-SOCIAL WORD.
(C carries cup to sink while holding it out for more juice) drink/	GENERAL NOMINAL or ACTION WORD Depending on the nonlinguistic context for the next utterance, this utterance could be referring to a general substance (GENERAL NOMINAL) or to an activity (ACTION WORD). The next utterance by the mom would determine how to code this utterance, presuming she accurately interprets the child's intent.

Continued on next page

Practice Examples—*Continued*

(C holds up larger half of cookie) big/	MODIFIER This utterance describes a property (attribute) of an object.
(M says, "What do you say?" as she holds out cookie; C says) please/	PERSONAL-SOCIAL WORD This utterance reflects a convention used in social relationships.
(clock on wall makes buzzing sound and C looks at M) what?/	FUNCTION WORD This utterance fulfills the grammatical function of requesting the label for something.

The translation of utterances previously coded using Bloom's One-Word Utterance Types into Nelson's categorization scheme is fairly straightforward. The category posing the greatest difficulty is probably FUNCTION WORD. In the practice examples, the types of words coded as such using Bloom's coding scheme were quite different from those using Nelson's coding scheme. Bloom's FUNCTION WORDS were more closely aligned with Nelson's MODIFIERS, although some of Bloom's FUNCTION WORDS overlap with Nelson's PERSONAL-SOCIAL WORDS category, and others overlap with Nelson's ACTION WORDS category. Keeping that in mind, return to the one-word utterances identified and categorized for Bridget's transcript using Bloom's One-Word Utterance Types. This time, code them on the *Nelson's One-Word Utterance Types* analysis sheet from Appendix A (page 230). Put each one-word utterance in the appropriate column. Again, if a particular word occurs more than once in the transcript, tally additional instances next to the original recording of the word. After you finish, check your analysis sheet against the completed sheet on page 46.

Calculating the Results Obtained Using Nelson's One-Word Utterance Types

Once again, the frequency of occurrence of each one-word utterance type needs to be calculated.

1. Count the number of words in each column, including additional instances of each word, and put the total for each utterance type in the blank provided.

2. Add all instances to obtain the total number of one-word utterances, and put that number in the blank provided. Double-check this number

Nelson's One-Word Utterance Types

Name of Child Bridget

Specific Nominals	General Nominals	Action Words	Modifiers	Personal-Social Words	Function Words
Bill	giraffe /	whoops	here /	no	huh ////
	bar	see	ick	yes	shh
	legs	gimme	more	yeah ~~////~~ ~~////~~ ~~////~~ /	else
	owie /		allgone	goodnight	
	stroller			allright	
	cow			welcome	
	plate			okay /	
	telephone /			hello	

1	Specific Nominals	=	1.9 %	of Total One-Word Utterances
11	General Nominals	=	21.2 %	of Total One-Word Utterances
3	Action Words	=	5.8 %	of Total One-Word Utterances
5	Modifiers	=	9.6 %	of Total One-Word Utterances
25	Personal-Social Words	=	48.1 %	of Total One-Word Utterances
7	Function Words	=	13.5 %	of Total One-Word Utterances

TOTAL NUMBER OF ONE-WORD UTTERANCES 52

TOTAL NUMBER OF UTTERANCES 100

52 **% OF TOTAL UTTERANCES**

by returning to the transcript and counting the one-word utterances.

3. Return to each one-word utterance type and compute the percentage of total one-word utterances accounted for by each type. This can be accomplished by dividing the number of instances of the type by the total number of one-word utterances, using the fourth decimal place to round up or down to the nearest thousandth, and multiplying that number by 100.

4. Determine the percentage of total utterances accounted for by one-word utterances. Do this by dividing the total number of one-word utterances by the total number of utterances.

Nelson specifies that yes/no responses (conversational devices) and routine responses (communication routines) should be included. Consequently, there will be no need to adjust for such one-word utterances and to recompute percentages as we did for Bloom's One-Word Utterance Types analysis.

In the sample transcript, there were 11 GENERAL NOMINALS, which when divided by 52 total one-word utterances, yielded .2115. After rounding this off and multiplying by 100 to convert to a percentage, this means that 21.2% of the one-word utterances were categorized as GENERAL NOMINALS. One instance of a SPECIFIC NOMINAL divided by 52 yielded 1.9%. There were 3 ACTION WORDS, which when divided by 52 total one-word utterances yielded 5.8% of the one-word utterances. Five MODIFIERS divided by 52 yielded 9.6%. Twenty-five PERSONAL-SOCIAL WORDS divided by 52 yielded 48.1%. There were 7 FUNCTION WORDS, which when divided by 52 yielded 13.5% of the one-word utterances. Again, the final step is to determine the percentage of total utterances accounted for by one-word utterances: Divide 52 by 100 total utterances, then multiply by 100 to obtain 52%.

Unlike Bloom's categorization scheme, normative data on the frequency of occurrence of Nelson's categories are available. Table 2.2 indicates the

TABLE 2.2

PERCENTAGE OF FIRST 50 WORDS ACCOUNTED FOR BY NELSON'S ONE-WORD UTTERANCE TYPES

(Computed from Nelson, 1973)

NOMINALS	
SPECIFIC	14%
GENERAL	51%
ACTION WORDS	14%
MODIFIERS	9%
PERSONAL-SOCIAL WORDS	9%
FUNCTION WORDS	4%

percentage of the child's first 50 words accounted for by each of Nelson's categories. Keep in mind that Nelson's data are based on types (i.e., the first 50 words used by each child). In other words, one word might have been used in 50% of all word attempts, yet in Nelson's data, it would contribute only 2% to a type category (i.e., 1 divided by 50 equals 2%). Data from Bridget's language sample are based on percentage tokens (i.e., how often a word type appeared in a sample of 100 utterances). Thus, it is not possible to compare these results directly to Nelson's data. To compare Nelson's normative data directly, a diary account of the first 50 words Bridget produced would be needed. (As previously mentioned, it may be productive to obtain diary accounts using Miller's, 1981, procedures.)

Interpretation of Results Obtained Using Nelson's One-Word Utterance Types

So how are our data to be interpreted? Cautiously. If one erroneously compared Bridget's frequency data directly to Nelson's, the distribution would be quite different. One might conclude that the sample is too limited and that diary analysis is needed. However, what the analysis does reveal is that approximately half of the utterances were longer than one word in length, warranting not a diary analysis but an analysis of the semantic content of the longer utterances.

In addition, the sample data can be considered in relation to a continuum similar to the nominal-pronominal continuum described by Bloom et al. (1975). Nelson refers to this continuum as a referential-expressive continuum. Children whose first 50-word lexicons consisted of a high percentage of NOMINALS were considered to be referential. In contrast, children whose first 50-word lexicons consisted of a high percentage of PERSONAL-SOCIAL WORDS and/or FUNCTION WORDS were considered to be expressive.

Again, these early preferences for types of words used may reflect different strategies for communicating and appear to persist beyond the one-word stage. From the sample transcript, it would be reasonable to conclude that Bridget is an expressive child since 61.6% of her one-word utterances were PERSONAL-SOCIAL WORDS and FUNCTION WORDS. Overall, the best judgment from the analysis performed would be to pursue additional analysis of more diverse aspects of the semantic content of Bridget's productions. As previously stated, Nelson's data were obtained from diary accounts and represent a first 50-word lexicon, but the data from Bridget's transcript represent a single, 100-utterance sampling; therefore, the comparison just made is like comparing apples to oranges. Nelson's categories are, however, helpful in analyzing children's first 50-word lexicons and can be useful in documenting changes in one-word utterance types over time. It is because a large number of Bridget's utterances in this 100-utterance sample are longer than one word that analysis of more diverse aspects of semantic content is warranted.

Because these one-word utterance analysis procedures do not result in scores or percentages unequivocally indicating the presence of delays, these procedures (and many of those that follow) must be considered as aspects of diagnostic therapy. That is, conclusions rarely can be drawn from a single sampling of the child's productions. Samplings obtained under a variety of conditions over time, as in the course of diagnostic therapy, yield the most valuable results. This is not said to postpone a decision, but rather to emphasize that these procedures must be considered as part of the ongoing process of hypothesis generation and testing through obtaining additional data.

Comparison of Bloom's and Nelson's One-Word Utterance Types

Bloom's and Nelson's One-Word Utterance Types are similar in some ways and different in others. Analysis of one-word utterances using Bloom's categories revealed the previously mentioned distinction between referential and relational aspects of semantic content. Bloom's SUBSTANTIVE WORDS and NAMING WORDS categories characterize a child's use of words to refer to specific and general instances of objects, people, and events, or to *referential* aspects of semantic content. Her FUNCTION WORDS capture the child's emerging ability to make note of the relations between objects and events. In fact, Bloom contends that a child's early two-word utterances grow out of greater explicitness in noting the relations between objects and events (e.g., "more" later becomes "more juice" or "more milk" as the context requires greater explicitness and as the child sees greater efficiency in the use of the longer utterance).

On the other hand, Nelson's categories appeared to reflect a quasi-grammatical function of individual words. Her categories more closely parallel a part-of-speech classification scheme beyond the individual meaning roles expressed and include routine forms. While more referential in nature than Bloom's scheme, Nelson's scheme may capture the transition toward two-word utterances as well as Bloom's scheme does. At the stage that a child's vocabulary includes approximately 50 words, Nelson contends that nouns, or NOMINALS, account for between 50% and 65% of the words. The child's vocabulary might be considered predominately referential. Later, words for describing actions increase (Leonard, 1976). These more verblike words parallel Nelson's ACTION WORDS. Then, words to describe attributes, locatives, and possessors of objects (Nelson's MODIFIERS) increase. It is about this time that two-word utterances emerge. Consequently, the transition to two-word utterances may be predicted more accurately with Nelson's categorization scheme. Overall, when using either Bloom's or Nelson's One-Word Utterance Types, if analysis of one-word utterances reveals approximately half or more of the utterances to be longer than one word in length, analysis of more diverse aspects of semantic content is warranted.

Analyzing Semantic Content of One-Word and Multiword Utterances

Two procedures will be used to analyze the semantic content of one-word and multiword utterances: (1) semantic roles analysis (Retherford et al., 1981) and (2) prevalent semantic relations analysis (Brown, 1973). Both of these procedures are based on semantic coding of all utterances within a production transcript. The first procedure employs a set of categories delineated by Retherford et al. (1981). Analysis of the frequency of occurrence of individual semantic roles within multiterm relations yields data interpretable as characteristic of children in Brown's Stage I or Stages II to III of linguistic development. The second procedure is based on the same semantic coding of one-word and multiword utterances but results in an analysis of frequently occurring multiterm combinations. Interpretation of data is accomplished by comparing data to reported frequencies of occurrence of Brown's

(1973) Prevalent Semantic Relations and expansions of his Prevalent Semantic Relations. Again, identification of combinations characteristic of children in Brown's Stage I versus Stage II or III is possible.

Semantic Roles

The 20 semantic roles described in Table 2.3 (beginning on page 51) are used to code utterances of children in Brown's (1973) Stages I–III. Included in this categorization scheme are semantic roles that correspond to those contained within Brown's (1973) eight Prevalent Semantic Relations, as well as categories that parallel those relations he specified as occurring with low frequency. In addition, many of the categories overlap with categories delineated by Greenfield and Smith (1976) for coding one-word utterances and by Bloom (1973) and Schlesinger (1971) for coding one-word and multiword utterances.

Detailed descriptions of nonlinguistic context, as described in Chapter 1, are crucial for determining the relational meanings expressed by children in the early stages of language acquisition. Many of the definitions that follow rely heavily on the nonlinguistic context for successful interpretation and coding.

The first step in semantically coding one-word and multiword utterances is to become familiar with the definitions and examples of the 20 semantic roles provided in Table 2.3. Not all utterances are "codable" using these 20 roles. The content of such utterances will be explained on pages 69–72 using the four broad categories of conversational devices, communication routines, complex utterances, and other.

For most utterances, the relationship between major semantic roles will be easily identifiable. In utterances longer than two semantic roles, some semantic roles are considered an expansion of one of the major roles in the semantic relation. Typically, these are expansions of the AGENT or OBJECT as described by Brown (1973). When a semantic role is an expansion of one of the major roles in the semantic relation, it may be helpful to set it off with parentheses to indicate this relationship. For example, the utterance "big boy jump" could be coded (ATTRIBUTE) AGENT-ACTION, indicating that AGENT-ACTION is the major semantic relation and ATTRIBUTE is an expansion of the AGENT in that relation. This is an optional coding scheme that some users may find helpful; however, it will not be used in *Guide*. Instead, all roles will be separated by hyphens.

The occurrence of grammatical morphemes—including number, tense, modal, and auxiliary aspects of the verb system; catenative verbs; articles; plural and possessive inflections; and prepositions—are coded within the semantic category of the major semantic role. For example, "is jumping" is coded as ACTION, as are "jumped," "can jump," and "jumps." An utterance containing "the doll" is coded ENTITY, unless it is in relationship with an ACTION, when it becomes the AGENT. In the utterance "Daddy's hat," "Daddy's" is coded POSSESSOR. The entire utterance "in the bed" is coded LOCATIVE. Thus, semantic roles may encompass more than one word and must be viewed as units of meaning not directly translated by single words. Examples of the use of this convention of using one semantic role for more than one word will be demonstrated in the practice examples beginning on page 55.

TABLE 2.3

20 Semantic Roles (Including Residual Grammatical Categories)

(Adapted from Retherford, Schwartz, and Chapman, 1981)

Individual Semantic Roles

The following 15 semantic roles are used for coding semantic content of mother (adult) and child speech. Additional content may be coded more appropriately using one of the 5 residual grammatical categories, which follow these definitions and mother-child examples. If those codes are not appropriate, it may be coded as conversational device or communication routine (described in Table 2.4, on pages 69–71), or as complex or other (see discussion on page 72).

ACTION — **A perceivable movement or activity engaged in by an agent (animate or inanimate).**

Mother: Can you *hit* the ball? (M addressing C)
Child: *Sit down.* (C plops standing bear into sitting position)

LOCATIVE — **The place where an object or action is located or toward which it moves.**

Mother: Put the flower *there.* (in response to C's query about where to set a flower)
Child: Milk *in cup.* (C pulling cup away from M)
Child: *Doctor.* (in response to M's question of where to take a broken doll)
Child: Jason *work.* (in response to M's question of where Jason is)

AGENT — **The performer (animate or inanimate) of an action. Body parts and vehicles, when used in conjunction with action verbs, are coded AGENT.**

Mother: *I'll* cover you. (C pretending to sleep)
Child: *You* do it. (C holding wind-up toy out to M)
Mother: That *car* went fast.

OBJECT — **A person or thing (marked by the use of a noun or pronoun) that receives the force of an action.**

Mother: Let's pick up your *blocks.* (M and C playing with blocks)
Child: Somebody ate *the cookies.* (M and C playing with toy tea set)

DEMONSTRATIVE — **The use of demonstrative pronouns or adjectives—*this, that, these, those*—and the words *there, here,* as well as *see* and *look* when stated for the purpose of pointing out a particular referent.**

Mother: *That* Santa Claus? (M pointing to picture)
Child: *There* are five girls. (in response to M's query about how many girls are in C's class)
Child: *See?* (C holding up picture)

Continued on next page

TABLE 2.3—Continued

RECURRENCE	**A request for or comment on an additional instance or amount, the resumption of an event, or the reappearance of a person or an object.** Mother: *Another* bead. (M referring to beads C is dropping in box) Child: I *more* hat mama. (C putting second hat through rungs of fence)
POSSESSOR	**A person or thing (marked by the use of a proper noun or pronoun) that an object is associated with or to which it belongs, at least temporarily.** Mother: Get *Baby's* puzzle. (M walking toward puzzle) Child: *My* fence fall down. (M and C playing with toy farm) Child: This is the leash *for the dog.* (C holding up leash) However, the use of the possessive pronoun *mine* in utterances like "That's mine" is unlike other possessive pronouns that don't really change in form when sentence position changes (e.g., *your yours). My* becomes *mine;* thus the child views *mine* as a different word, not a form of *my.*
QUANTIFIER	**A modifier that indicates amount or number of a person or an object. Prearticles and indefinite pronouns such as a *piece of, lots of, any, every,* and *each* are included.** Mother: There's sure *a lot of* mommies in that bus. (M referring to dolls C put in bus) Child: *Five* fingers. (C holding puppet's hand and tapping its fingers)
EXPERIENCER	**Someone or something that undergoes a given experience or mental state. This category often implies involuntary behavior on the part of the EXPERIENCER, in contrast to voluntary action performed by an AGENT. When used in conjunction with state verbs, body parts and vehicles, for example, are coded EXPERIENCER.** Mother: *I'd* like to see Ernie, please. (M referring to puppets C is playing with) Child: *She* feels better. (C hands baby doll to M) Child: My *tummy* hurts. (C puts head in M's lap)
RECIPIENT	**One who receives or is named as the recipient of an OBJECT (person or thing) from another.** Mother: Can you sing "Ring around the Rosie" *to her?* (M and C pretending Grandma is on toy telephone) Child: Give *me.* (C putting beads in container)
BENEFICIARY	**One who benefits from or is named as the beneficiary of a specified action.** Mother: I already dumped it out *for you.* (M dumps puzzle and hands board to C) Child: Do it *for me.* (C hands doll with untied shoe to M)

Continued on next page

TABLE 2.3—Continued

COMITATIVE	**One who accompanies or participates with an AGENT in carrying out a specified activity.** Mother: Come *with mommy.* (M standing, extending hand) Child: /ə/ go *mommy.* (M puts C in crib and starts to walk away; C stretches out arms, requesting to go with M)
CREATED OBJECT	**Something created by a specific activity; for example, a song by singing, a house by building, or a picture by drawing.** Mother: Can you draw *an apple?* (M and C playing with paper and crayons) Child: Write *tummy.* (same as above)
INSTRUMENT	**Something an AGENT uses to carry out or complete a specified action.** Mother: Don't write on the sofa *with that green pen.* (C writing on sofa) Child: Draw *with red.* (M helping C make a greeting card)
STATE	**A passive condition experienced by a person or object. This category often implies involuntary behavior on the part of the EXPERIENCER, in contrast to voluntary action performed by an AGENT.** Mother: You *want* some milk? (M and C playing with breakfast set) Child: She *feels* better. (M kisses baby doll and hands to C)

Residual Grammatical Categories

Five additional categories are used to code content for utterances not classified as conversational devices or communication routines when none of the preceding semantic roles fit. Although Retherford et al. felt it was more appropriate to label these "grammatical categories," throughout much of the discussion in text, these will be lumped into one broad category—the 20 semantic roles—and not referred to separately as the individual semantic roles and the residual grammatical categories.

ENTITY (one-term)	**Any labeling of a present person or object regardless of the occurrence or nature of action being performed on or by it. To be coded as a one-term ENTITY, the utterance must contain only one semantic role or grammatical category. The utterance may contain more than one word.** Mother: *The Piggy.* (M and C looking at picture book) Child: *Baby.* (M and C looking in fish tank) Child: *B.* (C pointing to letter on block)

Continued on next page

TABLE 2.3—Continued

ENTITY (multiterm)	**The use of an appropriate label for a person or an object in the absence of any action on it (with the exception of showing, pointing, touching, or grasping); or someone or something that causes or is the stimulus to the internal state specified by a state verb; or any object or person that is modified by a possessive form. ENTITY is used to code a possession if it meets any of the preceding criteria. The code multiterm ENTITY is used whenever an utterance contains more than the ENTITY category. There is no substantial difference between the two categories in terms of meaning. That is, each category describes a person or an object in the absence of action on it or by it. The only difference between the two categories is their occurrence in relation to other semantic roles and categories.** Mother: Dirty *diaper.* (M looking at diaper on floor) Child: That's *a baby.* (C pointing to doll)
NEGATION	**The expression of any of the following meanings with regard to someone or something, or an action or state: nonexistence, rejection, cessation, denial, disappearance.** Mother: I *didn't* have any eggs. (M and C playing with tea set) Child: *No* cookies. (C holding up empty bag)
ATTRIBUTE	**An adjectival description of the size, shape, or quality of an object or person; also, noun adjuncts that modify nouns for a similar purpose (e.g., gingerbread man). Excluded are the semantically coded categories of RECURRENCE and QUANTIFIER.** Mother: Where's the *little* ones? (M and C playing with toy animals) Child: *Big* animal. (same as above)
ADVERBIAL	**A modifier of an action indicating time, manner, duration, distance, or frequency. (Direction or place of action is coded separately as LOCATIVE; repetition is coded as RECURRENCE.)** Mother: You can dump it *the next time.* (M dumps puzzle, against C's protest) Child: *Now* go. (C pushing truck) **Also, a modifier indicating time, manner, quality, or intensity of a state, including predicate adjectives.** Mother: They've got their fancy socks on *today.* (M raises dolls' feet to show socks) Child: I'm *full.* (C puts fork down and looks at M)

A few other coding conventions need to be highlighted to assist in coding. As with aspects of the auxiliary system, separable, or two-part, action verbs are coded ACTION. Separable verbs that should be coded in this manner include *pick up, put away, get out, put down, put on, stand up, eat up, call up, put in, pull out, put back, turn over, sit down, fall down,* and *go back.* LOCATIVE is used with separable verbs only when the location is mentioned (e.g., "Mama sit down here"). State verbs typically coded STATE include *want, need, like, taste, wish, hurt, matter with, have on, smell, feel, fit,* and *hope. See* and *look* are coded STATE except when they occur at the beginning of an imperative pointing out something (e.g., "See the doggie?" meaning, "Look at the doggie"). A small number of verbs that might be considered part of the STATE verb category are coded ACTION because of their relation to specific intentional verbs also coded ACTION: *forget (remember), stay (leave), know (think).* When *being* is used as a main verb, as in "You are being silly," it is also coded ACTION; otherwise forms of *be* are coded STATE (e.g., "They are funny"). The main verb *have* is coded STATE when it implies possession, but coded ACTION in contexts in which an action verb synonym could be substituted (e.g., "What did you have for lunch?"). Changes in the state of an experiencer, where context makes the change clear, are coded ACTION; the EXPERIENCER or AGENT, in these cases, is coded AGENT. For example, "I go night-night," as the child moves to the bedroom, is coded AGENT-ACTION-LOCATIVE. In this coding scheme, an AGENT or EXPERIENCER can be either animate or inanimate. Thus, "the truck hit the wall" would be coded AGENT-ACTION-OBJECT and "the truck feels so sad" would be coded EXPERIENCER-STATE-QUANTIFIER-ADVERBIAL.

The examples in Table 2.3 can be helpful in determining the semantic role that individual words play in an utterance, but coding an entire utterance may be more difficult. Therefore, the following examples of fully coded utterances are provided for practice. Cover the right side of the page and code the utterances on the left. Check your codings with those provided in the shaded section. The explanations should help clear up any discrepancies.

Practice Examples for Semantic Roles

(C is pointing to picture in book) doggie jump/	AGENT-ACTION In this example, *doggie* is the AGENT of the ACTION, *jump.*
(C is pointing to picture in book) the doggie is jumping/	AGENT-ACTION The semantic code for this utterance is the same as that for the preceding utterance. Articles and auxiliary verbs are not assigned a separate semantic role; they are collapsed within the major role.

Continued on next page

Practice Examples—*Continued*

(M says, "What happened?" while pointing to picture) the boy kicked the ball/	AGENT-ACTION-OBJECT In this example, *the boy* is the AGENT of the ACTION, *kicked,* on the OBJECT, *the ball.* Again, articles are not assigned a separate semantic role.
(M says, "What happened?" while pointing to picture) that boy kick/	DEMONSTRATIVE-AGENT-ACTION The word *that* is a DEMONSTRATIVE indicating which AGENT, *boy,* is engaged in the ACTION, *kick.*
(C reaches for wind-up rabbit) more jump/	RECURRENCE-ACTION In this example, *more* reflects RECURRENCE of the ACTION, *jump.*

The preceding five examples demonstrated the semantic roles that typically combine with the semantic role ACTION. In addition, major semantic roles and expansions of major semantic roles were demonstrated. Remember that semantic roles may encompass more than one word and must be viewed as units of meaning, not directly translated by single words.

The following practice utterances will examine the use of another major semantic role, LOCATIVE. Cover the right side of the page and code the examples.

Practice Examples for Additional Semantic Roles

(C drops spoon in toy cup) spoon in/	MULTITERM ENTITY-LOCATIVE In this example, the *spoon* is a MULTITERM ENTITY situated *in* (LOCATIVE) something.

Continued on next page

Practice Examples—*Continued*	
(M asks, "Where is that spoon?") the spoon in the cup/	MULTITERM ENTITY-LOCATIVE The semantic coding for this utterance is the same as that for the preceding utterance for two reasons: First, as has already been demonstrated, articles are considered part of the major semantic relation. Second, *in the cup* and *in* both describe the location of the spoon and thus are coded LOCATIVE.
(M says, "Tell me about this," pointing to picture) the spoon is in the cup/	EXPERIENCER-STATE-LOCATIVE Although the overall meaning of this example is similar to that of the previous two examples, one striking difference is in the use of the copula, or main verb *is*. In this example, the semantic role STATE is used to reflect the use of the state verb. Consequently, the ENTITY becomes an EXPERIENCER. Ultimately, this utterance translates: *the spoon* (EXPERIENCER) *is* in the state (STATE) of being located *in the cup* (LOCATIVE).
(C points to spoons in a coffee pot) two spoon there/	QUANTIFIER-MULTITERM ENTITY-LOCATIVE *Two* (QUANTIFIER) indicates the number of the MULTITERM ENTITY, *spoon,* located (LOCATIVE) somewhere, *there.*
(C points to chair) sit down Mama/	ACTION-MULTITERM ENTITY In this example, the separable verb, *sit down,* is coded ACTION. Note that since the location is not mentioned, the semantic role LOCATIVE is not used.

The above examples demonstrate variations in the use of the semantic role LOCATIVE. They show how more than one word can be coded with only one semantic role. They also show how utterances with similar meaning are coded differently with the presence of an additional word(s). Now, for some practice with other semantic roles, cover the right side of the following page. Then code the practice utterances.

Practice Examples for Additional Semantic Roles

(C points to picture in book) big baby/	ATTRIBUTE-MULTITERM ENTITY Here, *big* is an ATTRIBUTE of the MULTITERM ENTITY, *baby.*
(C points to next picture) big baby cry/	ATTRIBUTE-AGENT-ACTION With the use of the ACTION verb, *cry,* the baby becomes an AGENT of that ACTION. In addition, now that a major semantic relation is expressed by the roles AGENT and ACTION in combination, the ATTRIBUTE, *big,* becomes an expansion of the major role, AGENT.
(C pulls baby doll away from M) my baby/	POSSESSOR-MULTITERM ENTITY In this example, the use of the pronoun, *my,* reflects the POSSESSOR of the MULTITERM ENTITY, *baby.*
(C holds up sock) this mine/	DEMONSTRATIVE-POSSESSOR In this example, *this* is a DEMONSTRATIVE and the pronoun, *mine,* is the POSSESSOR.
(C rocking baby doll in arms) my baby cry/	POSSESSOR-AGENT-ACTION With the use of the ACTION verb, *cry, baby* becomes an AGENT and the POSSESSOR role (for *my)* becomes an expansion of the AGENT.
(C pulls tiny doll out of bag) another baby/	RECURRENCE-MULTITERM ENTITY The word *another* reflects an additional instance (RECURRENCE) of the MULTITERM ENTITY, *baby.*
(C hears baby crying in another room) another baby cry/	RECURRENCE-AGENT-ACTION Once again, the use of the ACTION verb, *cry,* changes *baby* into an AGENT and the role of RECURRENCE (for *another)* becomes an expansion of the AGENT. RECURRENCE typically is a major role when forms of it occur in two-term utterances in conjunction with a MULTITERM ENTITY or an ACTION. When the role of RECURRENCE describes an AGENT or an OBJECT in a relationship with an ACTION, it is not considered a major role, but an expansion of a major role.

Continued on next page

Practice Examples—*Continued*

(M says, "What should we take to the other room?") that baby/	DEMONSTRATIVE-MULTITERM ENTITY The demonstrative pronoun, *that,* points out a particular instance of the MULTITERM ENTITY, *baby.*
that baby cry/	DEMONSTRATIVE-AGENT-ACTION Here the DEMONSTRATIVE role becomes an expansion of the AGENT with the addition of the ACTION, *cry.*

The examples clearly point out the different relationship between major semantic relations and expansions of major semantic roles. It is important to keep in mind the circumstances that account for a semantic role being used as a major role in one instance and not in another. Typically, if an ATTRIBUTE, POSSESSOR, RECURRENCE, or DEMONSTRATIVE is used alone with an ENTITY, then each role is considered a major role. If, however, an ACTION appears in the semantic relation, then the ATTRIBUTE, POSSESSOR, RECURRENCE, or DEMONSTRATIVE becomes an expansion of the AGENT or OBJECT. In addition, a demonstrative form used with an action verb will always be coded AGENT or OBJECT to reflect the major semantic role.

There are some exceptions to these circumstances; they will be demonstrated in the following practice examples. Cover the right side of the page and code the examples.

Practice Examples for Additional Semantic Roles

(C looks in bag where tiny dolls had been) no baby/	NEGATION-MULTITERM ENTITY The word *no* is an example of nonexistence, which is a type of NEGATION. Here, it refers to the nonexistence of the MULTITERM ENTITY, *baby.* *Continued on next page*

Practice Examples—*Continued*

(baby in other room stops crying) no cry/	NEGATION-ACTION Here the word *no* refers to the lack or cessation (a type of NEGATION) of the ACTION, *cry.*
(baby in other room stops crying) baby no cry/	AGENT-NEGATION-ACTION Now *baby* is the AGENT of the ACTION, *cry,* but the use of the word *no* relates to the entire semantic relation. Thus, NEGATION is considered a major semantic role.
(M is changing C's sister's diaper) baby wet/	MULTITERM ENTITY-ADVERBIAL The word *wet* describes the quality of the state the MULTITERM ENTITY, *baby,* is in. The state verb does not have to be present to use the ADVERBIAL role.
(C hands doll to M) baby is wet/	EXPERIENCER-STATE-ADVERBIAL However, as can be seen in this example, the STATE (in this case, *is)* can be present. And when the STATE (in this case, *wet)* is specified, the ENTITY (in this case, *baby)* becomes an EXPERIENCER.
(C runs into M's arms) run fast/	ACTION-ADVERBIAL The word *fast* describes the manner (ADVERBIAL) in which the ACTION, *run,* is performed.
(M and C looking at book) I can run fast/	AGENT-ACTION-ADVERBIAL Now there is an AGENT, *I,* performing an ACTION, *can run,* in a particular manner, *fast* (ADVERBIAL). Note that the modal verb *can* is coded ACTION along with the main verb *run.*

The above examples demonstrated the use of semantic roles and categories that can be used in combination with ENTITIES or AGENTS and ACTIONS. In addition, the ADVERBIAL category was demonstrated. Perhaps more importantly, the preceding practice items demonstrated the exceptions to the rule for determining when a semantic role is a major role or an expansion of a major role. In the preceding examples, each semantic role was considered to be a major role regardless of the presence of other semantic roles. NEGATION and ADVERBIAL are always considered to be major semantic roles, regardless of the presence of other semantic roles, as are AGENT, OBJECT, EXPERIENCER, ACTION, STATE, and LOCATIVE.

Some additional coding categories also are always considered to be major roles, but they occur less frequently than the preceding categories. The following practice examples are provided to demonstrate semantic coding using some of these less frequently occurring semantic roles.

Practice Examples for Additional Semantic Roles

(M and C are making cookies) I stir with spoon/	AGENT-ACTION-INSTRUMENT The pronoun, *I,* is the AGENT of the ACTION, *stir, with* the INSTRUMENT, *spoon.*
(C addressing M while the clinician, Anna, looks on) give Anna the cookies/	ACTION-RECIPIENT-OBJECT The ACTION, *give,* refers to an OBJECT, *the cookies,* presented to a RECIPIENT, *Anna.* RECIPIENTS receive the OBJECT of an ACTION.
(M and C are making clay cookies) the cookies are for Anna/	EXPERIENCER-STATE-BENEFICIARY *The cookies* (EXPERIENCER) are in the STATE of being, *are, for Anna* (BENEFICIARY).
(C looking in the toy bag) there is a doggie/	DEMONSTRATIVE-STATE-MULTITERM ENTITY The DEMONSTRATIVE pronoun, *there,* is in the STATE of being, *is.* Although used in conjunction with the STATE verb, *is, doggie* is the object of the sentence rather than the subject and so is coded MULTI-TERM ENTITY rather than EXPERIENCER.

Continued on next page

Practice Examples—*Continued*

(C crumbles clay on top of clay cookies) make chocolate-chip cookies/	ACTION-ATTRIBUTE-CREATED OBJECT The ACTION, *make,* creates the *chocolate-chip* (ATTRIBUTE) *cookies* (CREATED OBJECT).
(C turns to M, who is rocking baby) make cookies with me/	ACTION-CREATED OBJECT-COMITATIVE The ACTION, *make,* creates the *cookies* (CREATED OBJECT) and the AGENT (who is not specified) is to participate *with* the child, *me* (COMITATIVE).

The above examples contained some of the infrequently occurring semantic roles. Even though those roles may not occur in every transcript, it is important to be able to recognize them when they do occur. In addition, changes in frequency of use over time of the infrequently occurring roles may provide valuable diagnostic information. This will be discussed in more detail in the "Interpretation of Results Obtained Using Semantic Roles Analysis" section, beginning on page 82.

Question forms also can be coded using the preceding semantic roles. Questions are treated like any other utterance. However, before coding the question, turn it into a statement (e.g., "What is that?" becomes "That is what"). Then assign the semantic role that the *wh-* word in the question is querying using the following semantic roles based on context: ONE-TERM ENTITY, MULTITERM ENTITY, OBJECT, or CREATED OBJECT for *what;* ACTION for *what doing;* LOCATIVE for *where;* QUANTIFIER for *how many;* ADVERBIAL for *how, how long,* and *when;* ATTRIBUTE or DEMONSTRATIVE for *which;* AGENT, EXPERIENCER, ONE-TERM ENTITY, or MULTITERM ENTITY for *who;* and ATTRIBUTE for *what kind of.*

Keep in mind that presence of forms of the verb *to be* as a copula must be reflected in the semantic coding as STATE. Auxiliary verbs are coded with the main verb using the ACTION category. Remember to check (✓) the Question column on the coding sheet whenever a question is coded using one of the 20 semantic roles, because the coding of the utterances may not reflect the question form. The following practice examples demonstrate coding question forms using the semantic roles specified above.

Practice Examples for Additional Semantic Roles

(clock in room buzzes; C looks up from toy) what that?/	MULTITERM ENTITY-DEMONSTRATIVE In this example, the word *what* is querying the semantic role of MULTITERM ENTITY. It is querying the semantic role of a particular ENTITY, *that* (DEMONSTRATIVE).
(C digs in toy box) where's the ball?/	LOCATIVE-STATE-EXPERIENCER The *wh-* word, *where,* is asking where (LOCATIVE) the EXPERIENCER, *the ball, is* (STATE). The order of the words in the question was reversed to make the statement "the ball is where," so *the ball* is an EXPERIENCER of the STATE verb, *is.*
(C and M looking at book) what him doing?/	AGENT-ACTION Here the semantic role being queried is ACTION. The child is using the *what doing* form to query the ACTION of the AGENT, *him.*
(C and M looking at book) what are they doing?/	AGENT-ACTION Again, the semantic role being queried is ACTION. The child is using the *what doing* form to get a label for the ACTION *they* (AGENT) are engaged in. The auxiliary verb, *are,* is part of that ACTION.
(C hears talking in the hallway) who that?/	MULTITERM ENTITY-DEMONSTRATIVE In this case, it is impossible to know if *who* is an AGENT or a MULTITERM ENTITY, so the more neutral MULTITERM ENTITY is used. A particular ENTITY is being requested: *that* (DEMONSTRATIVE) entity.

Continued on next page

Practice Examples—*Continued*

(C, holding bag of marbles, looks at M) how many you got?/	QUANTIFIER-EXPERIENCER-STATE Here the semantic role being queried is QUANTIFIER. The child is using the QUANTIFIER to ask his mother, *you* (EXPERIENCER), *how many* marbles she's *got* (STATE). Because this is a question, the sentence form reverses to *you got how many* to explain why *you* is an EXPERIENCER.
(C putting pretend bandage on M's arm) how that feels?/	ADVERBIAL-DEMONSTRATIVE-STATE The child is asking for a description of the quality or intensity (ADVERBIAL) of his mother's STATE, *feels,* for a particular bandage, *that* (DEMONSTRATIVE) bandage.
(C and M are playing with model cars on a real track) what kinda car you driving?/	ATTRIBUTE-OBJECT-AGENT-ACTION The child is seeking a description, *what kinda* (ATTRIBUTE), of the *car* (OBJECT) that the mother, *you* (AGENT), is *driving* (ACTION).

Question forms are quite simple once it becomes possible to think in terms of semantic roles and not in words. Again, remember to indicate when a question form is coded by checking (✓) the Question column on the coding sheet. As can be seen in the preceding examples, once the question is semantically coded, it may be difficult to tell that the original utterance was in the form of a question. In the final analysis of semantic roles and relations, it is important to be able to differentiate question forms from other utterances because some comparison data exclude question forms from analysis.

The next step is to progress through Bridget's transcript and determine the appropriate combination of semantic roles for each utterance. Record the utterance number and semantic code for each utterance on the *Semantic Roles Coding Sheet* in Appendix A (page 231). If the utterance is a question, put a check (✓) in the Question column to differentiate it from nonquestions. For utterances that do not appear to be codable using the 20 semantic roles, record the utterance number but leave the Semantic Coding column blank. These utterances will be characterized using four additional categories—conversational devices, communication routines, complex utterances, and other—which will be discussed later in the chapter. Those utterances that can be semantically coded with what has been discussed so far are shown on the *Semantic Roles Coding Sheets* on pages 65–68.

Semantic Roles Coding Sheet

Name of Child Bridget

Utterance Number	Semantic Coding	Question
1		
2	Action	
3		
4		
5	State—Possessor—Multiterm Entity—Locative	
6	Demonstrative	✓
7	Multiterm Entity—Recurrence	✓
8	One-Term Entity	
9	One-Term Entity	
10		
11	Action—Adverbial	
12		
13	Locative	
14	Locative	
15	Agent—Action	
16	Multiterm Entity—Recurrence	✓
17	Action—Locative	
18	Demonstrative—State—Negation—Quantifier	
19	Multiterm Entity—Recurrence	✓
20	Experiencer—State—Negation—Locative	
21	Agent—Negation—Action	
22	Action—Object	
23	Locative—Experiencer—State	✓
24	Locative—Demonstrative—Experiencer—State	✓
25	One-Term Entity	

Semantic Roles Coding Sheet

Name of Child *Bridget*

Utterance Number	Semantic Coding	Question
26	Action	
27	One-Term Entity	
28	Action	
29		
30		
31	Agent—Action—Object—Adverbial	
32	Demonstrative—State—Multiterm Entity	
33	Experiencer—State—Adverbial	
34		
35	Locative—State—Recurrence—Experiencer	✓
36	Agent—Action—Object	
37		
38	Action	
39		
40	One-Term Entity	
41	One-Term Entity	
42		
43	Attribute—Adverbial	
44	Agent—Action	
45	Agent—Action—Object	
46	Action	
47		
48		
49		
50	One-Term Entity	

The form of this utterance doesn't indicate that the Recipient role is fully realized; "gimme" is often used as a one-word utterance.

Semantic Roles Coding Sheet

Name of Child Bridget

Utterance Number	Semantic Coding	Question
51		
52		
53		
54		
55		
56	Agent—Action—Object	
57		
58	One-Term Entity	
59		
60	Demonstrative—State—Multiterm Entity	✓
61	Demonstrative—State—Multiterm Entity	
62	Demonstrative—Possessor	
63		
64		
65	Demonstrative—State—Possessor	
66	Multiterm Entity—Recurrence	✓
67	Recurrence	
68		
69		
70	Recurrence	✓
71		
72	Action—Object	
73	Action—Object	
74		
75	State—Adverbial	

Semantic Roles Coding Sheet

Name of Child Bridget

Utterance Number	Semantic Coding	Question
76		
77		
78	Negation—Multiterm Entity	
79	Negation	
80		
81	Agent—Action—Object	
82		
83	Adverbial—Locative	
84	One-Term Entity	
85		
86	Action—Possessor	
87	Action—Object	
88	Action—Object	
89	Action—Object	
90	Action—Object	
91		
92		
93	One-Term Entity	
94	One-Term Entity	
95		
96	Object—Action	✓
97	Locative—Demonstrative	
98		
99	Multiterm Entity—Locative	
100	Agent—Action	

Typically, there are three reasons that an utterance is not semantically codable using the 20 semantic roles: (1) the utterance is a conversational device that may have been acquired as a whole unit rather than as individual roles; (2) the utterance is a communication routine that also may have been acquired as a whole unit, and semantically coding it may inflate the semantic complexity of the child's productions; or (3) the utterance is complex, requiring syntactic categories to reflect the complexity. (If the utterance is still not codable, it can be coded as OTHER [see page 72]). Identifying conversational devices and communication routines may be easier than semantically coding the utterances. The types of conversational devices and communication routines frequently occurring in child language transcripts are captured in Table 2.4.

TABLE 2.4

CONVERSATIONAL DEVICES AND COMMUNICATION ROUTINES

(Retherford, Schwartz, and Chapman, 1981)

Conversational Devices

The following categories are used to code utterances and parts of utterances that are not codable using the 20 semantic roles. These categories reflect pragmatic conventions governing conversation, rather than semantic intentions.

ATTENTION — **Use of an individual's name to gain attention.**

Mother: Abigail! (M calling C, who is climbing on sofa)
Child: Mama! (M dressing C while talking to another adult)

YES/NO RESPONSE — **Use of affirmative (or negative) terms or tags to assert that a previous utterance or behavior is correct (or incorrect) to indicate compliance with a request (or refusal of a request) made in a previous utterance.**

Mother: Okay. (following C's request for assistance in putting puzzle together)
Child: No. (in response to M's query if C wants a cracker)

POSITIVE EVALUATION — **Use of positive terms to evaluate an utterance or behavior of the other speaker.**

Mother: Right. (C manipulating puzzle, fits piece in correctly)
Child: Very good. (M places block on top of stack and C responds)

INTERJECTION — **Use of words like *um, oh,* etc. to hold a speaking turn and/or as a searching strategy for conversational contribution.**

Mother: Oh. (following C's affirmative response to M's question of activity)
Child: Um. (C looking at M, who has just queried C about doll's name)

Continued on next page

TABLE 2.4—Continued

POLITE FORM	**Use of terms like *please, thank you,* etc. in absence of other semantic content (e.g., "Please help me" = ADVERBIAL-ACTION-OBJECT).** Mother: Thank you. (C pouring M an imaginary cup of coffee) Child: Pretty please. (M offers imaginary plate of cookies to C)
REPETITION REQUEST	**Use of terms like *what, huh,* etc. to request repetition of another speaker's utterance.** Mother: What? (C describing toy people's activities) Child: Hmm? (following M's question)
ACCOMPANIMENT	**Use of *there* (in the absence of pointing or directional/locational intent), *there you go,* or *here* to accompany an action by one speaker.** Mother: There you go. (C attempting to wrap herself in blanket, finally succeeds) Child: There. (C giving doll to M)

Communication Routines

The following categories are used to code utterances not codable using semantic roles and residual grammatical categories. These categories are used to characterize utterances expressing typically occurring routinized forms.

ANIMAL	**Utterances used to engage in routines about animal sounds and behaviors. Also use of animal sounds with no referent present. When animal sounds are used to label an animal, the residual grammatical category of ENTITY is used.** Mother: The cow says, "Moo." (M and C playing with toy farm) Child: Moo. (same as above; C previously labeled toy cow appropriately) Child: Moo. (no referent present; C pretending to be cow)
STORY/SONG/POEM	**Utterances that consist of all or part of story text, songs, nursery rhymes, or poems.** Mother: Where is Thumbkin? Where is Thumbkin? (M and C singing along with finger play) Child: Here I am. (same as above)

Continued on next page

TABLE 2.4—Continued

COUNTING/ ALPHABET	**Utterances that consist of rote counting or recitation of all or part of alphabet. When context indicates counting of referents or labeling/identifying letters, the residual grammatical category ENTITY is used.** Mother: A, B, C, D. (M singing, no referent present) Child: One, two, three. (no referent present)
GREETING	**Use of greeting and leave-taking forms reflecting adherence to routines, rather than semantic intent.** Mother: How are you? (M and C talking on toy telephone) Child: Bye-bye. (C waving to M)
SAY X	**Requests for the other speaker to repeat specific information. Be sure *say* isn't being used to mean "Pretend..." or "Suppose...."** Mother: Say I'm sorry, Eugene. (following scolding C for pulling cat's tail) Child: Say good morning. (C picking up doll from baby bed)
SOUNDS ACCOMPANYING	**Noises and/or sounds used to replicate noises/sounds of vehicles or objects.** Mother: Whoops! (toy monkey falls off trapeze) Child: Vroom. (C moving toy car back and forth on floor)
NAME	**Routine forms requesting or specifying the name of something or someone.** Mother: What's your name? (M speaking to doll C is holding) Child: My name is Kiki. (C talking on telephone)

Identifying utterances appropriately labeled as COMPLEX may be more difficult than identifying conversational devices and communication routines. The decision to identify an utterance as COMPLEX when completing the semantic analysis is based on the presence of parallel semantic roles or categories within the same utterance. That is, it is not possible to have two AGENTS, ACTIONS, ENTITIES, or OBJECTS within the same utterance. If an utterance contains more than one of any type of major semantic role, the utterance is probably COMPLEX. (However, it could just be coded incorrectly.) This judgment of semantic complexity may be different than the judgment made when completing the syntactic analysis. In other words, an utterance could be classified as COMPLEX for the semantic analysis, but the same utterance would not necessarily be assigned a stage for complex sentence development when completing the syntactic analysis. The following examples of child utterances labeled COMPLEX may be helpful.

doggie barked and barked/	COMPLEX
doggie bite and I cried/	COMPLEX
I want the one what's big/	COMPLEX
my shoes and pants are dirty/	COMPLEX
'cuz he jumped/	COMPLEX

When complex utterances occur in a transcript, COMPLEX is written on the coding line of the *Semantic Roles Coding Sheet.* This permits efficient identification of the number of semantically complex utterances occurring in a transcript. Identification and analysis of semantically complex utterances will be completed in the syntactic analysis of a transcript (i.e., Chapter 3) using slightly different criteria.

Finally, utterances with ambiguous semantic content or that do not fit appropriately in any other category, should be coded OTHER. OTHER should be reserved for peculiar utterances and used rarely, as in this example:

Mother: Okay. (M and C putting paintbrushes into jars and mixing paint)

Mother: Let's pick one color to paint with.

Child: Yeah.

Mother: Hmm. (M looking at each jar of paint)

Child: What?

Mother: Which color should I choose?

In this example, the child's production of "what" is not to get the type of semantic information typically obtained from a *what* question. Neither is it a request for a repetition of a previous utterance. It appears to be functioning as a request for clarification of Mom's "hmm" and therefore is more pragmatic in its function.

One more convention in coding utterances needs to be discussed. This is the convention used for utterances that have semantic content and are codable using the 20 semantic roles, but that also contain a conversational device or a conjunction. For example, in the utterance "Mommy, big truck," the child is requesting the mother's attention and commenting on a big truck. The procedure used in this case is to indicate that a conversational device was used by recording CD in parentheses prior to the semantic code for the comment. The coding for this utterance would be (CD) ATTRIBUTE-MULTITERM ENTITY. The CD category is Attention.

Communication routines rarely occur within the context of a semantically codable utterance, because the communication routine is rarely tagged onto an utterance like a conversational device is. Conversational routines tend to be embedded into an utterance and then typically end up being coded as a CREATED OBJECT. For example, "One, two, three" said without counting some objects would be a counting routine. But if the child said, "I can count: one, two, three," the utterance would be coded AGENT-ACTION-CREATED OBJECT.

Now, from the coding sheet used earlier, identify the utterances that were left blank and the parts of utterances you didn't know how to code. Determine whether each is a conversational device, a communication routine, or a complex utterance, or other, and mark it appropriately. Then check your answers with those in the completed coding sheets on pages 73–76. (Note that for learning purposes, each CD or CR coded is followed in parentheses by the type of CD or CR.) In addition, the CD-ROM has practice worksheets for semantic roles analysis.

Calculating the Results Obtained Using Semantic Roles Analysis

Following the semantic coding of utterances in the sample transcript, tally the frequency of occurrence for each role or category. Using the *Total Use of 20 Semantic Roles* analysis sheet from Appendix A (page 232),

Semantic Roles Coding Sheet

Name of Child Bridget

Utterance Number	Semantic Coding	Question
1	CR (Sounds Accompanying)	
2	Action	
3	CD (Yes/No Response)	
4	CD (Yes/No Response)	
5	State—Possessor—Multiterm Entity—Locative	
6	Demonstrative	✓
7	Multiterm Entity—Recurrence	✓
8	One-Term Entity	
9	One-Term Entity	
10	CD (Accompaniment)	
11	Action—Adverbial	
12	CD (Yes/No Response)	
13	Locative	
14	Locative	
15	(CD Attention) Agent—Action	
16	Multiterm Entity—Recurrence	✓
17	Action—Locative	
18	Demonstrative—State—Negation—Quantifier	
19	Multiterm Entity—Recurrence	✓
20	Experiencer—State—Negation—Locative	
21	Agent—Negation—Action	
22	Action—Object	
23	Locative—Experiencer—State	✓
24	Locative—Demonstrative—Experiencer—State	✓
25	One-Term Entity	

Semantic Roles Coding Sheet

Name of Child *Bridget*

Utterance Number	Semantic Coding	Question
26	Action	
27	One-Term Entity	
28	Action	
29	CD (Repetition Request)	
30	CD (Yes/No Response)	
31	Agent—Action—Object—Adverbial	
32	Demonstrative—State—Multiterm Entity	
33	(CD Yes/No Response) Experiencer—State—Adverbial	
34	CD (Yes/No Response)	
35	Locative—State—Recurrence—Experiencer	✓
36	Agent—Action—Object	
37	CD (Yes/No Response)	
38	Action	
39	CR (Sounds Accompanying)	
40	One-Term Entity	
41	One-Term Entity	
42	CD (Yes/No Response)	
43	Attribute—Adverbial	
44	Agent—Action	
45	Agent—Action—Object	
46	Action (CD Sounds Accompanying)	
47	CD (Yes/No Response)	
48	CD (Yes/No Response)	
49	CD (Yes/No Response)	
50	One-Term Entity	

Semantic Roles Coding Sheet

Name of Child Bridget

Utterance Number	Semantic Coding	Question
51	CD (Yes/No Response)	
52	COMPLEX	
53	CR (Sounds Accompanying)	
54	CR (Greeting)	
55	CD (Yes/No Response)	
56	Agent–Action–Object	
57	CD (Yes/No Response)	
58	One-Term Entity	
59	CD (Repetition Request)	
60	Demonstrative–State–Multiterm Entity	✓
61	Demonstrative–State–Multiterm Entity	
62	Demonstrative–Possessor	
63	CD (Polite Form)	
64	CD(Yes/No Response)	
65	Demonstrative–State–Possessor	
66	Multiterm Entity–Recurrence	✓
67	Recurrence	
68	CD(Repetition Request)	
69	CD (Yes/No Response)	
70	Recurrence	✓
71	CD (Attention)	
72	Action–Object (CD Attention)	
73	Action–Object (CD Attention)	
74	CD (Repetition Request)	
75	State–Adverbial	

Semantic Roles Coding Sheet

Name of Child Bridget

Utterance Number	Semantic Coding	Question
76	CD (Yes/No Response)	
77	CD (Yes/No Response)	
78	Negation—Multiterm Entity	
79	Negation	
80	CD (Yes/No Response)	
81	Agent—Action—Object	
82	CD (Yes/No Response)	
83	Adverbial—Locative	
84	One-Term Entity	
85	CD (Yes/No Response)	
86	Action—Possessor	
87	Action—Object	
88	Action—Object	
89	Action—Object (CD Attention)	
90	Action—Object (CD Attention)	
91	CD (Repetition Request)	
92	CD (Yes/No Response)	
93	One-Term Entity	
94	One-Term Entity	
95	CD (Yes/No Response)	
96	Object—Action	✓
97	Locative—Demonstrative	
98	CR (Greeting)	
99	Multiterm Entity—Locative	
100	Agent—Action	

progress utterance by utterance through the coding sheets, tallying each semantic role in each utterance. For example, for the coded utterance AGENT-ACTION-OBJECT, mark one tally in the AGENT row, one tally in the ACTION row, and one tally in the OBJECT row. When all roles on the coding sheet have been tallied, count the number of instances of each semantic role and record that number in the # column of that row. For example, in Bridget's transcript, there were 25 instances of the ACTION role, 11 LOCATIVES, 11 ONE-TERM ENTITY roles, 11 MULTITERM ENTITY roles, and so on.

The next step is to compute the percentage of semantic roles accounted for by each role. To do this, add all totals in the # column and put this sum in the Total box at the bottom right corner of the analysis sheet. In the sample transcript, there was a total of 129 individual roles used. Divide each individual role total by 129 to obtain the percentage of total roles accounted for by each role. For ACTION, 25 divided by 129 yields .1937. Rounding this off to .194 and multiplying by 100 (to convert to a percentage) reveals that 19.4% of all semantic roles were coded ACTION. Progress through the analysis sheet, dividing each total by the overall total and multiplying by 100 to get the percentage for each semantic role. These percentages can be added together to double-check computations. If the total is more than .3% above or below 100%, a miscalculation may have occurred. A completed analysis sheet is provided on page 78 to check against your computations.

Before results of the percentage of total utterances accounted for by each semantic role can be interpreted, the percentage of total utterances that were semantically codable needs to be computed. Using the *Meaning Relationships in One-Word and Multiword Utterances* analysis grid in Appendix A (pages 233–234), progress through the coding sheets and put a check on the grid indicating whether each coded utterance is one of the following: one term, two terms, three terms, four terms or longer, a conversational device, a communication routine, a complex utterance, or other. If a semantically coded utterance also contains a conversational device (CD) or a communication routine (CR), the CD or CR column is not checked. Under the 100th utterance row, total each column from the entire grid. For example, in the first 25 utterances, there were 7 one-term utterances; in the second 25 utterances, 8 one-term utterances; in the third 25 utterances, 3 one-term utterances; and in the fourth 25 utterances, 4 one-term utterances. This totals 22 one-term utterances. Put 22 below the 100th row in the One-Term column. Tallies can be checked with those in the sample provided on page 80.

Totaling the one-term, two-term, three-term, and four-term-plus tallies in the sample transcript reveals that 64 utterances were coded semantically. Put this number in the appropriate blank of the *Semantic Roles Summary Form* from Appendix A (page 235). Now divide this number by 100 total utterances. The result should be .64, and after multiplying by 100 to convert to a percentage, note that 64.0% of Bridget's utterances in this transcript were semantically codable. Now transfer the percentage obtained for each semantic role to the *Semantic Roles Summary Form.* Finally, return to the meaning relationships grid and tally the number of utterances that were conversational devices, communication routines, complex utterances, and other. In Bridget's transcript, there were 30 utterances coded as conversational devices, indicating that 30.0% of her utterances were types of conversational devices. There were 5 utterances coded as communication routines, indicating that 5.0% of her utterances were types of communication routines. There was one instance of a complex utterance, indicating that 1.0% of her utterances were coded as COMPLEX. There were no instances of utterances coded as OTHER. A completed *Semantic Roles Summary Form* is provided on page 81.

Total Use of 20 Semantic Roles

Name of Child Bridget

ROLES	TALLY	#	%	ROLES	TALLY	#	%
Action	𝍸 𝍸 𝍸 𝍸 𝍸	25	19.4	Beneficiary		0	—
Locative	𝍸 𝍸 /	11	8.5	Comitative		0	—
Agent	𝍸 ////	9	7.0	Created Object		0	—
Object	𝍸 𝍸 //	12	9.3	Instrument		0	—
Demonstrative	𝍸 ////	9	7.0	State	𝍸 𝍸 //	12	9.3
Recurrence	𝍸 //	7	5.4	Entity (one-term)	𝍸 𝍸 /	11	8.5
Possessor	////	4	3.1	Entity (multiterm)	𝍸 𝍸 /	11	8.5
Quantifier	/	1	0.8	Negation	𝍸	5	3.9
Experiencer	𝍸	5	3.9	Attribute	/	1	0.8
Recipient		0	—	Adverbial	𝍸 /	6	4.7
				TOTAL		129	100.1

Meaning Relationships in One-Word and Multiword Utterances

Name of Child Bridget

Utterance Number	One-Term	Two-Term	Three-Term	Four-Term Plus	Conversational Device	Communication Routine	Complex	Other
1						✓		
2	✓							
3					✓			
4					✓			
5				✓				
6	✓							
7		✓						
8	✓							
9	✓							
10					✓			
11		✓						
12					✓			
13	✓							
14	✓							
15		✓						
16		✓						
17		✓						
18				✓				
19		✓						
20				✓				
21			✓					
22		✓						
23			✓					
24				✓				
25	✓							

Utterance Number	One-Term	Two-Term	Three-Term	Four-Term Plus	Conversational Device	Communication Routine	Complex	Other
26	✓							
27	✓							
28	✓							
29					✓			
30					✓			
31				✓				
32			✓					
33			✓					
34					✓			
35				✓				
36			✓					
37					✓			
38	✓							
39						✓		
40	✓							
41	✓							
42					✓			
43		✓						
44		✓						
45			✓					
46	✓							
47					✓			
48					✓			
49					✓			
50	✓							

Meaning Relationships in One-Word and Multiword Utterances

Name of Child *Bridget*

Utterance Number	One-Term	Two-Term	Three-Term	Four-Term Plus	Conversational Device	Communication Routine	Complex	Other
51					✓			
52							✓	
53						✓		
54						✓		
55					✓			
56			✓					
57					✓			
58	✓							
59					✓			
60			✓					
61			✓					
62		✓						
63					✓			
64					✓			
65			✓					
66		✓						
67	✓							
68					✓			
69					✓			
70	✓							
71					✓			
72		✓						
73		✓						
74					✓			
75		✓						

Utterance Number	One-Term	Two-Term	Three-Term	Four-Term Plus	Conversational Device	Communication Routine	Complex	Other
76					✓			
77					✓			
78		✓						
79	✓							
80					✓			
81			✓					
82					✓			
83		✓						
84	✓							
85					✓			
86		✓						
87		✓						
88		✓						
89		✓						
90		✓						
91					✓			
92					✓			
93	✓							
94	✓							
95					✓			
96		✓						
97		✓						
98						✓		
99		✓						
100		✓						
Total	22	25	11	6	30	5	1	0

Semantic Roles Summary Form

Name of Child Bridget

Total Number of Semantically Coded Utterances 64 = 64.0 % of Total Utterances

Percentage of Total Semantic Roles Accounted For by each Semantic Role:

ACTION	=	19.4	%
LOCATIVE	=	8.5	%
AGENT	=	7.0	%
OBJECT	=	9.3	%
DEMONSTRATIVE	=	7.0	%
RECURRENCE	=	5.4	%
POSSESSOR	=	3.1	%
QUANTIFIER	=	0.8	%
EXPERIENCER	=	3.9	%
RECIPIENT	=	—	%
BENEFICIARY	=	—	%
COMITATIVE	=	—	%
CREATED OBJECT	=	—	%
INSTRUMENT	=	—	%
STATE	=	9.3	%
ENTITY (one-term)	=	8.5	%
ENTITY (multiterm)	=	8.5	%
NEGATION	=	3.9	%
ATTRIBUTE	=	0.8	%
ADVERBIAL	=	4.7	%

Total Number of Utterances Coded **Conversational Device**	30	=	30.0	% of Total Utterances
Total Number of Utterances Coded **Communication Routine**	5	=	5.0	% of Total Utterances
Total Number of Utterances Coded **Complex**	1	=	1.0	% of Total Utterances
Total Number of Utterances Coded **Other**	0	=	0	% of Total Utterances

Interpretation of Results Obtained Using Semantic Roles Analysis

Begin by examining the percentage of total utterances that could be coded using combinations of semantic roles and grammatical categories. Brown (1973) found that 70% of children's utterances in Stages I–III of linguistic development could be semantically coded using a smaller set of semantic roles than Retherford et al.'s (1981). Based on Retherford, Schwartz, and Chapman's (1977) data, Retherford et al. (1981) found that between 64% and 85% of Stage I children's utterances were codable using the combination of semantic roles and grammatical categories described on pages 51–54. In addition, between 47% and 85% of utterances by children in Stages II and III were semantically codable. The sample analysis revealed 64% of Bridget's utterances were semantically codable. This percentage indicates that this child's productions encode meaning relations with frequencies typical of children in Brown's Stages I–III of linguistic development.

Next, the frequency of occurrence of individual semantic roles and residual grammatical categories should be examined. Summaries of Brown's data do not include frequency of occurrence of individual roles. Summaries of the Retherford et al. (1977) data were collected as Time 1 and Time 2. These data have been reorganized to provide a basis of comparison for results obtained from the sample transcript. Table 2.5 summarizes the frequency of occurrence of each semantic role as a percentage of total roles used by the children in the Retherford et al. (1977) study. Data are presented in Table 2.5 by stage of linguistic production: Stage I = Time 1 and Stages II and III = Time 2.

As can be seen in Table 2.5, the most striking change during the early stages of linguistic production is the decrease in the frequency of occurrence of the ONE-TERM ENTITY role. This, however, might be predicted on the basis of an increase in utterance length alone. In addition, substantial increases in the roles of AGENT, OBJECT, DEMONSTRATIVE, RECURRENCE, POSSESSOR, ATTRIBUTE, and ADVERBIAL were noted as the children advanced to higher stages of linguistic production. Comparing results of the sample transcript to these data indicates that Bridget's use of ONE-TERM ENTITY is more typical of Stages II and III than of Stage I. In addition, Bridget's use of the roles AGENT, OBJECT, DEMONSTRATIVE, RECURRENCE, POSSESSOR, NEGATION, and ADVERBIAL is more typical of children in Stages II and III. Overall, it can be said that this child's use of individual semantic roles in combination is typical of a child at least in Brown's Stages II and III. Because the sample size is so small for the Retherford et al. (1977) data (*N* = 3 for Stages II and III), the reader is cautioned not to overinterpret the normative data. The important change to look for in the child's use of individual semantic roles from Stage I to Stages II and III is the shift from between 30% and 7% use of ONE-TERM ENTITY to between 11 and 14% use for MULTITERM ENTITY. Obviously, this decrease in use of ONE-TERM ENTITY will be accompanied by increases in use of other roles, most often in the roles of AGENT, OBJECT, POSSESSOR, and ADVERBIAL.

Brown's Prevalent Semantic Relations

To identify Brown's (1973) Prevalent Semantic Relations, analysis will utilize data and theory summarized by Brown (1973) in his classic volume, *A First Language*. Brown contends that the eight Two-Term Prevalent Semantic Relations that he found to be frequently occurring in child language laid the foundation for longer utterances. The child, according to Brown, accomplished increases in utterance length by elaborating

TABLE 2.5
MEAN FREQUENCY OF OCCURRENCE OF 20 SEMANTIC ROLES OF CHILDREN IN BROWN'S STAGE I AND STAGES II AND III
(Computed from Retherford, Schwartz, and Chapman, 1977)

Role	Time 1 Stage I (*N* = 9)	Time 2 Stages II and III (*N* = 3)
ACTION	13.5	15.0
LOCATIVE	9.5	9.1
AGENT	3.8	6.9
OBJECT	2.0	5.7
DEMONSTRATIVE	2.9	5.6
RECURRENCE	1.8	2.8
POSSESSOR	1.1	3.9
QUANTIFIER	1.9	1.7
EXPERIENCER	2.4	1.5
RECIPIENT	0.2	0.3
BENEFICIARY	0.1	0.2
COMITATIVE	0.7	0.1
CREATED OBJECT	0.1	0.0
INSTRUMENT	0.0	0.0
STATE	1.6	1.8
ENTITY (One-Term)	30.3	6.8
ENTITY (Multiterm)	10.5	14.1
NEGATION	8.4	5.3
ATTRIBUTE	3.0	4.1
ADVERBIAL	1.4	2.8

on one of the roles in some of the basic two-term semantic relations. The role that the child was likely to expand was found to be predictable. Brown's eight Two-Term Prevalent Semantic Relations are listed on the *Brown's Prevalent Semantic Relations* analysis sheet (see example on page 85). A blank copy can be found in Appendix A (page 224). The roles that are underlined in five of the eight relations are the roles that the child is most likely to expand. Across the top right are the three types of expansions most likely to occur in children's productions during Stages I–III. These include DEMONSTRATIVE, which Brown called nomination; ATTRIBUTIVE, which Brown considered to also include RECURRENCE; and POSSESSIVE. The boxes that are crossed out represent impossible expansions. For example, in the two-term relation, DEMONSTRATIVE-ENTITY, ENTITY is underlined, indicating that ENTITY is the role likely to be expanded. But moving across the row, the DEMONSTRATIVE box is crossed out. This is because DEMONSTRATIVE-DEMONSTRATIVE-ENTITY (e.g., "that this ball") is not a likely combination. Keep in mind that Brown's POSSESSOR-POSSESSION would be coded POSSESSOR-ENTITY using Retherford et al.'s 20 semantic roles. In addition to Brown's eight Two-Term Prevalent Semantic Relations and the expansions of those relations, Brown suggests that some three-term relations do not represent expansions of his two-term relations. These three-term relations are listed at the bottom of *Brown's Prevalent Semantic Relations* analysis sheet.

To complete *Brown's Prevalent Semantic Relations* analysis sheet, progress through your *Semantic Roles Coding Sheets*, identifying coded utterances that coincide with Brown's Two-Term Prevalent Semantic Relations, expansions of Two-Term Prevalent Semantic Relations, and Three-Term Prevalent Semantic Relations. Record the utterance number in the appropriate box for each type of semantic relation. Carefully consider each coded utterance because variations in word order are possible.

Note that the first utterance on the coding sheets coinciding with one of Brown's multiterm combinations is utterance #7. This is an example of ATTRIBUTE-ENTITY even though it is listed as MULTITERM ENTITY-RECURRENCE. (Recall that Brown's ATTRIBUTE category includes the RECURRENCE category.) In addition, keep in mind that word order is irrelevant when identifying semantic relations. So, put a 7 in the Utterance Number column next to ATTRIBUTE-ENTITY. Moving on through the coding sheets, note that the next utterance that coincides with one of Brown's combinations is utterance #15. This is an example of AGENT-ACTION, so put a 15 in the Utterance Number column next to AGENT-ACTION. Continue through the coding sheets, looking for examples of Brown's Two-Term Prevalent Semantic Relations, expansions of Two-Term Prevalent Semantic Relations, and Three-Term Prevalent Semantic Relations. Once all utterances have been examined and identified as either being or not being examples of Brown's multiterm combinations, check your results with those provided on page 85.

Calculating the Results Obtained Using Brown's Prevalent Semantic Relations

After identifying each example of Brown's multiterm combinations, complete a *Brown's Prevalent Semantic Relations Summary Form.* A blank copy is provided in Appendix A (page 225), and a completed form is provided on page 86. Begin by counting each type of two-term and three-term relations and adding the numbers to the summary form. Then, add all instances of each type of two-term relation and put that total in the blank provided. In the sample transcript, there were 16 instances of Brown's Two-Term Prevalent Semantic Relations.

Next, add the totals for two-term, three-term, and four-term-plus utterances from the meaning relationships grid to get the total number of multiterm utterances. In the sample transcript, there were 42 multiterm utterances. Then add the one-term utterances to that number to get the total number of semantically coded utterances: 64. Add these numbers to the form. Divide the total number of instances of two-term relations by the total number of multiterm utterances and multiply by 100 to get the percentage of multiterm utterances accounted for by Brown's Two-Term Prevalent Semantic Relations. In the sample transcript, 16 instances of Brown's two-term relations divided by 42 multiterm utterances yielded .3809, which after multiplying by 100 indicated that 38.1% of Bridget's multiterm utterances were examples of Brown's Two-Term Prevalent Semantic Relations.

Brown's Prevalent Semantic Relations

Name of Child Bridget

		Utterance Number	Demonstrative	Attributive	Possessive
Two-Term	Agent-Action	15, 44, 100			
	Action-Object	22, 72, 73, 87, 88, 89, 90			
	Agent-Object		X	X	X
	Demonstrative-Entity		X		
	Entity-Locative	99			
	Action-Locative	17	X	X	X
	(-Entity)* Possessor-Possession				X
	(Recurrence-)* Attribute-Entity	7, 16, 19, 66	X	X	X
Three-Term	Agent-Action-Object	36, 45, 56, 81			
	Agent-Action-Locative				
	Action-Object-Locative				

*Per Retherford et al. (1981)

Brown's Prevalent Semantic Relations Summary Form Name of Child Bridget

TWO-TERM PREVALENT SEMANTIC RELATIONS		EXPANSIONS			
3	Agent-Action	0 Dem	0 Att	0 Poss	= 0
7	Action-Object	0 Dem	0 Att	0 Poss	= 0
0	Agent-Object				
0	Demonstrative-Entity		0 Att	0 Poss	= 0
1	Entity-Locative	0 Dem	0 Att	0 Poss	= 0
1	Action-Locative				
0	Possessor-Possession	0 Dem	0 Att		= 0
4	Attribute-Entity				0 **Total Expansions**
16	**Total Two-Term Utterances**				

THREE-TERM PREVALENT SEMANTIC RELATIONS

4	Agent-Action-Object
0	Agent-Action-Locative
0	Action-Object-Locative
4	**Total Three-Term Utterances**

16 Two-Term Utterances ÷ 42 Multiterm Utterances = 38.1 % of Multiterm Utterances Accounted For by Brown's Two-Term Semantic Relations

16 Two-Term Utterances ÷ 64 Semantically Coded Utterances = 25.0 % of Semantically Coded Utterances Accounted For by Brown's Two-Term Semantic Relations

0 Total Expansions ÷ 42 Multiterm Utterances = 0 % Semantically Coded Utterances Accounted For by Expansions of Brown's Prevalent Semantic Relations

4 Three-Term Utterances ÷ 42 Multiterm Utterances = 9.5 % of Multiterm Utterances Accounted For by Brown's Three-Term Semantic Relations

4 Three-Term Utterances ÷ 64 Semantically Coded Utterances = 6.3 % of Semantically Coded Utterances Accounted For by Brown's Three-Term Relations

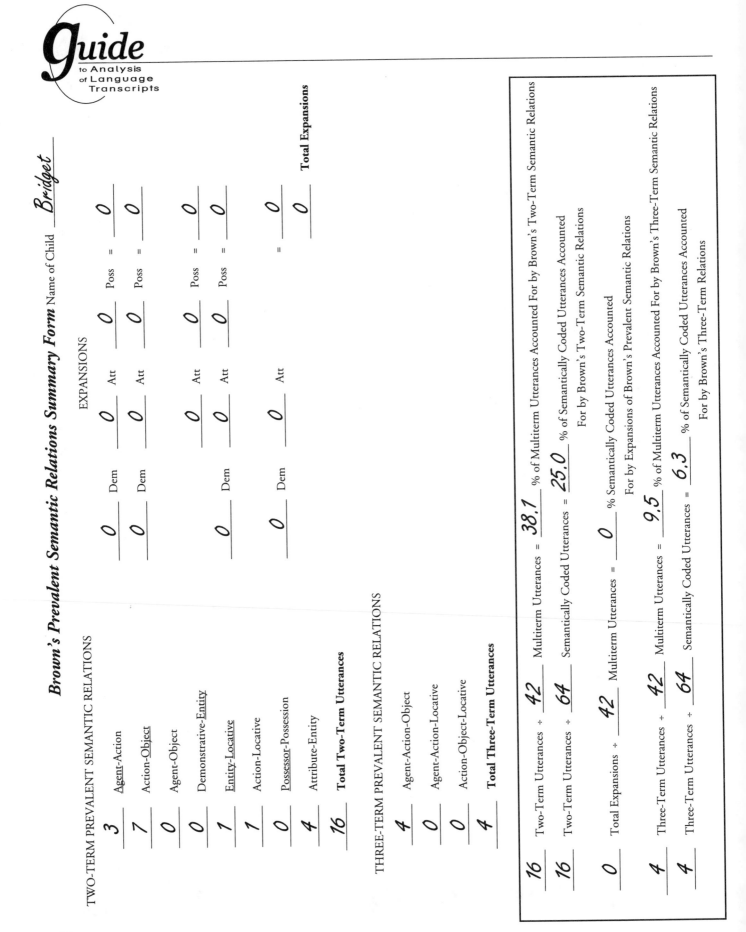

Next, calculate the percentage of semantically coded utterances accounted for by Brown's Two-Term Prevalent Semantic Relations. For the sample transcript, 16 was divided by 64 semantically coded utterances and then multiplied by 100 to get the percentage of semantically coded utterances accounted for by Brown's Two-Term Prevalent Semantic Relations: 25.0%.

The next step is to count and total all instances of each type of expansion of Brown's Prevalent Semantic Relations and add these numbers in the blanks provided. In the sample transcript, there were 0 instances of expansions. If there had been any, the total would have been divided by 42 multiterm utterances and multiplied by 100 to get the percentage of multiterm utterances accounted for by expansions of Brown's Two-Term Prevalent Semantic Relations. If there had been any, that same total would then have been divided by 64 semantically coded utterances and multiplied by 100 to get the percentage of semantically coded utterances accounted for by expansions of Brown's Two-Term Prevalent Semantic Relations.

The last step is to count all instances of each type of Three-Term Prevalent Semantic Relation and add these numbers in the blanks provided. Then add all instances of each type and put this total in the blank provided. In the sample transcript there were 4 examples of Brown's Three-Term Prevalent Semantic Relations. Dividing this by 42 multiterm utterances and multiplying by 100 revealed that 9.5% of this child's multiterm utterances were examples of Brown's Three-Term Semantic Relations. Then 4 was divided by 64 total semantically coded utterances and multiplied by 100 to get the percentage of semantically coded utterances accounted for by Brown's Three-Term Prevalent Semantic Relations: 6.3%.

TABLE 2.6

MEAN FREQUENCY OF OCCURRENCE OF BROWN'S PREVALENT SEMANTIC RELATIONS IN STAGES I, EARLY II, AND II AS PERCENTAGE OF TOTAL MULTITERM UTTERANCES

(Computed from Brown, 1973)

	Stage I* (*N* = 3) %	**Early Stage II*** (*N* = 8) %	**Stage II*** (*N* = 1) %
AGENT-ACTION	24.0	9.4	7.0
ACTION-OBJECT	7.0	9.3	16.0
AGENT-OBJECT	3.7	1.5	0.0
DEMONSTRATIVE-ENTITY	1.3	7.9	1.0
ENTITY-LOCATIVE	12.7	3.9	2.0
ACTION-LOCATIVE	2.3	3.6	5.0
POSSESSOR-POSSESSION	9.7	7.1	11.0
ATTRIBUTE-ENTITY	7.0	5.4	5.0
TOTAL	**67.7**	**48.1**	**47.0**
AGENT-ACTION-OBJECT	3.7	2.9	6.0
AGENT-ACTION-LOCATIVE	1.0	2.1	3.0
ACTION-OBJECT-LOCATIVE	0.3	1.0	0.0
TOTAL	**5.0**	**6.0**	**9.0**

*Based on MLUs reported by Brown, children were grouped according to stages redefined by Miller and Chapman (1981).

Interpretation of the Results Obtained Using Brown's Prevalent Semantic Relations

The first comparison in the interpretation of the summarized data is to Brown's (1973) reported frequency of occurrence of prevalent semantic relations for 12 children ranging in production abilities from Stage I to Stage II. Table 2.6 on page 87 displays the mean frequency of occurrence for each of the prevalent semantic relations and each three-term combination for three children at Stage I, eight children at Early Stage II, and one child at Stage II. Data represent a reorganization of individual child data presented by Brown. Frequencies are reported as percentages of total multiterm utterances.

Examination of Table 2.6 reveals increases across the three stages in ACTION-OBJECT and ACTION-LOCATIVE constructions. Decreases in AGENT-ACTION, AGENT-OBJECT, ENTITY-LOCATIVE, and ATTRIBUTE-ENTITY constructions and the total use of Brown's two-term semantic relations are present. In addition, increases in the total number of three-term semantic relations can be seen. Comparison of results obtained from analysis of Bridget's transcript and Brown's (1973) data suggest that Bridget is using constructions with frequencies most similar to Stage II. However, it cannot be determined if this child's use of Brown's Prevalent Semantic Relations is at a level higher than Stage II. Once again, the data cannot be overinterpreted. Variations in situations are likely to elicit differences in the frequency of occurrence of specific combinations. The conservative interpretation is that this child is capable of producing Brown's Prevalent Semantic Relations with frequencies similar to children at least in Stage II. Whether this child's productions truly are more typical of children in Stage III or higher cannot be determined.

It may be useful to examine the distribution of multiterm utterances into Brown's Prevalent Semantic Relations versus other combinations. Table 2.7 displays this distribution for Stages I–II for data reported by Brown (1973). Again, the data represent a reorganization of individual child data presented by Brown.

TABLE 2.7

Mean Percent of Total Multiterm Utterances Accounted For by Brown's Prevalent Semantic Relations and Additional Combinations of Semantic Roles

(Computed from Brown, 1973)

	Brown's Prevalent Semantic Relations* %	Additional Combinations* %
Stage I* (*N* = 3)	73.3	9.3
Early Stage II* (*N* = 8)	58.3	33.5
Stage II* (*N* = 1)	64.0	30.0

*Based on MLUs reported by Brown, children were grouped according to stages redefined by Miller and Chapman (1981); numbers do not total 100%, because Brown had a third category called "Uninterpretable" that is not reflected on this table.

To compare data obtained from the sample transcript to data presented in Table 2.7, one more computation is necessary. From the *Meaning Relationships in One-Word and Multiword Utterances* analysis grid, it has been shown that 42 of this child's 100 utterances were multiterm combinations of semantic roles. In addition, from the *Brown's Prevalent Semantic Relations Summary Form,* it is clear that a total of 20 utterances were Brown's Two-Term and Three-Term Prevalent Semantic Relations (16 + 4 = 20). That means that 48% (20 ÷ 42) of this child's utterances were examples of Brown's combinations and 52% were examples of additional combinations. This child had no examples of "uninterpretable" utterances. Now, comparing these percentages to those reported by Brown, no apparent match can be seen. This may have been predicted on the basis of an extended set of coding categories. That is, when a set of coding categories containing 20 semantic roles (Retherford et al., 1981) is used to code utterances, and results are compared to those obtained using a coding scheme containing far fewer categories, discrepancies are to be expected.

Let's compare Bridget's distribution of multiterm combinations to data reported by Retherford et al. (1977). The Retherford et al. data are summarized by percent of total semantically coded utterances rather than by percentage of total multiterm utterances. Table 2.8 displays the distribution of total semantically coded utterances into Brown's multiterm combinations versus additional combinations for children in Brown's Stages I–III. Keep in mind that the utterances in Bridget's transcript and the Retherford et al. (1977) data were coded using the 20 semantic roles previously described, and only those coinciding with Brown's categories in combination have been selected for comparison.

TABLE 2.8
Mean Percent of Total Semantically Coded Utterances Accounted For by Brown's Prevalent Semantic Relations and Additional Combinations
(Computed from Retherford, Schwartz, and Chapman, 1977)

	Brown's Prevalent Semantic Relations* %	Additional Combinations* %
Stage I* (*N* = 6)	55.4	21.9
Early Stage II* (*N* = 3)	50.9	20.9
Stage II* (*N* = 2)	38.2	31.8
Stage III* (*N* = 1)	64.0	22.4

*Numbers do not total 100%, because Retherford et al. (1977) had a third category called "Multi-term OTHER" that is not reflected on this table.

Bridget used similar percentages of Brown's combinations (48%) and additional combinations (52%), which is comparable to the distribution in Stage II in Table 2.8. Her percentages could also be interpreted as an indication that Bridget is using combinations characteristic of a more advanced stage of linguistic production.

Brown's own data in Table 2.7 reveal the percentage of multiterm combinations accounted for by his eight Prevalent Semantic Relations tends to decrease over the first three stages of linguistic production. In addition, the increase in the use of additional combinations suggests a greater attention on the part of the child to syntactic aspects of multiterm combinations. Again, overinterpretation of results is cautioned because of the small sample size. Taken together, these results suggest that Bridget's semantic productions are at or beyond Stage II. This finding indicates that analysis of syntactic aspects of the child's productions is warranted.

Analyzing Vocabulary Diversity

The last procedure that will be used to analyze semantic aspects of Bridget's productions analyzes the vocabulary diversity used in language transcripts. This procedure examines referential, rather than relational, aspects of production in that it analyzes vocabulary only, with no attention to the use of words in combination.

Templin's Type-Token Ratio

The procedure that will be used to analyze Bridget's vocabulary diversity in her 100-utterance language transcript is the Type-Token Ratio, described by Templin (1957). This procedure allows examination of the relationship between the total number of different words used and the total number of words used. For the 480 children that Templin studied, ratios of approximately 1:2 were obtained consistently for all age groups, gender groups, and socioeconomic groups, although the numbers composing these ratios varied at each level. Because of this consistency, this procedure is particularly useful in analyzing the diversity of a child's vocabulary. However, Templin's data are applicable only with children between the ages of 3 and 8 years.

In obtaining her language samples, Templin used an adult-child interaction format, with picture books and toys as stimulus materials. On-line recording of the children's spontaneous productions yielded transcripts sufficiently long to permit analysis of the middle 50 utterances. It is possible to use transcripts longer than 50 utterances; however, only 50 consecutive utterances should be used to compute the Type-Token Ratio. For example, since the sample transcript from Chapter 1 is 100 utterances in length, the middle 50 utterances of the transcript—utterances #26 to #75—will be used.

To compute the Type-Token Ratio, each word used by the child (except repetitions) in the sample transcript will be counted. In some cases, two or three words are used together as a familiar expression, and these are counted as one word (e.g., *a lot, all gone).* Table 2.9 delineates the rules used by Templin in counting words.

Although the child in the sample transcript is only 28 months old, her transcript will be used to practice Templin's TTR. To keep track of every word Bridget used, record each word on the *Templin's Type-Token Ratio* analysis sheet. A blank form can be found in Appendix A (pages 238–239). A parts-of-speech organizational scheme was selected for efficiency only and has no bearing on the final computation. To use this organizational scheme, progress through utterances #26 to #75 of the sample transcript, recording each word in the appropriate column according to its part of speech (either alphabetically or on the basis of first occurrence). If it is difficult to determine what part of speech a particular word represents, record it anywhere; final computations are not based on correct differentiation of parts of speech. Accurate tallying of each word is crucial

TABLE 2.9

Rules for Counting Number of Words to Complete Templin's Type-Token Ratio

1. Contractions of subject and predicate, like *it's* and *we're,* are counted as two words. Also, the contracted verb forms are counted as different words than their uncontracted forms. Thus, the *is* in "It's a big dog" is counted as a different word than the *is* in "It is a big dog."
2. Contractions of the verb and the negative, such as *don't,* are counted as one word. They can go in the Verbs or Negatives/Affirmatives category, but not both.
3. Each part of the verbal combination is counted as a separate word. Thus, *have been playing* is counted as three words.
4. Semiauxiliaries are counted as only one word. Even though *wanna* = *want to,* count it as only one type in the Verbs category.
5. Hyphenated words and closed compound nouns are one word. Thus, *blackboard* is counted as one word and *fire truck* is counted as two.
6. Expressions that function as a unit in the child's understanding are counted as one word. Thus, *oh boy, all right,* etc. are counted as one word, while a noun like *Christmas tree* is counted as two words.
7. Interjections, such as *um, oh,* and *huh* are counted as one word.
8. Articles (*the, a, an*) count as one word.
9. Bound morphemes and noun and verb inflections are not counted as separate words. Thus, *cats* and *walked* are each counted as one word.
10. Forms of the same verb with tense and/or number differences are counted as different words. Thus, *make, makes,* and *making* are counted as three different words, not as three types of the same token.

From "Certain Language Skills in Children: Their Development and Interrelationships," by M.C. Templin, 1957, *Institute of Child Welfare Monograph Series, 26.*

for final computation. If a particular word occurs more than once, tally additional instances of the word next to the original recording of the word (e.g., "ball ~~////~~ /" means the word *ball* occurred seven times in the transcript). When finished, compare your results with those in the completed *Templin's Type-Token Ratio* analysis sheet for Bridget on pages 92–93.

The parts-of-speech organizational scheme is maintained in Type-Token Ratio Analysis on the CD-ROM and is preceded by Parts of Speech Analysis. This parts-of-speech practice will be helpful in completing the Type-Token Ratio practice and in completing the various types of structural analysis in Chapter 3.

Calculating the Results Obtained Using Templin's Type-Token Ratio

To obtain the numbers needed for the final computation, count the number of different words in each column and put these totals in the bottom left of the columns. Transfer these totals to the spaces provided on the form. In Bridget's transcript, there were 7 different nouns, 11 verbs, 5 adjectives, 4 adverbs, 1 preposition, 5 others, 12 pronouns, 0 conjunctions, 4 negatives/affirmatives, 1 article, and 3 *wh-* words. Now add these totals to obtain the total number of different words used by Bridget. In the sample transcript, a total of 53 different words were used.

Templin's Type-Token Ratio

Name of Child Bridget

50 Utterances # 26–75

Nouns	Verbs	Adjectives	Adverbs	Prepositions
legs	stand /	heavy	up //	to
elephant	do	another	upside down	
owie /	's 𝍸	pretty	better	
stroller	kick /	else /	down	
cow	gimme	good		
ball /	fall /			
Bill //	go			
	sleep			
	wake			
	take /			
	taste			
7 11	11 20	5 6	4 6	1 1

Others
ick
boom
shh
good night
welcome
5 5

(to) In this instance, "to" is a sign of the infinitive, but since it is almost always a preposition, list it here.

(better) In this instance, "better" is an elliptical predicate adjective, but since it is almost always an adverb, list it here.

(pretty) In this instance, "pretty" is an adverb modifying an adjective, but since "pretty" is almost always an adjective, list it here so you won't miss it if it occurs again in the transcript.

Pronouns	Conjunctions	Negatives/Affirmatives	Articles	*Wh-* Words
you it / there // one I // him // he this yours / here more them /		yeah ~~||||~~ |||| no all right okay	a //	huh /// where what
12 21		4 13	1 3	3 6

Total Number of Different:

Nouns	7
Verbs	11
Adjectives	5
Adverbs	4
Prepositions	1
Others	5
Pronouns	12
Conjunctions	—
Negatives/Affirmatives	4
Articles	1
Wh- Words	3
TOTAL NUMBER OF DIFFERENT WORDS	53

Total Number of:

Nouns	11
Verbs	20
Adjectives	6
Adverbs	6
Prepositions	1
Others	5
Pronouns	21
Conjunctions	—
Negatives/Affirmatives	13
Articles	3
Wh- Words	6
TOTAL NUMBER OF WORDS	92

$\frac{\text{Total Number of Different Words}}{\text{Total Number of Words}}$ $\frac{53}{92}$ =.5760 = .58 = ____ Type-Token Ratio (TTR)

Next, count each instance of each word in the 11 columns, put the totals on the right side of each column, and transfer the totals to the spaces provided. In the sample transcript, there were 11 total instances of nouns used, 20 verbs, 6 adjectives, 6 adverbs, 1 preposition, 5 others, 21 pronouns, 0 conjunctions, 13 negatives/affirmatives, 3 articles, and 6 *wh-* words. Add these totals to obtain the total number of words used. A total of 92 words was obtained.

To complete the final computation and obtain the Type-Token Ratio, divide the total number of different words (53) by the total number of words (92). This results in a Type-Token Ratio of .5760, which rounds to .58.

Interpretation of the Results Obtained Using Templin's Type-Token Ratio

The interpretation of the obtained Type-Token Ratio is accomplished by comparing it to the normative data from Templin's analysis. Table 2.10 displays the mean and standard deviation of different words used, the mean and standard deviation of total words used, and the resulting Type-Token Ratio for various age groups between 3 and 8 years.

Comparison of Bridget's Type-Token Ratio of .58 to the 3-year-old Type-Token Ratios obtained by Templin reveals that Bridget's Type-Token Ratio is higher. This suggests that the child's vocabulary in the sample transcript is more diverse than would be expected for the total number of words used. Type-Token Ratios greater than .50 indicate more different words than typical for the total number of words. Is this an asset or a deficit? That is difficult to say. Type-Token Ratios significantly below .50 reflect a lack of diversity and may indicate language-specific deficiency (Miller, 1981). But greater diversity has not been implicated as a diagnostic indicator. In any event, results must be considered in greater detail before drawing a conclusion.

TABLE 2.10

CALCULATING VOCABULARY DIVERSITY USING TYPE-TOKEN RATIO (*N* = 480)

Age	Different Words		Total Words		Type-Token Ratio
	Mean	SD	Mean	SD	Different Words ÷ Total Words
3.0	92.5	26.1	204.9	61.3	0.45
3.5	104.8	20.4	232.9	50.8	0.45
4.0	120.4	27.6	268.8	72.6	0.45
4.5	127.0	23.9	270.7	65.3	0.47
5.0	132.4	27.2	286.2	75.5	0.46
6.0	147.0	27.6	328.0	65.9	0.45
7.0	157.7	27.2	363.1	51.3	0.43
8.0	166.5	29.5	378.8	80.9	0.44

From "Certain Language Skills in Children: Their Development and Interrelationships," by M.C. Templin, 1957, *Institute of Child Welfare Monograph Series, 26.* © 1957 by the University of Minnesota Press. © renewed 1985 by Mildred C. Templin. Reprinted with permission.

Although Type-Token Ratios were intended to be used only as normative data, valuable information can be gained by comparing total number of different words and total number of words to the means obtained by Templin. Reductions in the total number of different words and the total number of words have been implicated as potential indicators of developmental language delays or disorders (Miller, 1991). The sample transcript contained 53 different words. Compared to the mean obtained by Templin, this total is more than one standard deviation below the mean for 3-year-olds. In addition, the total of 92 words is also more than one standard deviation below the mean. In this case, the best interpretation is that Templin's data are not an appropriate comparison since the child in the sample transcript is younger than 3 years of age. However, given that Templin's TTR was used here, her vocabulary in this transcript was reasonably diverse.

Some data are available for children younger than 3 years of age. Phillips (1973) reports that the mean Type-Token Ratio for 10 children 8 months of age was .31; for 10 children 18 months of age, .34; and for 10 children 28 months of age, .41. Thus, these data further support the notion that Bridget's vocabulary was reasonably diverse for her age. However, Phillips does not report the number of different words and total number of words used to compute Type-Token Ratios. Until sufficient data are obtained on the diversity of a child's vocabulary before 3 years of age, direct application of Templin's norms is not appropriate.

Implications for Intervention

After the selected semantic analysis procedures have been completed, examination of the results is necessary to develop intervention goals. Data obtained from each of the analyses can lead to development of appropriate intervention goals if the results are considered in light of what is known about normal language acquisition. Based on the sequence of accomplishments in normal language acquisition, opportunities for the child to use new vocabulary expressing individual semantic roles and/or semantic relationships can be provided. Clinical experience has shown that the forms likely to emerge next in the acquisition sequence are predictable; consequently, opportunities for emergence can be provided. The suggestions delineated here are general considerations for intervention, not hard and fast rules.

When children at the one-word utterance stage are identified by percentages of one-word utterances exceeding 50% of total utterances, and the use of categories within Bloom's (1973) or Nelson's (1973) One-Word Utterance Types are documented, opportunities for the development of additional vocabulary within Bloom's or Nelson's utterance types can be provided. That does not mean that a specific set of vocabulary words is taught. It does mean that the child can be provided with repeated exposure to vocabulary that falls within Bloom's or Nelson's categories. Early in the one-word stage, the categories that the child is most likely to produce include SUBSTANTIVE and NAMING WORDS for Bloom's categories, and NOMINALS, MODIFIERS, and/or PERSONAL-SOCIAL WORDS for Nelson's categories. Later, children add FUNCTION WORDS for Bloom's categories and ACTION WORDS for Nelson's categories. Sufficient opportunities for children to acquire the new vocabulary types must be provided during intervention activities. The specific vocabulary representing these one-word utterance types should be determined by the interests of the child and the regular activities of the child.

When limited use of semantic roles has been identified for a particular child using Retherford et al.'s (1981) coding scheme, opportunities for encoding more diverse roles must be provided. Typically, goals and objectives related to semantic role use are combined with goals and objectives developed as a result of Brown's Prevalent Semantic Relations analysis. Clinical experience has shown that semantic roles encoding familiar objects and persons precede the production of verb relations such as AGENT-ACTION and ACTION-OBJECT. Appropriate objectives would include targeting object and person relations (DEMONSTRATIVE-ENTITY, ATTRIBUTE-ENTITY, ENTITY-LOCATIVE, POSSESSOR-POSSESSION) for the child early in the two-word period, and verb relations (AGENT-ACTION, ACTION-OBJECT, ACTION-LOCATIVE) for the child late in the two-word period. Three-term relations can be targeted next, as can the semantic roles identified by Retherford et al. as infrequently occurring, since they are likely to occur in three-term and expanded forms. Again, specific vocabulary should not be taught; opportunities for using targeted semantic relations within structured activities should be provided.

Results obtained from analysis of vocabulary diversity can be used to develop goals and objectives for increasing vocabulary. Type-Token Ratios one standard deviation below the norms provided suggest a lack of vocabulary diversity. Intervention should focus on increasing vocabulary, typically within developmentally appropriate semantic fields (e.g., noun categories such as vehicles, plants, animals; verb categories such as cooking, play, school; temporal terms; and polar adjectives). In this area, specific vocabulary can be taught, but the focus should be on developmentally appropriate semantic fields.

Overall, analysis of both referential aspects of semantic production and relational aspects of semantic production provides results that can be used to develop intervention goals and objectives. As the discussions in the following chapters will demonstrate, results obtained from semantic analysis can be combined with results obtained from syntactic and pragmatic analysis to develop comprehensive goals and objectives for intervention.

Syntactic Analysis

Chapter 3

Introduction

Analyzing syntactic aspects of language transcripts will help identify children beyond the one-word stage who have delays in language production. In addition, examining the developmental level of a variety of syntactic structures is essential to appropriately determine intervention goals and objectives. The syntactic analysis procedures described in this chapter are compatible with the semantic analysis procedures described in the previous chapter. However, these syntactic procedures are more appropriate for children whose language abilities have advanced beyond the one-word stage. It would be appropriate to analyze the semantic aspects of a child's language production using the multiterm procedures from Chapter 2 and then to analyze the syntactic aspects using the procedures in Chapter 3. Information obtained from analysis procedures could then be combined to diagnose language production delays and to develop intervention goals and objectives.

In addition to the procedures described in *Guide*, there are several procedures available to analyze syntactic aspects of language production: Lee's (1966, 1974) *Developmental Sentence Scoring (DSS)* and Lee's (1966) *Developmental Sentence Types (DST);* Tyack and Gottsleben's (1974) *Language Sampling, Analysis, and Training (LSAT);* Crystal, Fletcher, and Garman's (1976, 1991) *Language Assessment, Remediation, and Screening Procedure (LARSP);* and Miller's (1981) *Assigning Structural Stage (ASS),* among others. Although the procedures described in *Guide* do not differ demonstrably from those procedures developed by Miller (1981), the directions and interpretations are more explicit, and forms for analysis are provided. The intent is not to duplicate procedures nor to offer alternative procedures, but to provide experience both in determining the syntactic level of language production and in interpreting results obtained from such analysis. The experience gained here will be beneficial in using any of the aforementioned procedures, as all procedures are based on the analysis of documented aspects of syntactic production.

The procedures described here will have you identify a variety of syntactic structures and then document the developmental level of each structure. The most typical stage and the most advanced stage for each structure will be assigned in order to compare results to normative data to determine the presence or absence of syntactic delays. Once a delay has been documented, the stage assignments form the basis of decision rules for determining intervention goals and objectives.

Analyzing Mean Length of Utterance in Morphemes

The procedure that will be used to analyze utterance length is based on procedures described by Brown (1973) to examine the structural changes in children's productions on the basis of increases in utterance length. Brown documented changes in structural complexity concomitant to increases in utterance length as determined by meaning units, or morphemes. The rules for assigning morphemes to utterances have been presented in the literature (Bloom and Lahey, 1978; Brown, 1973; Miller, 1981; Owens, 1992) and appear fairly straightforward. Some inconsistencies in assigning morphemes do exist however. In addition, problems periodically arise from analysis of utterances produced by children with language delays or language disorders because their utterances may not follow a normal developmental sequence. A modification of Brown's rules will be used for assigning morphemes, and examples of utterances produced by children with language delays and language disorders will be provided. Table 3.1 summarizes the rules for assigning morphemes to utterances that have been used with the sample transcript from Chapter 1.

For practice, try to determine the number of morphemes in a few utterances before turning to the

TABLE 3.1
RULES FOR ASSIGNING MORPHEMES TO UTTERANCES
(Adapted from Brown, 1973)

1. Select a portion of the transcript that appears to be representative of the range of the child's abilities. Assign morphemes to 100 consecutive utterances, since selecting individual utterances for assigning morphemes can inflate the resulting MLU. However, be aware of transcripts with a high number of responses to yes/no questions, which can deflate the resulting MLU.
2. Assign morphemes only to utterances that are completely intelligible. Following the rules for numbering utterances in a transcript (see page 18), only assign morphemes to utterances that are numbered. Do not number or assign morphemes to any repeated, partially intelligible, unintelligible, or interrupted utterances.
3. Only assign morphemes to repetitions in the most complete form within an utterance as a result of stuttering or false starts (e.g., given the utterance "my dad dad is big," count only "my dad is big"). Occasionally, a child repeats a word for emphasis or part of a phrase for clarification. In these cases, count all words (e.g., given the utterance "my dad is big, big," count all words if the second *big* has more emphasis than the first).
4. Do not assign morphemes to fillers (e.g., *um, well, oh)* or to singsong repetitions. However, do assign morphemes to short words like *hi, yeah,* and *no.*
5. Treat compound words (e.g., *up-to-date, pocketbook, high school)* and closely related words like *all gone* as single words, even though they consist of two or more free morphemes. Likewise, assign one morpheme to indefinite and reflexive compound pronouns (e.g., *anything, somebody, nothing, everyone, herself)*. The reason for this is that children do not appear to have use of each constituent morpheme within these compounds and therefore treat them like single words.
6. Treat proper nouns (e.g., *Japanese, the Leaning Tower of Pisa, Mr. Smith)* and ritualized reduplications (e.g., *choo-choo, night-night, quack-quack)* as single words. If the child produces an utterance containing "choo-choo train" and there is evidence of the use of *train* separate from *choo-choo,* assign *choo-choo* and *train* one morpheme each.
7. Assign only one morpheme to diminutive forms of words (e.g., *doggie, mommy, Billy, funny)*. The reason for this is that children use many diminutive forms as the only form of the word produced, either because they do not have productive control over the suffix or because adults often use only the diminutive form of words when speaking with children.
8. Assign one morpheme to auxiliary verbs (e.g., *will, have, may)*.
9. Assign only one morpheme to catenative forms, even though they represent two to three morphemes in the expanded form (e.g., *gonna = going to; wanna = want to; hafta = have to)*.
10. Assign one morpheme to all inflectional affixes (i.e., plural *-s,* singular and plural possessive *-s,* present third person singular *-s,* regular past tense *-ed,* past participle *-ed* and *-en,* present participle *-ing,* comparative *-er,* and superlative *-est)*. (This is in addition to the morpheme[s] assigned to the word onto which the form is inflected.) An incorrect use of an inflection should not be counted as a separate morpheme. For example, *rided* would receive only one morpheme.

Continued on next page

TABLE 3.1—Continued

11. Inflections marked on gerunds and predicate adjectives are not counted as verb tense inflections (e.g., "*jogg**ing** is fun*"; "*I am bor**ed***"). Assign only one morpheme to the entire word.
12. Assign only one morpheme to irregular past tense and past participle forms (e.g., *rode, swum*). The reason for this is that children do not appear to have derived these from the present tense form. (An incorrect use of an inflection added to an irregular past tense or past participle form should not be counted as a separate morpheme. For example, *swummed* would receive only one morpheme.)
13. Assign two morphemes to negative contractions (e.g., *can't, don't, won't*) only if there is evidence within the transcript that the child uses each part of the contraction (e.g., *do* and *not*) separately. If the child does not use each part of the contraction separately, assign only one morpheme to the negative contraction. The reason for this is that until the child uses each part separately, the child does not appear to have productive control over the contraction.
14. Assign two morphemes to all nonnegative contractions (e.g., *I'm, he's, they've, you'll, she'd, they're*).
15. Common derivational affixes should be assigned their own morphemes. Common affixes include *re-, un-, -ly, -ful, -en.* Do not assign morphemes to such affixes as *al-* in *already* or *a-* in *around.*

sample transcript. As was done in the previous chapter, cover the right side of the page, determine the number of morphemes in the utterance, and then check your values with those provided in the shaded section. The explanations should help clear up any questions. In addition, the CD-ROM has practice worksheets you may wish to complete.

Practice Examples for Morpheme Assignment

(C points to picture in photo album) there Daddy/	morphemes = 2 In this utterance, each word is assigned one morpheme.
(C puts baby doll in crib and covers her) go night-night/	morphemes = 2 The word *night-night* is assigned only one morpheme. This is because it is assumed that *night-night* functions as a single concept for the child.

Continued on next page

Practice Examples—*Continued*

(C places empty juice cup on table) allgone juice/	morphemes = 2 Again, a word like *allgone* functions as a single word for most children and in most cases is written as one word in the transcript.
(C points to picture in picture book) two doggies/	morphemes = 3 The use of the plural inflection accounts for the addition of one morpheme. Remember, the diminutive form receives only one morpheme.
(C pulls circus train out of box) big choo-choo train/	morphemes = 2/3 Without any additional utterances, only two morphemes can be assigned to this utterance. If there is evidence that the child uses the word *train* separate from *choo-choo,* three morphemes could be assigned to this utterance. Two morphemes are never assigned to *choo-choo.*
(C picks up monkey that fell off bar) he fell down/	morphemes = 3 No credit is given for past tense of irregular verbs, since children appear not to have derived these from the present tense form.
(C watches baby brother eating raisins) he likes raisins/	morphemes = 5 The use of the third person singular present tense receives a morpheme, as does the plural *-s.*

Continued on next page

Practice Examples—*Continued*

(C shakes his head and says) I don't like raisins/	morphemes = 5/6 The negative contraction *don't* is assigned two morphemes only if there is evidence that each piece of the uncontracted form *(do, not)* is used separately or together elsewhere in the transcript.
(C kicks ball, then turns to M) I kicked the ball/	morphemes = 5 The regular past tense *-ed* receives a morpheme. Evidence of use in the uninflected form is not needed.
(M and C are racing cars around track) he's gonna catch me/	morphemes = 5 Since *he's* is a nonnegative contraction, it receives two morphemes. The catenative form of *going to* receives only one morpheme. Brown indicated that catenatives were assigned two morphemes in older children, but for consistency in these analyses, one morpheme will always be assigned to catenatives.
(M says to crying C, "Did she hurt you?") yeah she hit me/	morphemes = 4 With no boundary marker indicating a pause between *yeah* and the rest of this utterance, one morpheme is assigned to each word in this utterance. If there had been a pause between *yeah* and the rest of the utterance, it would have been segmented into two utterances.
(C pulls large stuffed dog from surprise box) oh that's a big doggie/	morphemes = 5 The filler *oh* does not receive a morpheme in the count. The diminutive form of *dog* receives one morpheme only. The contractible copula is a nonnegative contraction, so *that's* is assigned two morphemes.

Continued on next page

Practice Examples—*Continued*

(C sets dog next to middle-sized dog) that is a big doggie/	morphemes = 5 In this utterance, the uncontracted form of the copula is used. This does not change the morpheme count, but the example is provided to demonstrate a pragmatic convention of "uncontracting" the copulas used for emphasis.
(C puts handful of popcorn in mouth) I am eating popcorn/	morphemes = 5 The present progressive form of *eat* receives a morpheme, so that *eating* receives a total of two morphemes. The compound word *popcorn* receives only one morpheme.
(C is explaining why he was late) she couldn't find her pocketbook/	morphemes = 5/6 *Couldn't* is assigned two morphemes only if there is evidence that each piece of the uncontracted form *(could, not)* is used separately or together elsewhere in the transcript. The compound word *pocketbook* receives only one morpheme.
(C is relating story to M) she didn't say hi/	morphemes = 4/5 *Didn't* is assigned two morphemes only if there is evidence that each piece of the contracted form *(did, not)* is used separately or together elsewhere in the transcript. Greeting terms are not treated as fillers and are assigned one or more morphemes.
(C points to arm) he hitted me/	morphemes = 3 Assigning a morpheme to incorrect use of the regular past tense *-ed* inflates MLU. Thus, no morpheme is assigned. Valuable information is obtained if attempts by the child to mark past tense are noted.

Continued on next page

Practice Examples—*Continued*

(C holds up picture) look it Mommy/	morphemes = 2/3 In most cases, the child's use of *lookit* functions as one word. Thus, only one morpheme is assigned. If there is evidence that the child uses *look* and *it* independently of one another, then each is counted as a separate morpheme. The use of *Mommy* as an attention-getter does receive a morpheme.
(C points to picture in book) that's a silly one/	morphemes = 5 The contractible copula and the pronoun onto which it is contracted each are assigned a morpheme. The adjective *silly* is assigned only one morpheme.
(C hands cars to M) Mommy do it/	morphemes = 2/3 The use of *do it* also typically functions as one word. If there is evidence that the child uses *do* and *it* independently of one another, then each is counted as a separate morpheme.
(C pours milk from pitcher) I didn't spilled it/	morphemes = 4/5 In this utterance, the child is attempting to mark the past tense but has not realized that the rule for marking the past tense is to mark it on the auxiliary verb. Therefore, the child has marked past tense on both the main verb *spill* and the auxiliary *did.* Counting double marking of past tense in auxiliary and main verb inflates MLU, so the past tense *-ed* on *spilled* is not counted. The rule for assigning morphemes to negative contractions holds here as in previous examples, resulting in four or five total morphemes.
(M asks, "And who knocked the cart over?") the man the man the big man/	morphemes = 3 The use of false starts in an utterance is disregarded. Count only the most complete form.
(C pulls truck away from other child) that's my big my big truck/	morphemes = 5 Again, false starts, even if they occur within an utterance, are disregarded. Count only the most complete form.

Continued on next page

Practice Examples—*Continued*

(C continues arguing with other child) that's my new one my new truck/	morphemes = 8 This utterance is different from the previous two in that the repetition is not considered a false start but a clarification of an unclear sentence constituent. The child apparently decided that the listener might not know what *one* referred to and therefore provided additional information. This is not considered a false start, and as a result each word in the repetition receives a morpheme.

With that practice, assigning morphemes to the utterances in Bridget's transcript should be easier. In addition, a completed syntactic analysis of a transcript obtained from a conversation with an older child (Sara) is provided in Appendix B to provide experience in making some of the more difficult judgments. Using the transcript of Bridget (from Chapter 1) and a blank *Structural Stage Analysis Grid* from Appendix A (pages 240–241), record the number of morphemes for each utterance in the Number of Morphemes column. When the number of morphemes for all of the child's utterances have been recorded, add the morphemes for each utterance to obtain the total number of morphemes. To obtain the mean length of utterance (MLU) in morphemes, divide this total by the total number of utterances (in Bridget's case, 100). (Note that if any utterance is not assigned one or more morphemes, the total number of utterances may be less than 100 [e.g., if an utterance is a filler, it would not be assigned a morpheme and therefore would reduce the total number of utterances]). For Bridget's transcript, compare your morpheme assignments, the total morpheme computation, and the resulting MLU in morphemes with those in the sample provided on pages 105–106.

For Bridget's transcript, an MLU of 2.00 morphemes should have been obtained. This value provides very little information without additional analyses. One mechanism for analyzing this MLU is to compare it to data provided by Miller and Chapman (1981) on the predicted MLU ranges for 123 children. Table 3.2, on page 107, summarizes the predicted MLUs, MLU ranges, and standard deviations for the children in their study.

The following computation permits evaluation of the MLU obtained from Bridget's transcript (in Chapter 1) or for any obtained MLU:

$$\frac{\text{obtained MLU} - \text{predicted MLU}}{\text{predicted SD}} = \text{SD below the mean for CA}$$

$$\frac{2.00 - 2.23}{.510} = -.45 \text{ SD below the mean for 27 months}$$

Although Bridget is 28 months of age, the values for 27-month-olds are used. The MLU for the sample transcript fell .45 standard deviations below the mean for children 27 months of age. This MLU clearly reflects utterances that would be considered within normal limits in terms of mean length of morpheme. But this is a cursory analysis. Therefore, the next step is to examine variations in utterance length by completing a length distribution analysis, which can add to the interpretation of the obtained MLU. After

Structural Stage Analysis Grid

Name of Child Bridget

"It" and "do" appear separately as part of other utterances.

Utterance Number	Number of Morphemes	Negation	Yes/No Question	*Wh-* Question	Noun Phrase Elaboration	Verb Phrase Elaboration	Complex Sentence
1	1						
2	2						
3	1						
4	1						
5	4						
6	1						
7	2						
8	1						
9	1						
10	1						
11	3						
12	1						
13	1						
14	1						
15	4						
16	2						
17	4						
18	4						
19	2						
20	4						
21	4						
22	2						
23	3						
24	4						
25	2						
26	2						
27	2						
28	2						
29	1						
30	1						
31	5						
32	4						
33	4						
34	1						
35	4						
36	3						
37	1						
38	1						
39	1						
40	1						
41	1						
42	1						
43	2						
44	2						
45	3						
46	3						
47	1						
48	1						
49	1						
50	1						
Subtotal 1	105						

Structural Stage Analysis Grid

Name of Child *Bridget*

Utterance Number	Number of Morphemes	Negation	Yes/No Question	*Wh-* Question	Noun Phrase Elaboration	Verb Phrase Elaboration	Complex Sentence
51	1						
52	3						
53	1						
54	1						
55	1						
56	4						
57	1						
58	1						
59	1						
60	4						
61	4						
62	(3)						
63	1						
64	1						
65	(4)						
66	2						
67	1						
68	1						
69	1						
70	1						
71	1						
72	3						
73	3						
74	1						
75	2						

Based on possessive "s" morpheme added to possessive pronoun.

[105] + [95] = 200

No. of Morphemes (Subtotal 1) + No. of Morphemes (Subtotal 2) = Total Number of Morphemes

Utterance Number	Number of Morphemes	Negation	Yes/No Question	*Wh-* Question	Noun Phrase Elaboration	Verb Phrase Elaboration	Complex Sentence
76	1						
77	1						
78	3						
79	1						
80	1						
81	5						
82	1						
83	3						
84	1						
85	1						
86	2						
87	3						
88	3						
89	(3)						
90	(3)						
91	1						
92	1						
93	1						
94	1						
95	1						
96	3						
97	3						
98	1						
99	2						
100	2						
Subtotal 2	95						

Note that in the preceding utterance, she elaborates the directive, so it makes sense to give credit for both morphemes in "look it" in these utterances.

$$\frac{\text{Total Number of Morphemes}}{\text{Total Number of Utterances}} = \frac{[\ 200\ ]}{[\ 100\ ]} = 2.00 \text{ MLU}$$

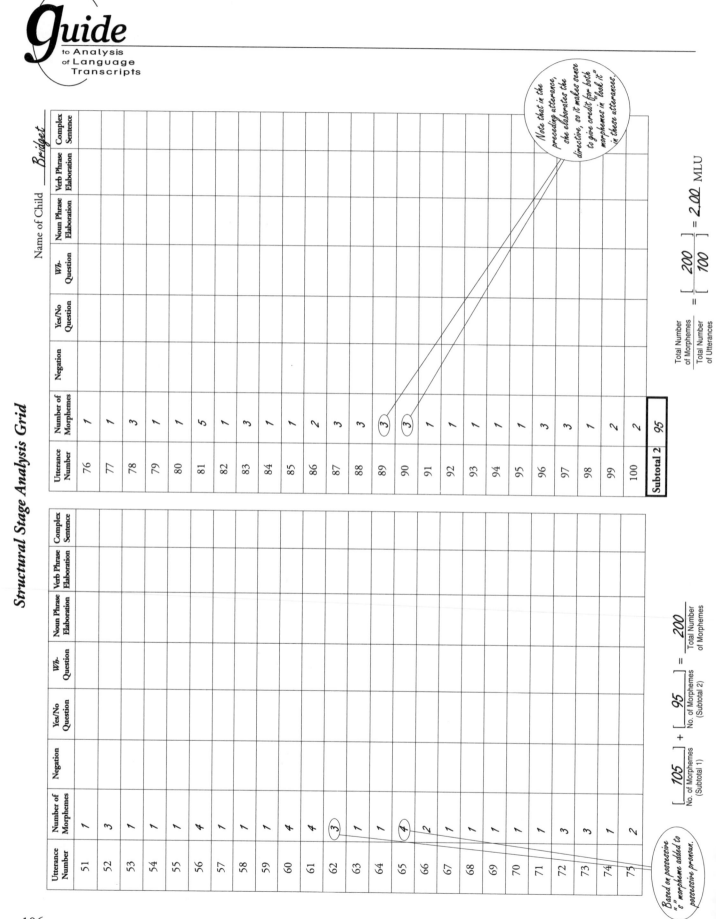

TABLE 3.2

PREDICTED MLU RANGES AND LINGUISTIC STAGES OF CHILDREN WITHIN ONE PREDICTED STANDARD DEVIATION OF PREDICTED MEAN

Age ± 1 Mo.	Predicted MLU[a]	Predicted SD[b]	Predicted MLU ± 1 SD (Middle 68%)	Brown's Stages within 1 SD of Predicted MLU							
				EI	LI	II	III	EIV	LIV/EV	LV	Post V
18	1.31	.325	.99 - 1.64	X	X						
21	1.62	.386	1.23 - 2.01	X	X	X					
24	1.92	.448	1.47 - 2.37	X	X	X					
27	2.23	.510	1.72 - 2.74		X	X	X				
30	2.54	.571	1.97 - 3.11		X	X	X	X			
33	2.85	.633	2.22 - 3.48			X	X	X			
36	3.16	.694	2.47 - 3.85			X	X	X	X		
39	3.47	.756	2.71 - 4.23				X	X	X	X	
42	3.78	.817	2.96 - 4.60				X	X	X	X	X
45	4.09	.879	3.21 - 4.97					X	X	X	X
48	4.40	.940	3.46 - 5.34					X	X	X	X
51	4.71	1.002	3.71 - 5.71						X	X	X
54	5.02	1.064	3.96 - 6.08						X	X	X
57	5.32	1.125	4.20 - 6.45							X	X
60	5.63	1.187	4.44 - 6.82							X	X

[a]MLU is predicted from the equation MLU = -.548 + .103 (AGE).
[b]SD is predicted from the equation SD MLU = -.0446 + .0205 (AGE).
From "The Relation between Age and Mean Length of Utterance in Morphemes," by J.F. Miller and R.S. Chapman, 1981, *Journal of Speech and Hearing Research, 24*(2), p. 158. © 1981 by the American Speech-Language-Hearing Association. Reprinted with permission.

you analyze variations in utterance length and identify grammatical morphemes, you will fill in the remaining columns of the *Structural Stage Analysis Grid.*

ANALYZING VARIATIONS IN UTTERANCE LENGTH

In this analysis procedure, the utterances in Bridget's transcript (from Chapter 1) will be tallied by length in morphemes. This will allow you to examine the distribution of utterances by length and to determine the range of utterance lengths within this transcript. Using the partially completed *Structural Stage Analysis Grid* and a blank *Length Distribution* analysis sheet from Appendix A (page 242), progress utterance by utterance through the Number of Morphemes column of the *Structural Stage Analysis Grid.* Mark each utterance in the Tally column on the *Length Distribution* analysis sheet in the row next to the number of morphemes that each utterance contains. For example, in the sample transcript, utterance #1 contains one morpheme, so mark a tally next to the box indicating one morpheme length. Utterance #2 contains two morphemes, so mark a tally next to the box indicating two morpheme lengths. Proceed through the *Structural Stage Analysis Grid* until all 100 utterances have been tallied. Then count the tallies in each row and record that number in the Total box for the corresponding row. Then check

Length Distribution Name of Child Bridget

Length in Morphemes	Tally	Total
1	𝍸 𝍸 𝍸 𝍸 𝍸 𝍸 𝍸 𝍸 𝍸 𝍸 /	51
2	𝍸 𝍸 𝍸 /	16
3	𝍸 𝍸 𝍸 //	17
4	𝍸 𝍸 ////	14
5	//	2
6		0
7		0
8		0
9		0
10		0
11		0
12		0
13		0
14		0
15		0

This appears inconsistent with Bloom's and Nelson's One-Word Utterance Types analyses in Chapter 2 in which 52 one-word utterances were counted, but note that utterance #27, "legs," is a one-word utterance with two morphemes.

Upper Bound Length = 5 morpheme(s)

Lower Bound Length = 1 morpheme(s)

your tallies and totals with those in the sample provided on page 108.

Totals obtained should be 51 utterances that were one morpheme in length, 16 utterances two morphemes in length, 17 utterances three morphemes in length, 14 utterances four morphemes in length, and the 2 longest utterances were five morphemes in length. Upper bound length and lower bound length are reported at the bottom of the *Length Distribution* analysis sheet; they provide analysis of variability in utterance length. To determine the upper bound length, check the Total column for the longest utterance in morphemes. In the sample transcript, there were 2 utterances that were five morphemes in length. Thus, in this transcript, the upper bound length, or the longest utterance, was five morphemes. Put a 5 in the blank next to "Upper Bound Length." To determine the lower bound length, check the Total column for the shortest utterance in morphemes. In this sample, there were 51 utterances that were one morpheme in length. Thus, the lower bound length, or the shortest utterance, was one morpheme. Put a 1 in the blank next to "Lower Bound Length."

This analysis may not appear to provide information substantially different from the MLU in morphemes. But, in fact, it does. A length distribution analysis is necessary for interpretation of an obtained MLU. The analysis may confirm the obtained MLU by indicating that there is appropriate variation in length of utterance around the mean length. Brown (1973) has provided expected upper bound lengths significantly higher than the target MLU for each of his five stages. His target values were data sampling points for each stage. He used these values to compare children's productions at each stage. These target values are not to be interpreted as midpoints or boundaries for stages. Table 3.3 summarizes the target values and the upper bound length for each stage of Brown's five stages of linguistic development.

As can be seen in Table 3.3, the upper bound length for each stage is substantially longer than the mean might indicate. Completing a length distribution analysis provides insight into the variation in length of utterances that a particular child is capable of producing. The obtained MLU can be validated by completing a length distribution analysis. The MLU of 2.00 morphemes

TABLE 3.3

Brown's (1973) Target MLU in Morphemes and Upper Bound Lengths for Each Stage

Stage	MLU	Upper Bound Length
I	1.75	5
II	2.25	7
III	2.75	9
IV	3.50	11
V	4.00	13

From *A First Language: The Early Stages* (p. 56), by R. Brown, 1973, Cambridge, MA: Harvard University Press. © 1973 by the President and Fellows of Harvard College. Reprinted with permission.

from the sample transcript, which is midway between Stage I and Stage II in Table 3.3, implies that this child should produce utterances five to seven morphemes in length. This child produces utterances five morphemes in length, the upper bound length for Stage I. Are we to conclude that Bridget is incapable of producing utterances as long as her MLU would predict? That would be too strong a conclusion. The conservative conclusion would be that for this particular sample, Bridget produced utterances that did not vary around the mean as much as would be expected for her MLU.

The length distribution analysis also can confirm sample representativeness. Had Bridget produced a great number of responses to yes/no questions, as observed directly by a preponderance of yes/no responses in the sample transcript, a lower MLU would have been obtained and the length distribution analysis would have revealed restricted length variation. Such a finding would suggest a need for obtaining another sample of this child's language under more natural interactional conditions. In contrast, a very high MLU with little variation in length around the mean may be the result of obtaining a sample under narrative or storytelling conditions. Obtaining another sample under conversational conditions or using another part of the transcript would be indicated in this case as well.

Reductions in variation in utterance length also may be indicative of additional problems beyond sample representativeness. A child with utterances clustering closely around the mean may have a specific deficit in production abilities. For example, children with apraxic-like behaviors or speech motor control problems tend to produce utterances resulting in low MLUs and minimal variation in utterance length around the mean. Children who are learning language in a very rote manner tend to produce utterances resulting in MLUs of varying lengths but with minimal variation around the mean. Children with autistic-like behaviors present profiles such as this. Chapman (as cited in Miller, 1981) provides an excellent discussion on the importance of completing a length distribution analysis and the implications of its results. The appropriate interpretation of the length distribution results for the sample transcript would be that this sample seems reasonably representative, and that there may be a restriction in the amount of variation in utterance length around the obtained mean length. There also may be concern in regard to the large number of one-morpheme utterances (51). This may have brought the MLU down, resulting in a less-than-typical profile of variability about the mean.

Analyzing Use of Grammatical Morphemes

The next analysis procedure that will be used results in a stage assignment reflecting mastery of grammatical morphemes. The stage assignments are based on data reported by de Villiers and de Villiers (1973) and indicate the stage at which each of the 14 grammatical morphemes studied by Brown (1973) are used correctly in 90 percent of the utterances where a particular grammatical morpheme is necessary (i.e., obligatory context). Brown designated 90 percent correct use in obligatory contexts as mastery level. Using this 90 percent criterion, de Villiers and de Villiers reported the stage at which each of the 14 grammatical morphemes typically is mastered. Table 3.4 (see pages 111–112) summarizes the development for a variety of linguistic structures throughout Brown's stages of linguistic

Production Characteristics of Linguistic Development Organized by Brown's Stages

	Stage	MLU	Age (months)	Grammatical Morphemes	Negation	Yes/No Questions	*Wh*-Questions	Noun Phrase Elaboration[d]	Verb Phrase Elaboration[d]	Complex Sentences
I[d]	**Early I**	1.01–1.49	19–22[a] 16–26[b]	Occasional use	*no* as single-word utterance (but not as a negative response to a yes/no question)	Marked with rising intonation	*what* + *this/that*	NP □ (M) + N[e] Elaborated NPs occur only alone	Main Verb: uninflected; occasional use of *-ing* Auxiliary: not used Copula: not used Verb + Particles: occasional use	None used
	Late I/ Early II	1.50–1.99	23–26 18–31	Occasional use	*no* + noun or verb *not* + noun or verb		*what* + NP or VP *where* + NP or VP			
II[d]	**II**	2.00–2.49	27–30 21–35	1. Present progressive tense of verb *-ing*[c] 2. Regular plural *-s* 3. Preposition *in*				NP same as Stage I Object NP elaboration appears: V + NP	Main Verb: occasionally marked Auxiliary: 1. Semiauxiliary appears 2. Use of present progressive *-ing* without auxiliary Copula: appears without tense/number inflection	Semiauxiliary appears: *gonna, gotta, wanna, hafta*
III[d]	**III**	2.50–2.99	31–34 24–41	4. Preposition *on* 5. Possessive *-s*	NP + (negative) + VP		*Wh*- word + sentence *why, who,* and *how* questions appear	NP □ {(demonstrative) (article)} + (M) + N Subject NP elaboration appears: NP + V	Main Verb: 1. Obligatory 2. Overgeneralization of regular past *-ed* Auxiliary: Present tense forms appear: *can, will, be, do*	Object NP complement; full sentence takes the place of object of the verb
	Early IV	3.00–3.49	35–38 28–45		NP + auxiliary + (negative) + VP NP + copula + (negative) + VP	Inversion of auxiliary verb and subject noun	Inconsistent auxiliary inversion *when* questions appear			Simple infinitive phrases appear Simple *wh*-clauses appear Conjoined sentences with conjunction *and*

Continued on next page

TABLE 3.4—Continued

Stage	MLU	Age (months)	Grammatical Morphemes	Negation	Yes/No Questions	*Wh-* Questions	Noun Phrase Elaboration	Verb Phrase Elaboration	Complex Sentences
Late IV/ Early V	3.50–3.99	39–42 31–50	No others mastered	No change	No change	No change	NP □ { (demonstrative) (article) } { (M) (possessive) } + (adjective) + N Subject NP obligatory; noun or pronoun always appears in subject position	Main Verb: regular past *-ed* (double marking of main verb and auxiliary for past in negative sentences) Auxiliary: 1. Past modals appear, including *could, would, should, must, might* 2. *be* + present progressive *-ing* appears Verb Phrase: semi-auxiliary complements take NP	Multiple embeddings Conjoined and embedded clauses in the same sentence
Late V	4.00–4.49	43–46 37–52	6. Regular past tense of verb *-ed* 7. Irregular past tense of verb 8. Regular third person singular present tense *-s* 9. Definite and indefinite articles 10. Contractible copula	Past tense modals and *be* in contracted and uncontracted form		See Grammatical Morphemes column (6–14)	NP □ same as Stage IV Number agreement between subject and predicate verb phrase continues to be a problem beyond Stage V	See Grammatical Morphemes column (6–10)	Relative clauses appear Infinitive phrases with subjects different from that of main sentence Conjunction *if* used
V+	4.50–4.99	47–50 41–59	11. Contractible auxiliary 12. Uncontractible copula 13. Uncontractible auxiliary 14. Irregular third person singular	No data	No data			See Grammatical Morphemes column (11–14) Main Verb/Aux. 1. Past tense *be* appears as main verb and auxiliary 2. Infrequent use of present perfect tense with auxiliary marked	Gerund phrases appear *Wh-* infinitive phrases appear Unmarked infinitive phrases appear Conjunction *because* used
V++	5.00–5.99	51–67 43–67	No data	No data	No data	No data			Conjunctions *when* and *so* appear

[a]Predicted age range
[b]Age range within one SD of predicted values
[c]Based on 90% use in obligatory contexts, except stages EI–LI/EII

[d]Stages I, II, and III have been used to describe developments within only noun phrase elaboration and verb phrase elaboration based on sources of these data

[e]The following are definitions of sentence notation:
□ is expanded, or elaborated, as — S □ NP + VP; VP □ V + NP
(x) the item within the parentheses is optional
{(x) (y)} either one of the items must occur

Adapted from *Assessing Language Production in Children: Experimental Procedures* by J. Miller, 1981, Baltimore: University Park Press.

production, including grammatical morphemes. The fourth column indicates the stage at which each of the 14 grammatical morphemes is used in 90 percent of obligatory contexts. The other structures in Table 3.4 are reported at their emergence level and will be discussed individually in the following six sections describing the analysis procedures for each. It may be useful to photocopy the table at this time, instead of having to flip back and forth as each analysis procedure is discussed.

To determine mastery of the 14 grammatical morphemes in Bridget's transcript, the obligatory contexts for and the use of each grammatical morpheme will be identified. Instances of correct use of the grammatical morphemes are easier to identify than instances of obligatory contexts where the grammatical morphemes are not used. With practice, it should be possible to identify each obligatory context with ease.

Before beginning the grammatical morphemes analysis, examine the practice utterances provided. These will provide experience both in identifying the 14 grammatical morphemes and in determining obligatory contexts when the grammatical morphemes are not used. Again, cover the right side of the page, identify the use of and/or the obligatory contexts for each of the 14 grammatical morphemes, and then check your results with those provided in the shaded section. The explanations provided should help clear up any discrepancies.

Practice Examples for Grammatical Morphemes

(C points to picture in book) two puppies/	This is an example of the correct use of the regular plural *-s*. Therefore, there is an obligatory context for and a correct use of a regular plural *-s* grammatical morpheme.
(C pulls second tiny doll from bag) two baby/	In this utterance, there is an obligatory context for the regular plural *-s*, but the child has not used the plural inflection.
(C points to box in corner) puppy in box/	This is an example of an obligatory context for and a correct use of the preposition *in*. Determining the obligatory context for many of the grammatical morphemes, especially prepositions, requires that the transcript include detailed description of the nonlinguistic context. This utterance also contains an obligatory context for articles preceding the nouns, but the articles are not used. In addition, this utterance contains an obligatory context for the contractible copula, and, again, that grammatical morpheme is not used.

Continued on next page

Practice Examples—*Continued*

(C hears baby crying in another room) baby cry/	If the context notes indicate that the child is describing an ongoing activity, this utterance can be considered an obligatory context for the present progressive tense of the verb *(-ing)*. Obviously, it was not used in this utterance. In addition, there is an obligatory context for the contractible auxiliary without use. There also is questionable obligatory context for an article without use. The reason this would be considered questionable is that many times children use the word *baby* as a proper name, and an article would not be required.
(C points to puppy still in box) puppy there/	The context notes for this utterance indicate that the child was pointing out one of the puppies that was still in the box. Therefore, this would be an obligatory context for the preposition *in.* In addition, there is an obligatory context for an article and a contractible copula *(a/the* puppy *is* in there).
(C hands M's hat to clinician) mommy hat/	Again, from the context notes it can be seen that the child is talking about his mother's hat. Thus, there is an obligatory context for the possessive *-s* without use of that grammatical morpheme.
(clinician asks, "Where's your owie?" and C holds out hand) on finger/	This utterance contains an obligatory context for and a correct use of the preposition *on.*
(C dances doll across toy piano keys) Mommy singing/	This is an instance of an obligatory context for and a correct use of the present progressive tense of the verb *(-ing)*. This utterance also contains an obligatory context for the contractible auxiliary, but the auxiliary is not used. Note that the auxiliary does not have to be present to give the child credit for correct use of *-ing.*

Continued on next page

Practice Examples—*Continued*

(C hands book to M) Daddy's book/	This utterance contains an obligatory context for and a correct use of the possessive *-s.*
(C knocks doll off barn) she falled down/	This utterance contains an obligatory context for the irregular past tense of the verb. However, the child's use is of the regular form, and thus there is incorrect use of the irregular past. This is simply an obligatory context for the irregular past.
(puppy knocks C down) puppy jumped on me/	This utterance contains an obligatory context for and the correct use of the regular past tense of the verb. It also contains an obligatory context for and a correct use of the preposition *on.* In addition, it contains an obligatory context for an article.
(C points to puppy) that a puppy/	This utterance contains an obligatory context for the contractible copula, but the copula is not used. In addition, there is an obligatory context for and a correct use of the article *a.*
(C points to one of the puppies) he barks/	This is an example of an obligatory context for and a correct use of the regular third person singular present tense of the verb. The regular form is easy to identify by looking for the use of proper names or singular pronouns. These are often followed by the regular third person singular present tense of the verb.
(C points to another puppy) that's my puppy/	This utterance contains an obligatory context for and a correct use of the contractible copula. The possessive pronoun *my* does not require use of the possessive *-s* grammatical morpheme and therefore this utterance does not contain an obligatory context for the possessive *-s.*

Continued on next page

Practice Examples—*Continued*

(C scoops raisins into a pile) these are my ones/	This utterance contains obligatory contexts for and correct use of two grammatical morphemes: the uncontractible copula (plural form) and the regular plural *-s*.
(M says, "You need to hurry," as C puts toys in bag) I'm hurrying/	This utterance, too, contains obligatory contexts for and correct use of two grammatical morphemes: the contractible auxiliary and the present progressive tense of the verb *(-ing)*.
(C makes doll jump up and down) him jumping/	This utterance contains an obligatory context for the contractible auxiliary without the correct use. It also contains an obligatory context for and a correct use of the present progressive tense of the verb.
(M says, "Who's ready for ice cream?") I am/	This utterance is in response to a question, and in this elliptical form, the copula is uncontractible *(I'm* cannot be said as a response). Thus, this is an obligatory context for and a correct use of the uncontractible copula.
(M says, "Who's making all that noise?") he is/	This utterance is also in response to a question, and again, as a response, *he's* isn't possible. The preceding utterance makes this an obligatory context for and a correct use of the uncontractible auxiliary.
(C shows M a new toy) do you like it↑/	This utterance contains no obligatory contexts. *Do* is an auxiliary but not a form of the verb, *to be,* that Brown studied in the contractible and uncontractible forms.

Continued on next page

Practice Examples—*Continued*	
(C walks dolls away from toy piano) they were singing/	This utterance contains an obligatory context for and a correct use of the present progressive tense of the verb. In addition, since using the contracted form of the auxiliary eliminates the tense information (e.g., *They are singing* and *They were singing* both contract to *They're singing),* this is an example of an uncontractible auxiliary. De Villiers and de Villiers (1978) indicate that uncontractible forms typically are syllabic, as in this example. The previous two examples are uncontractible in the elliptical form.
(C points to puppy climbing out of box) he does that every time/	This is an example of an obligatory context for and a correct use of the irregular third person singular present tense of the verb.

For additional practice, you may wish to complete the worksheets on the CD-ROM at this time. Then return to Bridget's transcript and examine each utterance for the use of and/or the obligatory context for each of the 14 grammatical morphemes. Remember, there may be more than one instance of the use of and/or the obligatory context for any grammatical morpheme in each utterance. Using a blank *Grammatical Morphemes* analysis sheet from Appendix A (page 243), record the utterance number for each obligatory context for the 14 grammatical morphemes in the Obligatory Context column. If the grammatical morpheme was used correctly in the obligatory context, record the utterance number in the Use column too. It may be easier to consider each of the 14 grammatical morphemes individually as you examine each utterance for the obligatory context for and/or the use of a particular grammatical morpheme. This means that it will be necessary to go through the transcript 14 times. It is possible to examine each utterance once for the obligatory context for and/or the use of all 14 grammatical morphemes; however, it is more likely that some will be missed that way.

Once all the obligatory contexts for and uses of the 14 grammatical morphemes have been identified, add the number of uses of each grammatical morpheme and divide this total by the total number of obligatory contexts for that grammatical morpheme. Multiply this number by 100 to get the percentage of use for that grammatical morpheme. Put this number in the % Use column. Check your results with those in the sample on page 118.

As can be seen from the completed *Grammatical Morphemes* analysis sheet, several of the grammatical morphemes were not present in the sample transcript, nor were the obligatory contexts present. For these grammatical morphemes, no statement can be made regarding mastery. In addition, several of the grammatical morphemes occurred so infrequently that the resulting percentages are questionable. Both of these problems point to the need for obtaining samples that are

Grammatical Morphemes

Name of Child Bridget

Grammatical Morpheme	Obligatory Context	Use	% Use
1. *-ing*	—	—	—
2. plural *-s*	27, 78, 81	27, 78, 81	100
3. *in*	17, 97	17, 97	100
4. *on*	13	—	0
5. possessive *-s*	62, 65	62, 65	100
6. regular past *-ed*	36, 45, 96	96	33
7. irregular past	2, 5, 44, 46, 56, 81, 86	5, 81, 86	43
8. regular third person singular	75	—	0
9. articles *a, an, the*	8, 9, 13, 17, 25, 27, 32, 40, 41, 50, 58, 60, 61, 81, 84, 93, 94	17, 25, 32, 60, 61, 81	35
10. contractible copula	18, 20, 32, 33, 35, 60, 61, 65	18, 20, 32, 33, 35, 60, 61, 65	100
11. contractible auxiliary	21, 24	21	50
12. uncontractible copula	23, 62	23	50
13. uncontractible auxiliary	—	—	—
14. irregular third person singular	—	—	—

relatively lengthy. As discussed in Chapter 1, a sample of 100 utterances is the absolute minimum length.

So what conclusions can be drawn from the grammatical morphemes analysis of Bridget's transcript? First, in spite of few instances of each, this child apparently has mastered the regular plural *-s,* the preposition *in,* and the possessive *-s.* In addition, the contractible copula appears to have been mastered. We are more confident of Bridget's mastery of this last grammatical morpheme because there were eight instances of correct use. It can also be concluded that five grammatical morphemes do not appear to have been mastered: the regular past tense *-ed* (with 33% correct use in obligatory contexts), the irregular past tense of the verb (with 43% correct use in obligatory contexts), indefinite and definite articles (with 35% correct use in obligatory contexts), the contractible auxiliary (with 50% correct use in obligatory contexts), and the uncontractible copula (with 50% correct use in obligatory contexts). In addition, one obligatory context was noted for each of two grammatical morphemes (the preposition *on* and the regular third person singular present tense *-s).* Only one obligatory context for each with no use yielded 0% correct use for these two grammatical morphemes. No conclusions can be drawn for the grammatical morphemes *-ing,* uncontractible auxiliary, and irregular third person singular. Stages will be assigned reflecting mastery of grammatical morphemes in the "Summary and Interpretation" section, beginning on page 152.

Analyzing Complexity of Negation

Negation analysis results in a stage assignment reflecting its structural complexity within a transcript. The stage assignments are based on data reported by Klima and Bellugi (1966); Chapman (1978, as cited in Miller, 1981); and Chapman, Paul, and Wanska (1981). Changes in the child's ability to incorporate negative elements into an utterance typically occur with increases in utterance length. The fifth column in Table 3.4 (see pages 111–112) indicates the changes in structural complexity of negation and the stage at which those changes emerge. Keep in mind that the stage assignments reflect emergence of a new way of producing negation and not mastery of this new form. In addition, note that changes do not occur at every stage.

To determine the stage that characterizes the child's level of negation, analyze each utterance within the transcript for developmental complexity. The first step is to identify negative elements within the transcript. Identifying negative elements is easier than identifying some syntactic structures because there are a limited number of ways in which negation can be incorporated into an utterance at these developmental levels. These include the use of *no* as a single-word utterance (except in response to a question) or adding *no* to a noun or verb, as well as the use of *not* in contracted and uncontracted forms in various sentence positions. After identifying utterances with negation, determine the stage that best characterizes each negative element. This second step may be more difficult. To increase your ability to make such judgments, use the practice utterances provided on the next few pages. Cover the right side of the page, compare the utterance to the descriptions provided in the fifth column of Table 3.4 (see pages 111–112), assign a stage, and then check your results with those provided. The explanations in the shaded section should help clear up any questions. You may wish to turn to the CD-ROM for additional practice.

Practice Examples for Negation

(M and C are playing with circus set; M says, "Do you want me to put him in the wagon?") no/	No Stage Assigned This is not an example of *no* as a negative sentence. It is a one-word response to a yes/no question, so no stage is assigned. A transcript that contains many responses to yes/no questions will erroneously report the stage for negation. A transcript such as this would be rejected on the basis of a lack of representativeness prior to beginning analysis of structural complexity.
(C pushes M's hand away as she tries to wipe his mouth) no/	Early Stage I (EI) The use of *no* as a single-word utterance is the earliest type of negative sentence. Assigning Early Stage I to this utterance in a transcript with utterances considerably longer than one word may distort the assignment of an overall stage for negation, but it represents the accurate stage assignment.
(C hits doll with teddy bear, then looks at M and says) no hit/	Late Stage I/Early Stage II–Stage II (LI/EII–II) This utterance is an example of a *no* + verb sentence form. This form is characteristic of Late Stage I/Early Stage II, but it continues to be used through Stage II.
(C pulls on M's arm) not go/	Late Stage I/Early Stage II–Stage II (LI/EII–II) This utterance is an example of a *not* + verb sentence form, also characteristic of Late Stage I/Early Stage II through Stage II.
(as M leaves room, C shakes head and looks at M) me no go/	Stage III (III) This utterance is an example of a negative sentence in the form NP (noun phrase) + (negative) + VP (verb phrase), with the negative element integrated into the sentence. This form emerges in Stage III.

Continued on next page

Practice Examples—*Continued*

(C puts girl doll in car) Daddy not go/	Stage III (III) This is another example with the negative element integrated into the sentence. In this case, the negative element is *not* instead of *no.* This utterance and the preceding one are characteristic of the same stage.
(C opens box of people and animals) there aren't any kikis here/	Early Stage IV–Late Stage IV/Early Stage V (EIV–LIV/EV) This utterance is an example of the verb *be,* in the plural present tense negative contracted form. This form appears in Early Stage IV, at the same time as auxiliary elements in contracted and uncontracted forms.
(C picks up a toy dog and shakes her head) not a kiki/	Late Stage I/Early Stage II–Stage II (LI/EII–II) This utterance is an example of *not* + noun with an article included. As discussed in the third example on page 120, assigning Late Stage I/Early Stage II to the utterance appears to underestimate the child's abilities to produce negative structures. Therefore, the best stage assignment that can be made is to assign the range of stages.
(puppy jumps on clinician and C looks at her) he no bite you/	Stage III (III) This utterance contains a negative element integrated within the sentence between the NP and the VP.
(C's baby brother is babbling and C says to M) he isn't silly/	Early Stage IV–Late Stage IV/Early Stage V (EIV–LIV/EV) This negative sentence contains the present tense of the verb *be,* in the negative contracted form. It is typical of examples provided in the literature for Early Stage IV.

Continued on next page

Practice Examples—*Continued*

(M holds up dirty socks) those aren't mine/	Late Stage V (LV) This utterance contains the plural form of the verb *be* in the form of a negative contraction.
(M says from other room, "Did you find your hat?") it wasn't there/	Late Stage V (LV) This utterance contains a negative contraction of the past tense form of the verb *be.*
(C turns cup upside down on table) no juice/	Late Stage I/Early Stage II–Stage II (LI/EII–II) This utterance is an example of the *no* + noun form of negation. It is characteristic of Late Stage I/Early Stage II, but the range of stages is recorded.
(C pushes blue crayon away) I don't want that one/	Early Stage IV–Late Stage IV/Early Stage V (EIV–LIV/EV) This utterance contains an auxiliary (the dummy *do)* in the negative contracted form, which appears in Early Stage IV.
(clinician drops box of little bears and begins to pick them up) you shouldn't do that/	Late Stage V (LV) This utterance contains the modal auxiliary verb *should* in the negative contracted form. Modals in contracted and uncontracted form appear in negative sentences at this stage.
(C turns puzzle piece around and around) this one doesn't fit/	Early Stage IV–Late Stage IV/Early Stage V (EIV–LIV/EV) Again, there is an auxiliary, *does,* in the negative contracted form.
(C hugs teddy bear after pulling it out of box) I couldn't find him/	Late Stage V (LV) This utterance contains the past tense modal auxiliary *could* in the negative contracted form.

The practice you just completed should help you identify negative elements and assign stages to the developmental complexity of each. Now, return to the sample transcript and examine each utterance for the presence of negative elements. If there is no negative element in the utterance, mark a dash (—) for that utterance in the Negation column on the *Structural Stage Analysis Grid* used earlier to record the number of morphemes for each of Bridget's utterances. When an utterance with a negative element is identified, compare that utterance to the descriptions of increases in complexity provided in the fifth column of Table 3.4 (see pages 111–112) to determine the stage that best characterizes the complexity of the negative element within the utterance. Then record the stage number for that utterance in the Negation column on the *Structural Stage Analysis Grid.* When each utterance has been examined for the presence of negative elements and stage assignments have been recorded, compare your results with those provided on pages 124–125.

Bridget's transcript contained four negative utterances, ranging in complexity from Late Stage I/Early Stage II–Stage II to Early Stage IV–Late Stage IV/Early Stage V. Utterances #3 and #33 pose some problems and therefore are not included in the total of the four negative utterances. Utterance #3 is simply a negative response to the mother's question; therefore, it is not included in the total of negative utterances. Utterance #33 includes a negative response to the mother's question, "Do you want to put him up there?" The child responds, "No [I don't want to put him up there because] it's heavy." The utterance is not a negative utterance in terms of the presence of negative elements incorporated into the utterance structure. It is a negative response that is elliptical in relation to the mother's utterance and is a clarification of that negative response. Therefore, it is not appropriate to include it in the total of negative utterances.

The stage assignments for individual utterances recorded on the *Structural Stage Analysis Grid* will be used to complete the *Production Characteristics Summary Form* (see page 156) in the "Summary and Interpretation" section, beginning on page 152. Before tallying these instances of negation on the summary form, the complexity of five other syntactic structures will be analyzed. The tallying of stage assignments for individual utterances will allow for examination of the most frequently occurring stage for negation as well as the most advanced stage. These data can only be interpreted in relation to stage assignments for other structures.

Analyzing Complexity of Yes/No Questions

Analyzing the complexity of yes/no questions yields a stage assignment reflecting that complexity. Such analysis is done in the same manner as we used for grammatical morphemes and negation. The developmental sequence of changes in complexity and stage assignments is based on data reported by Klima and Bellugi (1966) and Chapman et al. (1981). The sixth column in Table 3.4 (see pages 111–112) summarizes the sequence of developmental changes for yes/no questions. As with negation, stage assignments reflect appearance of changes in producing yes/no questions and not mastery of the changes. And like the preceding syntactic structure, changes in complexity of yes/no questions do not occur at every stage.

To determine the stage that characterizes Bridget's level of yes/no question production, each yes/no question in the sample transcript will be examined for developmental complexity. First, identify the yes/no questions and then examine the way in which the questions were formed. To determine the stage that describes each

Structural Stage Analysis Grid

Name of Child Bridget

response to yes/no question (utterance 3)

response to yes/no question plus explanation (utterance 33)

Utterance Number	Number of Morphemes	Negation	Yes/No Question	Wh-Question	Noun Phrase Elaboration	Verb Phrase Elaboration	Complex Sentence
1	1	–					
2	2	–					
3	1	(–)					
4	1	–					
5	4	–					
6	1	–					
7	2	–					
8	1	–					
9	1	–					
10	1	–					
11	3	–					
12	1	–					
13	1	–					
14	1	–					
15	4	–					
16	2	–					
17	4	–					
18	4	EIV–LIV/EV					
19	2	–					
20	4	EIV–LIV/EV					
21	4	EIV–LIV/EV					
22	2	–					
23	3	–					
24	4	–					
25	2	–					

Utterance Number	Number of Morphemes	Negation	Yes/No Question	Wh-Question	Noun Phrase Elaboration	Verb Phrase Elaboration	Complex Sentence
26	2	–					
27	2	–					
28	2	–					
29	1	–					
30	1	–					
31	5	–					
32	4	–					
33	4	(–)					
34	1	–					
35	4	–					
36	3	–					
37	1	–					
38	1	–					
39	1	–					
40	1	–					
41	1	–					
42	1	–					
43	2	–					
44	2	–					
45	3	–					
46	3	–					
47	1	–					
48	1	–					
49	1	–					
50	1	–					
Subtotal 1	105						

Structural Stage Analysis Grid

Name of Child Bridget

Utterance Number	Number of Morphemes	Negation	Yes/No Question	*Wh-* Question	Noun Phrase Elaboration	Verb Phrase Elaboration	Complex Sentence
51	1	—					
52	3	—					
53	1	—					
54	1	—					
55	1	—					
56	4	—					
57	1	—					
58	1	—					
59	1	—					
60	4	—					
61	4	—					
62	3	—					
63	1	—					
64	1	—					
65	4	—					
66	2	—					
67	1	—					
68	1	—					
69	1	—					
70	1	—					
71	1	—					
72	3	—					
73	3	—					
74	1	—					
75	2	—					

Utterance Number	Number of Morphemes	Negation	Yes/No Question	*Wh-* Question	Noun Phrase Elaboration	Verb Phrase Elaboration	Complex Sentence
76	1	—					
77	1	—					
78	3	LI/EII—II					
79	1	—					
80	1	—					
81	5	—					
82	1	—					
83	3	—					
84	1	—					
85	1	—					
86	2	—					
87	3	—					
88	3	—					
89	3	—					
90	3	—					
91	1	—					
92	1	—					
93	1	—					
94	1	—					
95	1	—					
96	3	—					
97	3	—					
98	1	—					
99	2	—					
100	2	—					
Subtotal 2	95						

[105] + [95] = 200

No. of Morphemes (Subtotal 1) + No. of Morphemes (Subtotal 2) = Total Number of Morphemes

$$\frac{\text{Total Number of Morphemes}}{\text{Total Number of Utterances}} = \frac{[\ 200\ ]}{[\ 100\ ]} = 2.00 \text{ MLU}$$

individual yes/no question, compare each question to the descriptions provided in Table 3.4. Before identifying the yes/no questions and determining the developmental complexity of each question in the sample transcript, complete the practice examples below. The following utterances have been selected to demonstrate some of the problems that are frequently encountered when describing the developmental complexity of yes/no questions. The practice gained in assigning stages to these utterances will be helpful when such analysis is performed on the sample transcript. Cover the right side of the page, compare the utterance to the descriptions of developmental changes in Table 3.4 (see pages 111–112), and assign a stage. Then check your results with those in the shaded section. The explanations provided should help clear up any questions.

Practice Examples for Yes/No Questions

(C picks up an apple) ball≠/	Early Stage I–Stage III (EI–III) Yes/No questions are marked only with rising intonation during these four stages. It is impossible to differentiate among these stages in the child's productions, so the best way to assign a stage is to assign a range. When this information is put together with other stage assignments, the adequacy of the child's productions can be determined.
(C shows cow to M) see≠/	Early Stage I–Stage III (EI–III) This yes/no question is of the same form as the previous one, and the four stages cannot be differentiated at this point.
(C turns empty cookie box upside down) more≠/	Early Stage I–Stage III (EI–III) Again, this is a yes/no question marked only with rising intonation, and, as in the preceding two examples, these four stages cannot be differentiated.
(C hands empty cup to M) more juice≠/	Early Stage I–Stage III (EI–III) Although this utterance is longer than the preceding three, it is of the same form. Therefore, these four stages cannot be differentiated.
(C talking to toy monkey) do like monkeys≠/	Early Stage I–Stage III (EI–III) This utterance contains the "dummy *do,*" an auxiliary form used to invert the auxiliary and subject noun phrase. But the subject noun phrase is omitted. It would be inappropriate to assign Early Stage IV–Late Stage V, so we must assign Early Stage I–Stage III.

Continued on next page

Practice Examples—*Continued*

(C hands puzzle piece to M) da no go≠/	Early Stage I–Stage III (EI–III) Again, this is a yes/no question marked only with rising intonation. No differentiation of stages is possible.
(C picks up doll from doll bed) baby wet≠/	Early Stage I–Stage III (EI–III) This is one more example of a yes/no question marked only with rising intonation.
(C turns to M as she leaves the room) am I gonna go≠/	Early Stage IV–Late Stage V (EIV–LV) Finally, this is an example of a yes/no question with inversion of the auxiliary and the subject noun. This form emerges in Early Stage IV.
(C looks on as M dumps cookie out of box) is that the only one≠/	Early Stage IV–Late Stage V (EIV–LV) This also is an example of a yes/no question with the inversion necessary to form a question. In this utterance, the main verb, *be,* is inverted. The ability to invert all or part of the verb phrase with the noun phrase appears in Early Stage IV.
(C picks up last cupcake) can I eat this one≠/	Early Stage IV–Late Stage V (EIV–LV) This yes/no question also contains auxiliary inversion. Although assigning the same stage to each of these three utterances seems to distort the apparent differences in complexity, it appears to be the best alternative. The differences in complexity will be captured in the verb phrase analysis.
(C hands wind-up toy to M) will you fix this≠/	Early Stage IV–Late Stage V (EIV–LV) This yes/no question is of the same auxiliary inversion form. The obviously higher level of complexity will be credited to the child in the verb phrase analysis.

These practice utterances should have clarified the two ways in which children construct yes/no questions. Although other changes in complexity are apparent within yes/no questions, such changes reflect changes in structures other than the formation of the question. Now, return to the sample transcript and examine each utterance for the presence of rising intonation or verb phrase inversion. Progress through the transcript, recording a dash (—) for each utterance that is not a type of yes/no question in the Yes/No Question column on the *Structural Stage Analysis Grid* used earlier. If the utterance is a type of yes/no question, compare that utterance to the descriptions provided in the sixth column of Table 3.4 (see pages 111–112) to determine the stage that best describes the complexity of that yes/no question. Then record the stage number or range of stages for that utterance in the Yes/No Question column on the *Structural Stage Analysis Grid.* After each yes/no question in the sample transcript has been analyzed, compare your results with those in the partially completed *Structural Stage Analysis Grid* on pages 129–130.

Three utterances should have been identified as types of yes/no questions in the sample transcript. Each of these yes/no questions was formed using rising intonation and thus each was typical of Early Stage I–Stage III. Although these utterances appear to be a minimal amount of data for analysis of the developmental level of yes/no questions, it is not uncommon to find that only a small percentage of the utterances are question forms. These instances of yes/no questions will be tallied on the *Production Characteristics Summary Form* after analyzing the complexity of four other syntactic structures. Final interpretation of the level of complexity of yes/no questions can be made only after summarizing the developmental level of all other syntactic structures to be analyzed.

Analyzing Complexity of *Wh-* Questions

Analysis of the developmental level of *wh-* questions results in a stage assignment reflecting the complexity of the questions. Unlike the preceding analyses, the analysis of *wh-* questions considers two aspects of the structure to be analyzed. The first consideration in determining the developmental level of a *wh-* question is the type of *wh-* question. For example, *what* questions appear early in the developmental sequence and *when* questions appear much later. A stage is assigned to a particular *wh-* question on the basis of which type of *wh-* question it is. The second consideration in determining the developmental level of a *wh-* question is the form of the question. For example, "*what* + NP" question forms occur early in the developmental sequence, while questions with auxiliary inversion occur considerably later in the sequence. The form of the question and the type of *wh-* word are to refine the judgments about stage assignment. A *what* question with auxiliary inversion is assigned a higher stage than a *what* question without auxiliary inversion.

Both aspects of the *wh-* question are considered in assigning a stage to each utterance. The changes in type and form of the *wh-* questions are summarized in the seventh column of Table 3.4 (see pages 111–112). The stage assignments are based on data reported by Klima and Bellugi (1966); Ervin-Tripp (1970); Tyack and Ingram (1977); and Chapman et al. (1981). Changes in type and form reflect the appearance of these changes and not mastery of the changes.

To determine the stage that characterizes the child's level of *wh-* question development, analyze each *wh-* question within the sample transcript for type and

Structural Stage Analysis Grid

Name of Child Bridget

Utterance Number	Number of Morphemes	Negation	Yes/No Question	*Wh*-Question	Noun Phrase Elaboration	Verb Phrase Elaboration	Complex Sentence
1	1	—	—				
2	2	—	—				
3	1	—	—				
4	1	—	—				
5	4	—	—				
6	1	—	EI—III				
7	2	—	—				
8	1	—	—				
9	1	—	—				
10	1	—	—				
11	3	—	—				
12	1	—	—				
13	1	—	—				
14	1	—	—				
15	4	—	—				
16	2	—	—				
17	4	—	—				
18	4	EIV—LIV/EV	—				
19	2	—	—				
20	4	EIV—LIV/EV	—				
21	4	EIV—LIV/EV	—				
22	2	—	—				
23	3	—	—				
24	4	—	—				
25	2	—	—				

Utterance Number	Number of Morphemes	Negation	Yes/No Question	*Wh*-Question	Noun Phrase Elaboration	Verb Phrase Elaboration	Complex Sentence
26	2	—	—				
27	2	—	—				
28	2	—	—				
29	1	—	—				
30	1	—	—				
31	5	—	—				
32	4	—	—				
33	4	—	—				
34	1	—	—				
35	4	—	—				
36	3	—	—				
37	1	—	—				
38	1	—	—				
39	1	—	—				
40	1	—	—				
41	1	—	—				
42	1	—	—				
43	2	—	—				
44	2	—	—				
45	3	—	—				
46	3	—	—				
47	1	—	—				
48	1	—	—				
49	1	—	—				
50	1	—	—				
Subtotal 1	105						

Structural Stage Analysis Grid

Name of Child Bridget

Utterance Number	Number of Morphemes	Negation	Yes/No Question	Wh-Question	Noun Phrase Elaboration	Verb Phrase Elaboration	Complex Sentence
51	1	—	—				
52	3	—	—				
53	1	—	—				
54	1	—	—				
55	1	—	—				
56	4	—	—				
57	1	—	—				
58	1	—	—				
59	1	—	—				
60	4	—	EI—III				
61	4	—	—				
62	3	—	—				
63	1	—	—				
64	1	—	—				
65	4	—	—				
66	2	—	—				
67	1	—	—				
68	1	—	—				
69	1	—	—				
70	1	—	EI—III				
71	1	—	—				
72	3	—	—				
73	3	—	—				
74	1	—	—				
75	2	—	—				

Utterance Number	Number of Morphemes	Negation	Yes/No Question	Wh-Question	Noun Phrase Elaboration	Verb Phrase Elaboration	Complex Sentence
76	1	—	—				
77	1	—	—				
78	3	LI/EII—II	—				
79	1	—	—				
80	1	—	—				
81	5	—	—				
82	1	—	—				
83	3	—	—				
84	1	—	—				
85	1	—	—				
86	2	—	—				
87	3	—	—				
88	3	—	—				
89	3	—	—				
90	3	—	—				
91	1	—	—				
92	1	—	—				
93	1	—	—				
94	1	—	—				
95	1	—	—				
96	3	—	—				
97	3	—	—				
98	1	—	—				
99	2	—	—				
100	2	—	—				
Subtotal 2	95						

[105] No. of Morphemes (Subtotal 1) + [95] No. of Morphemes (Subtotal 2) = 200 Total Number of Morphemes

Total Number of Morphemes / Total Number of Utterances = [200] / [100] = 2.00 MLU form. To increase your ability to identify changes in type and form, complete the following practice utterances. Cover the right side of the page, make the stage assignment, and then check your assignments with those provided in the shaded section. The explanations should help clear up any discrepancies.

Practice Examples for *Wh-* Questions

(M tells C to pick up toys quickly) what?/	No Stage Assigned This child is simply asking for a repetition of the statement or has learned to say *what* as a stalling technique. Repetition requests are not coded as *wh-* questions.
(C points to doughnut and looks at M) wazit?/ [what this?]	Early Stage I (EI) This probably is the most basic type of *wh-* question in that it functions as a generic question type. It is a *what* question type and is in the form of a reduced *what* + *this.*
(clock makes noise and C looks to M) what that?/	Early Stage I (EI) This question is characteristic of the same stage as the preceding example, even though it is more complex.
(C holds up small plastic animal) what this one?/	Late Stage I/Early Stage II–Stage II (LI/EII–II) Although this is the same type of question as the preceding two *(what),* it is in a more complex form: *what* + NP. Consequently, it is assigned a more advanced stage range.
(C hears voices outside door and asks M) where Daddy?/	Late Stage I/Early Stage II–Stage II (LI/EII–II) This question is of a different type *(where)* than the preceding questions, but it is in the same form: *where* + NP. Thus, it is assigned the same stage.
(C is drawing with marking pens) where the green one is?/	Stage III (III) This question is the same type of question as the preceding one *(where),* but it is in a more complex form: *wh-* word + sentence. This form emerges in Stage III.
(C is digging through toy box) where's the big one?/	Early Stage IV–Late V (EIV–LV) Again, this is a *where* question, but this one reflects inversion of the verb and noun phrase. This form emerges in Early Stage IV.

Continued on next page

Practice Examples—*Continued*

(clinician enters room and adjusts remote control camera) what him doing?/	Late Stage I/Early Stage II–Stage II (LI/EII–II) This is an example of a simple *what doing* question that emerges in Late Stage I/Early Stage II and does not change in form through Stage II.
(C searching through bag of small plastic animals) where that elephant?/	Late Stage I/Early Stage II–Stage II (LI/EII–II) This is another *where* + NP question form that emerges in Late Stage I/Early Stage II and does not change in form through Stage II.
(clinician enters room to adjust camera) who that is?/	Stage III (III) The *who* question type emerges in Stage III, and the form of this particular *who* question is typical of Stage III (*wh-* word + sentence).
(someone shouts in hallway) who is that?/	Early Stage IV–Late V (EIV–LV) This *who* question shows evidence of inversion of the verb and noun phrase. So even though it is a Stage III question type, it is in the Early Stage IV form.
(C pushes puppy away) why him bite me?/	Stage III (III) This type of question emerges in Stage III, and it is in the Stage III form (no inversion).
(C fitting blocks together) how this one go?/	Stage III (III) This is another question type to emerge in Stage III, and the uninverted form continues.
(C looks at clinician) when is my mom coming?/	Early Stage IV–Late V (EIV–LV) *When* questions emerge in Early Stage IV, so the assignment is simple on those grounds. But notice that this utterance also contains an example of auxiliary inversion, which also emerges at this stage. Consequently, it is assigned Early Stage IV on the basis of type and form.

This practice should be helpful in assigning stages on the basis of both the type and the form of the *wh-* question. Now return to the sample transcript and determine the stage that best characterizes the type and form of each *wh-* question. Progress through the transcript, recording a dash (—) for each utterance that is not a *wh-* question and the appropriate stage for each *wh-* question in the *Wh-* Question column on the *Structural Stage Analysis Grid* used earlier. When a dash or a stage has been recorded for all 100 utterances, compare your results with those in the sample on pages 134–135.

The sample transcript contained eight *wh-* questions ranging in complexity from Late Stage I/Early Stage II–Stage II to Late Stage V. These *wh-* questions will be recorded on the *Production Characteristics Summary Form.*

Before moving on to the analysis of other structures, one type of *wh-* question not included in the total needs to be examined. Five questions might have been assigned Early Stage I. All of these were a type of *what* question and all were in the form of "huh?" Although these are *what* questions, and the only information to use when assigning a stage to them is the type, tallying these in Early Stage I may distort the child's level of *wh-* question development. These *what* questions are different from other Early Stage I *what* questions in that they are not querying a specific semantic role. Typically, children use Early Stage I *what* questions to query the label of an object. The five *what* questions in this transcript appear to have been used to request repetition of the mother's utterance, not to obtain the label for an object. This use of *what?* or *huh?* serves a pragmatic function, not a semantic one. Analysis of the syntactic form of these questions underestimates the child's syntactic abilities. Therefore, these five questions will be eliminated from the syntactic analysis. They will be considered in the next chapter when pragmatic aspects of this child's productions are examined.

Thus, the total number of *wh-* questions is eight. But one more type of *wh-* question should be re-examined. Utterances #7, #16, #19, and #66 are all examples of a routine form for this child (i.e., "What else?"). She appears to use this form in various places in conversation when she wants to move on to play with and talk about other toys. If she had used the fully elaborated form, "What else is in the box?" or "What else should we do?" Early Stage IV would be the more appropriate assignment. Given the abbreviated form of her utterances, Late Stage I/Early Stage II–Stage II was judged to be the best stage assignment. Before the developmental level of *wh-* questions in this child's productions can be interpreted, the complexity of three more syntactic structures must be analyzed. Only after all aspects of syntactic production have been analyzed can each structure be appropriately interpreted.

Analyzing Complexity of Noun Phrases

As in the analysis of each of the preceding syntactic structures, analysis of the complexity of the noun phrase results in a stage assignment. Stage assignments reflect the type and amount of elaboration of the noun phrase as well as the position of the noun phrase within the utterance. Stage assignments are based on data reported by Brown and Bellugi (1964), Cazden (1968), Ingram (1972), de Villiers and de Villiers (1973), Brown (1973), and Chapman (1978, as cited in Miller, 1981). Increases in complexity of the noun phrase occur with increases in utterance length, but the increases in complexity of the noun phrase are not simply increases in length. The eighth column of Table 3.4 (see pages 111–112) summarizes the changes in the noun phrase with increases in utterance length. The summaries reflect emergence of new ways to increase the complexity of the noun phrase and not mastery of the forms.

Structural Stage Analysis Grid

Name of Child Bridget

Utterance Number	Number of Morphemes	Negation	Yes/No Question	*Wh*-Question	Noun Phrase Elaboration	Verb Phrase Elaboration	Complex Sentence
1	1	—	—	—			
2	2	—	—	—			
3	1	—	—	—			
4	1	—	—	—			
5	4	—	—	—			
6	1	—	EI—III	—			
7	2	—	—	LI/EII—II			
8	1	—	—	—			
9	1	—	—	—			
10	1	—	—	—			
11	3	—	—	—			
12	1	—	—	—			
13	1	—	—	—			
14	1	—	—	—			
15	4	—	—	—			
16	2	—	—	LI/EII—II			
17	4	—	—	—			
18	4	EIV—LIV/EV	—	—			
19	2	—	—	LI/EII—II			
20	4	EIV—LIV/EV	—	—			
21	4	EIV—LIV/EV	—	—			
22	2	—	—	—			
23	3	—	—	III			
24	4	—	—	III			
25	2	—	—	—			

Utterance Number	Number of Morphemes	Negation	Yes/No Question	*Wh*-Question	Noun Phrase Elaboration	Verb Phrase Elaboration	Complex Sentence
26	2	—	—	—			
27	2	—	—	—			
28	2	—	—	—			
29	1	—	—	— (circled: repetition request)			
30	1	—	—	—			
31	5	—	—	—			
32	4	—	—	—			
33	4	—	—	—			
34	1	—	—	—			
35	4	—	—	LV			
36	3	—	—	—			
37	1	—	—	—			
38	1	—	—	—			
39	1	—	—	—			
40	1	—	—	—			
41	1	—	—	—			
42	1	—	—	—			
43	2	—	—	—			
44	2	—	—	—			
45	3	—	—	—			
46	3	—	—	—			
47	1	—	—	—			
48	1	—	—	—			
49	1	—	—	—			
50	1	—	—	—			
Subtotal 1	105						

Structural Stage Analysis Grid

Name of Child Bridget

repetition request

Utterance Number	Number of Morphemes	Negation	Yes/No Question	Wh-Question	Noun Phrase Elaboration	Verb Phrase Elaboration	Complex Sentence
51	1	—	—	—			
52	3	—	—	—			
53	1	—	—	—			
54	1	—	—	—			
55	1	—	—	—			
56	4	—	—	—			
57	1	—	—	—			
58	1	—	—	—			
59	1	—	—	—			
60	4	—	EI—III	—			
61	4	—	—	—			
62	3	—	—	—			
63	1	—	—	—			
64	1	—	—	—			
65	4	—	—	—			
66	2	—	—	LI/EII—II			
67	1	—	—	—			
68	1	—	—	—			
69	1	—	—	—			
70	1	—	EI—III	—			
71	1	—	—	—			
72	3	—	—	—			
73	3	—	—	—			
74	1	—	—	—			
75	2	—	—	—			

repetition request

Utterance Number	Number of Morphemes	Negation	Yes/No Question	Wh-Question	Noun Phrase Elaboration	Verb Phrase Elaboration	Complex Sentence
76	1	—	—	—			
77	1	—	—	—			
78	3	LI/EII—II	—	—			
79	1	—	—	—			
80	1	—	—	—			
81	5	—	—	—			
82	1	—	—	—			
83	3	—	—	—			
84	1	—	—	—			
85	1	—	—	—			
86	2	—	—	—			
87	3	—	—	—			
88	3	—	—	—			
89	3	—	—	—			
90	3	—	—	—			
91	1	—	—	—			
92	1	—	—	—			
93	1	—	—	—			
94	1	—	—	—			
95	1	—	—	—			
96	3	—	—	LV			
97	3	—	—	—			
98	1	—	—	—			
99	2	—	—	—			
100	2	—	—	—			
Subtotal 2	95						

[105] + [95] = 200

No. of Morphemes (Subtotal 1) + No. of Morphemes (Subtotal 2) = Total Number of Morphemes

$$\frac{\text{Total Number of Morphemes}}{\text{Total Number of Utterances}} = \frac{[\ 200\ ]}{[\ 100\ ]} = 2.00 \text{ MLU}$$

Judgments about the developmental complexity of the noun phrase are more difficult to make than those for some of the preceding structures. One reason for this is that the vast majority of utterances contain a noun phrase. In addition, there is greater variability in the specificity of the noun phrase. Pragmatic requirements are such that not all utterances containing a noun phrase are in the most complex form that the child is capable of producing. In addition, many utterances contain only a noun phrase because the child is responding to a question from the other speaker or clarifying a previous utterance. Assignment of a stage to these utterances may underestimate the child's abilities. For these reasons, a greater number of practice utterances are provided to obtain experience in making these more difficult judgments. Cover the right side of the page, compare the noun phrases within the utterances to the descriptions provided in the Noun Phrase Elaboration column of Table 3.4 (see pages 111–112), and assign a stage. Remember for Stages I, II, and III to use the broad stages as indicated by white lettering on the far left side of Table 3.4. Then check your judgments with those provided in the shaded section. The explanations should help clarify differences.

Practice Examples for Noun Phrase Elaboration

(C reaches for box of cookies)
more cookie/

Stage I–Stage II (I–II)
This utterance is an example of an elaborated noun phrase that includes an optional modifier (M) *more.* Because the noun phrase does not change in form from Stage I to Stage II, the range of stages is used.

(C points to picture in book)
kitty/

Stage I–Stage II (I–II)
Because the modifier is optional in Stage I and the form of the noun phrase does not change in Stage II, the stage range is the best assignment.

(C points to another picture in book)
pretty kitty/

Stage I–Stage II (I–II)
This utterance includes the optional modifier that typifies the form of the elaborated noun phrase in Stage I and Stage II. The stage range is the best assignment.

(C reaches for box of crackers on counter)
want more cracker/

Stage II (II)
This utterance contains an elaborated noun phrase but the type of elaboration is not one of those specified in Stage III. As indicated in Stage II, this elaborated noun phrase occurs only in the object position.

(C sees clinician roll ball to M)
that ball/

Stage III (III)
This utterance is an example of an elaborated noun phrase also, but it includes an optional demonstrative form, *that,* which emerges in Stage III.

Continued on next page

Practice Examples—*Continued*

(C points to picture in book) that a baby/	Stage III (III) This utterance contains an elaborated noun phrase with two optional forms, a demonstrative, *that,* and an article, *a.* It is presumed that the demonstrative represents a subject noun phrase and the article plus noun represents the object noun phrase. The verb is omitted. Utterances of this type and form emerge in Stage III. Consequently, Stage III is assigned to this utterance.
(C pulls tiny doll from bag) that a tiny baby/	Stage III (III) This utterance contains an article plus a modifier, *tiny,* plus a noun in the object noun phrase position with the demonstrative form in the subject noun phrase position. Noun phrases in this form appear in Stage III.
(C points to bus with toy kittens in it) that alotta kitties/	Stage III (III) The use of *alotta* in this utterance represents an article and the optional modifier in the object position. A verb is not necessary to assign Stage III.
(C points to juice box) orange juice/	Stage I–Stage II (I–II) Noun phrase elaboration occurs only alone with no verb present.
(C takes juice glass from M) drink juice/	Stage I–Stage II (I–II) This utterance has a noun phrase with no elaboration.
(C puts cup to doll's mouth) drink orange juice/	Stage II (II) This utterance has a noun phrase in the object position with elaboration.
(C holds puppy out to clinician) kiss the puppy/	Stage III (III) Although this utterance contains a verb, the constituent that is the most significant is the object noun phrase, *the puppy.* This noun phrase comprises an article plus a noun. This form is characteristic of Stage III.

Continued on next page

Practice Examples—*Continued*

(C pushes puppy away) hit that naughty puppy/	Stage III (III) The noun phrase in this utterance is in the object position. It contains a demonstrative, *that,* and a modifier, *naughty,* before the noun, *puppy.* Noun phrases of this type are characteristic of Stage III.
(puppy jumps out of box) that puppy jump/	Stage III (III) The noun phrase in this utterance is in the subject position. Subject noun phrases appear in Stage III. This is the best cue for stage assignment. But the form of this noun phrase also is consistent with Stage III in that there is a demonstrative, *that,* with the noun. No modifier is present, but the modifier is optional at this stage.
(C pushes puppy away) that puppy licked my face/	Late Stage IV/Early Stage V (LIV/EV) There are two noun phrases in this utterance: a subject noun phrase, *that puppy,* and an object noun phrase, *my face.* The presence of a subject noun phrase suggests at least Stage III. However, the possessive pronoun *my* in the object noun phrase of a NP + VP complete utterance indicates Late Stage IV/Early Stage V. The possessive is one of the optional constituents in Late Stage IV/Early Stage V.
(M asks, "Where should we put the sprinkles?") on that cookie/	Stage III (III) The noun phrase in this utterance contains a demonstrative, *that,* and a noun, *cookie,* in the object position. Noun phrases of this type and in this position are characteristic of Stage III.
(C points to cookie on plate) I want that cookie/	Late Stage IV/Early Stage V (LIV/EV) There are two noun phrases in this utterance: a subject noun phrase, *I,* and an object noun phrase, *that cookie.* The object noun phrase is in Stage III form (demonstrative plus noun). The subject noun phrase is in the form of a pronoun, but stage assignment is more difficult. To assign Late Stage IV, the subject noun phrase is obligatory where pragmatically appropriate, and a noun or a pronoun appears in the subject position. Because it was necessary for the child to include the subject noun phrase in his utterance due to pragmatic convention, and he did, Late Stage IV/Early Stage V is assigned.

Continued on next page

Practice Examples—*Continued*

(M points to picture in book and says "What is that?") a baby crying/	Stage III (III) The noun phrase in this utterance is in the subject position and consists of an article plus a noun. Both of these are indicative of Stage III.
(C shows finger to clinician) hurt my little finger/	Late Stage IV/Early Stage V (LIV/EV) Although there is only one noun phrase and it is in the object position, the presence of the possessive pronoun, *my,* with the adjective, *little,* makes this noun phrase typical of Late Stage IV/Early Stage V.
(C pushes puppy away) he eated my cookie/	Late Stage IV/Early Stage V (LIV/EV) The two noun phrases in this utterance are indicative of Late Stage IV/Early Stage V. The subject noun phrase pronoun, *he,* and the object noun phrase possessive pronoun, *my,* confirm Late Stage IV/Early Stage V.
(C reaches for cookie on plate) eat my big cookie/	Late Stage IV/Early Stage V (LIV/EV) This utterance contains only an object noun phrase, which could result in a lower stage assignment. But this noun phrase contains a possessive pronoun and an adjective preceding the noun. Noun phrases with these constituents are characteristic of Late Stage IV/Early Stage V.
(C points to box in corner) lotta doggies goes in there/	Late Stage IV/Early Stage V (LIV/EV) The most significant thing to note in this utterance is the lack of number agreement between the subject and the verb. Although this lack of number agreement continues to be a problem beyond Stage V, the presence of a subject noun phrase and an object noun phrase indicate at least Late Stage IV/Early Stage V. And with no further data on which to base a judgment, Late Stage IV/Early Stage V is assigned. This would indicate that assigning a stage higher than Late Stage IV/Early Stage V is not probable when analyzing noun phrases.

Now, with the experience gained from the practice utterances, return to the sample transcript and examine each utterance for the presence of one or more noun phrases. If there is no noun phrase in the utterance, mark a dash (—) for that utterance in the Noun Phrase Elaboration column on the *Structural Stage Analysis Grid* used earlier. When an utterance that contains a noun phrase is identified, compare that noun phrase to the descriptions of noun phrases in the eighth column of Table 3.4 (see pages 111–112) to determine the stage that best characterizes the complexity of the noun phrase or phrases in the utterance. Then record the stage number for that utterance in the Noun Phrase Elaboration column on the *Structural Stage Analysis Grid.* When each utterance has been examined for the presence of noun phrases and stage assignments have been recorded, compare your results with those in the sample on pages 141–142.

Forty-six utterances containing noun phrases should have been identified. The noun phrases in this transcript ranged in complexity from Stage I–Stage II to Late Stage IV/Early Stage V. These utterances will be tallied on the *Production Characteristics Summary Form* after the complexities of two more syntactic structures have been analyzed.

Analyzing Complexity of Verb Phrases

The stage assignments that are made for verb phrase development are based on data reported by Klima and Bellugi (1966); Cazden (1968); Brown (1973); de Villiers and de Villiers (1973); and Chapman et al. (1981). The ninth column of Table 3.4 (see pages 111–112) summarizes the changes in complexity of the verb phrase and the stage at which those changes emerge. Changes in complexity of verb phrases overlap with developments in other structures more than some of the other structures analyzed. Most notably, increases in complexity of the verb phrase coincide with advances in the development of grammatical morphemes. Final interpretation of the developmental complexity of the verb phrase will depend on the child's mastery of grammatical morphemes.

To determine the stage that best characterizes the child's level of verb phrase development, examine each utterance for the presence of a verb phrase. Then compare each verb phrase to the developments summarized in the ninth column of Table 3.4 (see pages 111–112) and assign a stage to the verb phrase in that utterance. For Stages I, II, and III, use the broad stages as indicated by white lettering on the far left side of Table 3.4. Like the judgments made in analyzing noun phrase development, making judgments about verb phrases is more difficult than with some of the other syntactic structures. Therefore, a greater number of practice utterances are provided for verb phrases than for some of the other structures. Cover the right side of the page, compare the utterance to the developments described in Table 3.4, and assign a stage. Then check your stage assignments with those provided in the shaded section. The explanations provided should help clear up any questions.

Then return to the sample transcript and examine each utterance for the presence of a verb phrase. As with the preceding structures, if there is no verb phrase in the utterance, mark a dash (—) for that utterance in the Verb Phrase Elaboration column on the *Structural*

Structural Stage Analysis Grid

Name of Child Bridget

Utterance Number	Number of Morphemes	Negation	Yes/No Question	Wh-Question	Noun Phrase Elaboration	Verb Phrase Elaboration	Complex Sentence
1	1	—	—	—	—		
2	2	—	—	—	—		
3	1	—	—	—	—		
4	1	—	—	—	—		
5	4	—	—	—	LIV/EV		
6	1	—	EI—III	—	—		
7	2	—	—	LI/EII—II	—		
8	1	—	—	—	I—II		
9	1	—	—	—	I—II		
10	1	—	—	—	—		
11	3	—	—	—	—		
12	1	—	—	—	—		
13	1	—	—	—	I—II		
14	1	—	—	—	—		
15	4	—	—	—	LIV/EV		
16	2	—	—	LI/EII—II	—		
17	4	—	—	—	III		
18	4	EIV—LIV/EV	—	—	III		
19	2	—	—	LI/EII—II	—		
20	4	EIV—LIV/EV	—	—	LIV/EV		
21	4	EIV—LIV/EV	—	—	LIV/EV		
22	2	—	—	—	III		
23	3	—	—	III	LIV/EV		
24	4	—	—	III	III		
25	2	—	—	—	III		

Utterance Number	Number of Morphemes	Negation	Yes/No Question	Wh-Question	Noun Phrase Elaboration	Verb Phrase Elaboration	Complex Sentence
26	2	—	—	—	—		
27	2	—	—	—	I—II		
28	2	—	—	—	—		
29	1	—	—	—	—		
30	1	—	—	—	—		
31	5	—	—	—	LIV/EV		
32	4	—	—	—	III		
33	4	—	—	—	LIV/EV		
34	1	—	—	—	—		
35	4	—	—	LV	LIV/EV		
36	3	—	—	—	LIV/EV		
37	1	—	—	—	—		
38	1	—	—	—	—		
39	1	—	—	—	—		
40	1	—	—	—	I—II		
41	1	—	—	—	I—II		
42	1	—	—	—	—		
43	2	—	—	—	—		
44	2	—	—	—	LIV/EV		
45	3	—	—	—	LIV/EV		
46	3	—	—	—	—		
47	1	—	—	—	—		
48	1	—	—	—	—		
49	1	—	—	—	—		
50	1	—	—	—	I—II		
Subtotal 1	105						

based on its abbreviated form, only VP was assigned.

Structural Stage Analysis Grid

Name of Child Bridget

greeting

Utterance Number	Number of Morphemes	Negation	Yes/No Question	Wh-Question	Noun Phrase Elaboration	Verb Phrase Elaboration	Complex Sentence
51	1	–	–	–	–		
52	3	–	–	–	–		
53	1	–	–	–	–		
54	1	–	–	–	–		
55	1	–	–	–	–		
56	4	–	–	–	LIV/EV		
57	1	–	–	–	–		
58	1	–	–	–	I–II		
59	1	–	–	–	–		
60	4	–	EI–III	–	III		
61	4	–	–	–	III		
62	3	–	–	–	III		
63	1	–	–	–	–		
64	1	–	–	–	–		
65	4	–	–	–	III		
66	2	–	–	LI/EII–II	–		
67	1	–	–	–	–		
68	1	–	–	–	–		
69	1	–	–	–	–		
70	1	–	EI–III	–	–		
71	1	–	–	–	I–II		
72	3	–	–	–	I–II		
73	3	–	–	–	I–II		
74	1	–	–	–	–		
75	2	–	–	–	–		

Utterance Number	Number of Morphemes	Negation	Yes/No Question	Wh-Question	Noun Phrase Elaboration	Verb Phrase Elaboration	Complex Sentence
76	1	–	–	–	–		
77	1	–	–	–	–		
78	3	LI/EII–II	–	–	I–II		
79	1	–	–	–	–		
80	1	–	–	–	–		
81	5	–	–	–	LIV/EV		
82	1	–	–	–	–		
83	3	–	–	–	–		
84	1	–	–	–	I–II		
85	1	–	–	–	–		
86	2	–	–	–	I–II		
87	3	–	–	–	I–II		
88	3	–	–	–	I–II		
89	3	–	–	–	I–II		
90	3	–	–	–	I–II		
91	1	–	–	–	–		
92	1	–	–	–	–		
93	1	–	–	–	I–II		
94	1	–	–	–	I–II		
95	1	–	–	–	–		
96	3	–	–	LV	–		
97	3	–	–	–	III		
98	1	–	–	–	–		
99	2	–	–	–	I–II		
100	2	–	–	–	LIV/EV		
Subtotal 2	95						

[105] No. of Morphemes (Subtotal 1) + [95] No. of Morphemes (Subtotal 2) = 200 Total Number of Morphemes

Total Number of Morphemes / Total Number of Utterances = [200] / [100] = 2.00 MLU

Practice Examples for Verb Phrase Elaboration

(C falls down and looks at M) fall down/	Stage I–Stage II (I–II) This utterance contains a verb plus a particle. Verb phrases of this form are used occasionally in Stage I but do not change in form through Stage II. The best stage assignment is the range of stages.
(puppy jumps out of box) puppy jump/	Stage I–Stage II (I–II) This utterance contains a noun phrase and a verb phrase, with the verb phrase containing a main verb in an uninflected form. This form of the verb is consistent with Stage I through Stage II. The presence of the noun phrase has no bearing on the stage assignment.
(C curls up in doll bed, then sits up) I is sleeping/	Stage III (III) The verb phrase in this utterance contains a main verb in the present progressive tense. The auxiliary is included, and even though it is in an incorrect form for first person, the inclusion of the auxiliary requires the assignment of Stage III.
(M and C looking at picture book) he could hit you/	Late Stage IV/Early Stage V (LIV/EV) The most significant thing to note for stage assignment is the presence of the modal auxiliary *could.* This type of auxiliary is characteristic of Late Stage IV/Early Stage V.
(C points to picture in book) baby cry/	Stage I–Stage II (I–II) The verb phrase in this utterance is in an uninflected form. Thus, the most appropriate stage assignment is Stage I–Stage II.

Continued on next page

Practice Examples—*Continued*

(another child is crying in the hall) baby crying/	Stage I–Stage II (I–II) The reason for the difficulty in assigning a stage to this utterance is that the present progressive *-ing* is used occasionally in Stage I and more consistently in Stage II. The best solution is to assign the range of stages.
(puppy crawls in clinician's lap) her gonna bite/	Stage II (II) The use of the semiauxiliary *gonna* in this verb phrase indicates Stage II. The only time Stage II would be assigned as opposed to the range of Stage I–Stage II is when the semiauxiliary or the copula is included without other information that could influence a higher stage assignment.
(C points to one of the puppies) she can jump/	Stage III (III) This utterance contains an obligatory main verb. The presence of the present tense auxiliary *can* preceding the verb in this verb phrase also indicates Stage III.
(puppy puts front paws up on edge of box) puppy'll jump/	Stage III (III) This utterance contains an obligatory main verb. The verb phrase in this utterance also contains an auxiliary, *will,* but in this utterance it is in the contracted form.
(puppy chases heels of clinician) she's gonna bite you/	Late Stage IV/Early Stage V (LIV/EV) The verb phrase in this utterance contains the auxiliary *is,* the semiauxiliary *gonna,* and the main verb *bite.* But the most important thing to take note of is that the semiauxiliary complement *gonna bite* takes a noun phrase. Verb phrases of this type appear in Late Stage IV/Early Stage V.

Continued on next page

Practice Examples—*Continued*

(clinician picks up puppy) she bites/	Late Stage V (LV) The verb phrase in this utterance only contains a main verb. But the main verb includes correct number agreement in the use of regular third person singular present tense. This is the eighth grammatical morpheme and it is mastered in Late Stage V. The consistent use of this grammatical morpheme results in the assignment of Late Stage V.
(C gestures toward puppy in box) she was a a naughty puppy/	Stage V+ (V+) The verb phrase in this utterance consists of the copula, or the verb *be,* as a main verb. It is in the past tense, a form that emerges in Stage V+. In addition, it is an uncontractible copula, which, as a grammatical morpheme, is mastered in Stage V+.
(C pulls toys out of toy box) is big!/	Stage II (II) This utterance also contains a copula, *is,* but without tense or number inflection. The copula appears in this form in Stage II.
(as clinician leaves the room, C turns to M) she eated my cookie/	Stage III (III) The main verb in this utterance is an irregular verb, but the child has marked the past tense of the verb by using the regular past tense *-ed* inflection. Overgeneralization of the past tense *-ed* occurs in Stage III.
(C relating story to M) she was jumping on the couch/	Stage V+ (V+) The verb phrase in this utterance contains the past tense form of the verb *be* as an auxiliary. This form appears in Stage V+.
(C and M playing with cars and toy gas station) you need gas↑/	Stage III (III) This utterance contains an uninflected verb, and no auxiliary verbs are present. The verb is obligatory to hold this utterance together. The main verb becomes obligatory in Stage III.

Continued on next page

Practice Examples—*Continued*

(C makes horse bump car and says to M) horsie bumped the car/	Late Stage V (LV) The main verb in this utterance includes the regular past tense *-ed* inflection used correctly. Although Stage III is assigned for incorrect or overgeneralized use and Late Stage IV/Early Stage V is assigned for double marking, Late Stage V is assigned for correct use. This is due to the fact that the *-ed* inflection is mastered in Late Stage V as a grammatical morpheme.
(C relating story to M) he should go night-night/	Late Stage IV/Early Stage V (LIV/EV) This utterance contains a past tense modal auxiliary in the verb phrase. Modals of this type appear in Late Stage IV/Early Stage V.
(clinician puts cookie toppings on table) I have eaten those kind/	Stage V+ (V+) The verb phrase in this utterance is in the present perfect tense, and the child has correctly marked the tense on the auxiliary verb. This is a relatively infrequently occurring form in adult conversation, and it is reported to be marked correctly only after reaching Stage V+.
(C referring to puppy) I might get one/	Late Stage IV/Early Stage V (LIV/EV) The presence of the modal auxiliary in the verb phrase is the best cue for stage assignment. Modals of this type appear in Late Stage IV/Early Stage V.
(clinician enters room and C points to mat) I was jumping on that/	Stage V+ (V+) This utterance contains the past tense form of the verb *be* as an auxiliary verb. The verb *be* emerges in this form in Stage V+.

Stage Analysis Grid used earlier. For those utterances that do contain a verb phrase, record the stage number for the verb phrase's complexity in that utterance in the Verb Phrase Elaboration column on the *Structural Stage Analysis Grid.* When each utterance has been examined for the presence of a verb phrase and stage assignments have been recorded, compare your results with those in the sample on pages 148–149.

The sample transcript contained 39 utterances with verb phrases. The verb phrases in the utterances in the sample transcript ranged in complexity from Stage I–Stage II to Late Stage V. These verb phrases will be tallied on the *Production Characteristics Summary Form* after the complexity of one more syntactic structure is analyzed.

Analyzing Complexity of Complex Sentences

The last aspect of syntactic development that will be analyzed is the complex sentence. The frequency of occurrence of complex sentences is very low in transcripts obtained from children within Brown's stages of linguistic production. At the upper end of Brown's stages, typically less than 20 percent of the child's utterances are complex (Paul, 1981). And in the early stages, complex sentences are rarely used.

The stage assignments that will be made for complex sentence development are based on data provided by Limber (1973) and Paul (1981). The data reported by Paul provide stage assignments on the basis of the stage at which 50 percent of the children in her sample used the structure and the stage at which 90 percent of the children in her sample used the structure. The data summarized in the tenth column of Table 3.4 (see pages 111–112) reflect the stage at which 50 percent of the children used the structure. The decision was made that data on complex sentence development will be at the emergence level rather than the mastery level, because this plan was followed for data on all other structures except grammatical morphemes.

First identify the complex sentences in the transcript. This may be more difficult than making the stage assignments. Some practice in doing this was gained in the preceding chapter on semantic analysis (see page 72), where a few utterances were provided as examples of complex sentences. However, the practice provided here will be more extensive and will provide explanations for stage assignments.

There are two main reasons that an utterance is considered syntactically complex. First, the utterance is considered complex if it contains two or more sentences within the utterance that are connected by conjunctions. These usually take the form of two or more full-sentence propositions connected by *and, but, so, or, because, before,* or *after.* Second, an utterance is considered complex if it contains a dependent clause (i.e., a sentencelike segment that contains a main verb) (Paul, 1981). These dependent clauses are embedded within the sentence and take a variety of forms, including infinitive phrases, *wh-* clauses, relative clauses, full propositional complements, and gerunds.

Although the identification of types of complex sentences becomes easier with practice, some practice utterances will be helpful before returning to the sample transcript. Cover the right side of the page, compare each utterance with the descriptions provided in the tenth column of Table 3.4 (see pages 111–112), and assign a stage. Then check your assignments with those provided in the shaded section. The explanations given should help clear up any discrepancies.

Structural Stage Analysis Grid

Name of Child Bridget

Utterance Number	Number of Morphemes	Negation	Yes/No Question	Wh- Question	Noun Phrase Elaboration	Verb Phrase Elaboration	Complex Sentence
1	1	—	—	—	—	—	
2	2	—	—	—	—	I—II	
3	1	—	—	—	—	—	
4	1	—	—	—	—	—	
5	4	—	—	—	LIV/EV	III	
6	1	—	EI—III	—	—	I—II	
7	2	—	—	LI/EII—II	—	—	
8	1	—	—	—	I—II	—	
9	1	—	—	—	I—II	—	
10	1	—	—	—	—	—	
11	3	—	—	—	—	I—II	
12	1	—	—	—	—	—	
13	1	—	—	—	I—II	—	
14	1	—	—	—	—	—	
15	4	—	—	—	LIV/EV	III	
16	2	—	—	LI/EII—II	—	—	
17	4	—	—	—	III	III	
18	4	EIV—LIV/EV	—	—	III	LV	
19	2	—	—	LI/EII—II	—	—	
20	4	EIV—LIV/EV	—	—	LIV/EV	LV	
21	4	EIV—LIV/EV	—	—	LIV/EV	III	
22	2	—	—	—	III	III	
23	3	—	—	III	LIV/EV	LV	
24	4	—	—	III	III	III	
25	2	—	—	—	III	—	

Utterance Number	Number of Morphemes	Negation	Yes/No Question	Wh- Question	Noun Phrase Elaboration	Verb Phrase Elaboration	Complex Sentence
26	2	—	—	—	—	I—II	
27	2	—	—	—	I—II	—	
28	2	—	—	—	—	I—II	
29	1	—	—	—	—	—	
30	1	—	—	—	—	—	
31	5	—	—	—	LIV/EV	III	
32	4	—	—	—	III	LV	
33	4	—	—	—	LIV/EV	LV	
34	1	—	—	—	—	—	
35	4	—	—	LV	LIV/EV	LV	
36	3	—	—	—	LIV/EV	III	
37	1	—	—	—	—	—	
38	1	—	—	—	—	I—III	
39	1	—	—	—	—	—	
40	1	—	—	—	I—II	—	
41	1	—	—	—	I—II	—	
42	1	—	—	—	—	—	
43	2	—	—	—	—	—	
44	2	—	—	—	LIV/EV	III	
45	3	—	—	—	LIV/EV	III	
46	3	—	—	—	—	I—II	
47	1	—	—	—	—	—	
48	1	—	—	—	—	—	
49	1	—	—	—	—	—	
50	1	—	—	—	I—II	—	
Subtotal 1	105						

No inflection on main verb, but

Structural Stage Analysis Grid

Name of Child __Bridget__

Utterance Number	Number of Morphemes	Negation	Yes/No Question	Wh-Question	Noun Phrase Elaboration	Verb Phrase Elaboration	Complex Sentence
51	1	—	—	—	—	—	
52	3	—	—	—	—	///	
53	1	—	—	—	—	—	
54	1	—	—	—	—	—	
55	1	—	—	—	—	—	
56	4	—	—	—	LIV/EV	///	
57	1	—	—	—	—	—	
58	1	—	—	—	I–II	—	
59	1	—	—	—	—	—	
60	4	—	EI–III	—	///	LV	
61	4	—	—	—	///	LV	
62	3	—	—	—	///	—	
63	1	—	—	—	—	—	
64	1	—	—	—	—	—	
65	4	—	—	—	///	LV	
66	2	—	—	LII/EII–II	—	—	
67	1	—	—	—	—	—	
68	1	—	—	—	—	—	
69	1	—	—	—	—	—	
70	1	—	EI–III	—	—	—	
71	1	—	—	—	I–II	—	
72	3	—	—	—	I–II	I–II	
73	3	—	—	—	I–II	I–II	
74	1	—	—	—	—	—	
75	2	—	—	—	—	I–II	

$$\left[\ \frac{105}{\text{No. of Morphemes (Subtotal 1)}}\ \right] + \left[\ \frac{95}{\text{No. of Morphemes (Subtotal 2)}}\ \right] = \left[\ \frac{200}{\text{Total Number of Morphemes}}\ \right]$$

Utterance Number	Number of Morphemes	Negation	Yes/No Question	Wh-Question	Noun Phrase Elaboration	Verb Phrase Elaboration	Complex Sentence
76	1	—	—	—	—	—	
77	1	—	—	—	—	—	
78	3	LII/EII–II	—	—	I–II	—	
79	1	—	—	—	—	—	
80	1	—	—	—	—	—	
81	5	—	—	—	LIV/EV	LV	
82	1	—	—	—	—	—	
83	3	—	—	—	—	—	
84	1	—	—	—	I–II	—	
85	1	—	—	—	—	—	
86	2	—	—	—	I–II	LV	
87	3	—	—	—	I–II	///	
88	3	—	—	—	I–II	///	
89	3	—	—	—	I–II	///	
90	3	—	—	—	I–II	///	
91	1	—	—	—	—	—	
92	1	—	—	—	—	—	
93	1	—	—	—	—	—	
94	1	—	—	—	I–II	—	
95	1	—	—	—	—	—	
96	3	—	—	LV	—	LIV/EV	
97	3	—	—	—	///	—	
98	1	—	—	—	—	—	
99	2	—	—	—	I–II	—	
100	2	—	—	—	LIV/EV	///	
Subtotal 2	**95**						

$$\frac{\text{Total Number of Morphemes}}{\text{Total Number of Utterances}} = \left[\ \frac{200}{100}\ \right] = \underline{2.00}\ \text{MLU}$$

Practice Examples for Complex Sentences

(C relating event to clinician)
doggie barked and barked/

Early Stage IV (EIV)
This utterance contains the conjunction *and.* It is conjoining the two sentences *the doggie barked* and *the doggie barked.*

(C continuing story)
doggie bite and I cried/

Early Stage IV (EIV)
This utterance also contains the conjunction *and.* In this example, the two utterances that are conjoined are more obvious.

(C points to cookie on plate)
I want the one what's big/

Late Stage V (LV)
This utterance contains a relative clause, but the child has used a *wh*-word to introduce the clause. Even though the form is incorrect, Late Stage V is assigned. The relative clause modifies the noun *one.*

(C brushes flour off pants)
my shoes and pants are dirty/

Early Stage IV (EIV)
This utterance is an example of another type of conjoined complex utterance. The two sentences that are conjoined are *my shoes are dirty* and *my pants are dirty.*

(C pulls on door)
I want to go/

Early Stage IV (EIV)
This utterance contains a simple infinitive phrase. To assign this stage, the child must use the full infinitive, not the catenative form *(wanna)* or a reduction *(go* for *to go).*

(C picks up plastic animal)
pretend he's a monster/

Stage III (III)
This utterance contains a full propositional complement. The complement *he's a monster* is a full sentence and may or may not be introduced by the word *that.*

(C looking for M to drive up)
I gotta go when Mom comes/

Stage V++ (V++)
This utterance contains the conjunction *when*, which appears at Stage V++.

Continued on next page

Practice Examples—*Continued*

(C pulls plastic animal out of bag) I know what that is/	Early Stage IV (EIV) This example contains a simple *wh-* clause. The sentence *that is* is linked to the main sentence with a *wh-* word.
(C holds up doll dress) this is for her to wear/	Late Stage V (LV) This utterance contains an infinitive phrase with a subject different than the subject of the main verb.
(C gestures to cupcakes on rack) the ones what have hats on are mine/	Late Stage V (LV) This utterance contains a relative clause, *what have hats on.* The relative clause modifies the noun *ones.* Again, the relative clause introducer does not have to be correct to give the child credit for use of the relative clause.
(M asks, "Why did you do that?" after C eats handful of cookie dough) I felt like eating it/	Stage V+ (V+) This utterance contains a gerund clause, *eating it.* Gerund clauses include a verb plus *-ing* used within a noun clause.
(C picks up marking pen) help me draw/	Stage V+ (V+) This utterance contains an unmarked infinitive phrase. These are usually introduced by one of the following: *let, help, watch, make, need, see, hear,* and *feel.* This utterance implies "Help me to draw."
(C opens game box) I'll show you how to do it/	Stage V+ (V+) This utterance contains a *wh-* infinitive phrase. These are marked with both a *wh-* word and *to.*
(C starts to search toy box) I think I know where it is/	Late Stage IV/Early Stage V (LIV/EV) This is an example of double embedding. It contains an embedded clause, *where it is,* that is embedded within another clause, *I know,* that is embedded within the main proposition *I think.*

These examples of types of complex sentences should be helpful in identifying complex sentences within the sample transcript. In addition, the explanations as to why each is considered complex should help in making stage assignments. Now, return to the sample transcript and examine each utterance to determine if it is an example of a complex sentence. If an utterance is not a complex sentence, mark a dash (—) in the Complex Sentence column on the *Structural Stage Analysis Grid* used earlier. If an utterance is complex, compare it to the descriptions in the tenth column of Table 3.4 (see pages 111–112) and assign a stage to the utterance. After each utterance has been examined to determine if it is complex and each stage assignment has been recorded, compare your results to those in the sample provided on pages 153–154.

The sample transcript contained only one utterance that was an example of a complex sentence. This complex sentence will be tallied on the *Production Characteristics Summary Form* later. With practice, transcripts can be scanned for examples of complex sentences very quickly, since very few complex sentences occur in transcripts of children within Brown's stages of linguistic production. Also, identifying complex sentences is easier to do after a verb phrase analysis has been completed. Judgments about the verb phrase typically illuminate the clause structure of the utterance, so the decision about whether the utterance is a complex sentence is made during verb phrase analysis. You may find the practice set on the CD-ROM helpful in identifying various types of complex sentences.

Now that all the boxes on the *Structural Stage Analysis Grid* have been filled in, the data obtained from analyzing the preceding seven syntactic structures must be analyzed. The data obtained from analysis of these seven aspects of syntactic production will be combined with the MLU data and length distribution analysis to provide an interpretation of the structural complexity of this child's productions.

Summary and Interpretation

To summarize the analysis of syntactic structures, results from the analysis of each structure must be transferred to the *Production Characteristics Summary Form* from Appendix A (page 244). This tally sheet will display the range of performance by the child for each of the syntactic structures and the relationship between each. The visual display can be helpful in understanding the assignment of the Most Typical Stage and the Most Advanced Stage for each structure.

The first step in summarizing the analysis data is to transfer the percent use computations for each grammatical morpheme from the *Grammatical Morphemes* analysis sheet into the appropriate stage box on the *Production Characteristics Summary Form.* The percent use for the present progressive tense of the verb *-ing* is entered next to the number 1 in the box for Stage II under the Grammatical Morphemes column. Since there were no instances of the present progressive tense (i.e., present tense progressive aspect) in the sample transcript, put a dash (—) next to number 1. The percent use for the regular plural *-s* is recorded next to number 2 in the box for Stage II under the Grammatical Morphemes column. In the sample transcript, 100% correct use of the regular plural *-s* in obligatory contexts was obtained, so record 100% next to number 2. Now proceed through the *Grammatical Morphemes* analysis sheet and enter the remaining percentages for grammatical morpheme use next to the appropriate numbers on the summary form.

Structural Stage Analysis Grid

Name of Child Bridget

Utterance Number	Number of Morphemes	Negation	Yes/No Question	*Wh-* Question	Noun Phrase Elaboration	Verb Phrase Elaboration	Complex Sentence
1	1	—	—	—	—	—	—
2	2	—	—	—	—	I—II	—
3	1	—	—	—	—	—	—
4	1	—	—	—	—	—	—
5	4	—	—	—	LIV/EV	III	—
6	1	—	EI—III	—	—	I—II	—
7	2	—	—	LI/EII—II	—	—	—
8	1	—	—	—	I—II	—	—
9	1	—	—	—	I—II	—	—
10	1	—	—	—	—	—	—
11	3	—	—	—	—	I—II	—
12	1	—	—	—	—	—	—
13	1	—	—	—	I—II	—	—
14	1	—	—	—	—	—	—
15	4	—	—	—	LIV/EV	III	—
16	2	—	—	LI/EII—II	—	—	—
17	4	—	—	—	III	III	—
18	4	EIV—LIV/EV	—	—	III	LV	—
19	2	—	—	LI/EII—II	—	—	—
20	4	EIV—LIV/EV	—	—	LIV/EV	LV	—
21	4	EIV—LIV/EV	—	—	LIV/EV	III	—
22	2	—	—	—	III	III	—
23	3	—	—	III	LIV/EV	LV	—
24	4	—	—	III	III	III	—
25	2	—	—	—	III	—	—
26	2	—	—	—	—	I—II	—
27	2	—	—	—	I—II	—	—
28	2	—	—	—	—	I—II	—
29	1	—	—	—	—	—	—
30	1	—	—	—	—	—	—
31	5	—	—	—	LIV/EV	III	—
32	4	—	—	—	III	LV	—
33	4	—	—	—	LIV/EV	LV	—
34	1	—	—	—	—	—	—
35	4	—	—	LV	LIV/EV	LV	—
36	3	—	—	—	LIV/EV	III	—
37	1	—	—	—	—	—	—
38	1	—	—	—	—	I—III	—
39	1	—	—	—	—	—	—
40	1	—	—	—	I—II	—	—
41	1	—	—	—	I—II	—	—
42	1	—	—	—	—	—	—
43	2	—	—	—	—	—	—
44	2	—	—	—	LIV/EV	III	—
45	3	—	—	—	LIV/EV	III	—
46	3	—	—	—	—	I—II	—
47	1	—	—	—	—	—	—
48	1	—	—	—	—	—	—
49	1	—	—	—	—	—	—
50	1	—	—	—	I—II	—	—
Subtotal 1	105						

Structural Stage Analysis Grid

Name of Child Bridget

Utterance Number	Number of Morphemes	Negation	Yes/No Question	Wh-Question	Noun Phrase Elaboration	Verb Phrase Elaboration	Complex Sentence
51	1	–	–	–	–	–	–
52	3	–	–	–	–	///	E/V
53	1	–	–	–	–	–	–
54	1	–	–	–	–	–	–
55	1	–	–	–	–	–	–
56	4	–	–	–	L/V/EV	///	–
57	1	–	–	–	–	–	–
58	1	–	–	–	/–//	–	–
59	1	–	–	–	–	–	–
60	4	–	E/–///	–	///	LV	–
61	4	–	–	–	///	LV	–
62	3	–	–	–	///	–	–
63	1	–	–	–	–	–	–
64	1	–	–	–	–	–	–
65	4	–	–	–	///	LV	–
66	2	–	–	L/E//–//	–	–	–
67	1	–	–	–	–	–	–
68	1	–	–	–	–	–	–
69	1	–	–	–	–	–	–
70	1	–	E/–///	–	–	–	–
71	1	–	–	–	/–//	–	–
72	3	–	–	–	/–//	/–//	–
73	3	–	–	–	/–//	/–//	–
74	1	–	–	–	–	–	–
75	2	–	–	–	–	/–//	–

[105] No. of Morphemes (Subtotal 1) + [95] No. of Morphemes (Subtotal 2) = 200 Total Number of Morphemes

Utterance Number	Number of Morphemes	Negation	Yes/No Question	Wh-Question	Noun Phrase Elaboration	Verb Phrase Elaboration	Complex Sentence
76	1	–	–	–	–	–	–
77	1	–	–	–	–	–	–
78	3	L//E//–//	–	–	/–//	–	–
79	1	–	–	–	–	–	–
80	1	–	–	–	–	–	–
81	5	–	–	–	L/V/EV	LV	–
82	1	–	–	–	–	–	–
83	3	–	–	–	–	–	–
84	1	–	–	–	/–//	–	–
85	1	–	–	–	–	–	–
86	2	–	–	–	/–//	LV	–
87	3	–	–	–	/–//	///	–
88	3	–	–	–	/–//	///	–
89	3	–	–	–	/–//	///	–
90	3	–	–	–	/–//	///	–
91	1	–	–	–	–	–	–
92	1	–	–	–	–	–	–
93	1	–	–	–	/–//	–	–
94	1	–	–	–	/–//	–	–
95	1	–	–	–	–	–	–
96	3	–	–	LV	–	L/V/EV	–
97	3	–	–	–	///	–	–
98	1	–	–	–	–	–	–
99	2	–	–	–	/–//	–	–
100	2	–	–	–	L/V/EV	///	–
Subtotal 2	95						

$$\frac{\text{Total Number of Morphemes}}{\text{Total Number of Utterances}} = \frac{[\ 200\ ]}{[\ 100\ ]} = 2.00 \text{ MLU}$$

If there are no instances of a particular grammatical morpheme in the transcript and no obligatory contexts for that grammatical morpheme, put a dash (—) next to the number for that grammatical morpheme. If there were no instances of use, but some number of obligatory contexts for a particular grammatical morpheme, put a zero next to the number for that grammatical morpheme. This notation differentiates those grammatical morphemes that were not used in the obligatory contexts from those grammatical morphemes for which no data could be obtained.

The next step in summarizing analysis data is to tally the occurrences of each stage for each of the syntactic structures analyzed. Using the *Structural Stage Analysis Grid,* record the stage number assigned to each instance of negation on the summary form. If a particular utterance was assigned a range of stages (e.g., "*no* + noun" = Late Stage I/Early Stage II–Stage II), be certain to record that range on the summary form. When all negations have been tallied, tally the stage number assigned to each yes/no question on the summary form. Again record a range of stages if that is the notation on the *Structural Stage Analysis Grid.* Next, tally the stage number assigned to each *wh*-question on the summary form. Then tally the stage number assigned to each noun phrase and the stage number assigned to each verb phrase. Finally, tally the stage number assigned to each complex sentence. Remember that for some structures, a tally is entered only at one particular stage. For other structures, a range of stages is tallied. This is indicated by drawing a vertical line through as many boxes as necessary and then marking the tally in the top left of the box at the end of that line.

Once a stage has been tallied for each instance of each structure, check your tallies with those in the sample summary form on page 156. The summary form provides a visual display to compare the developmental complexity of the structures analyzed for this particular child. Initial examination of this visual display reveals a great deal of variability in the developmental complexity of the structures analyzed for this child. Although this may seem inappropriate, considerable variation in the developmental complexity of a particular structure and across structures is expected. In fact, the developmental level of a particular structure may vary as much as two stages on either side of the most frequently occurring level of that structure (Miller, 1981). This variability is the result of the ongoing nature of linguistic development. Most children do not master a single form of a particular structure (e.g., subject noun phrase elaboration) before going on to work on the production of another form of that structure (e.g., subject noun phrase pronouns). Rather, the child works on the production of a variety of forms at the same time, and a sampling of the child's production abilities at a single point in time will reveal many forms to be at a particular level of complexity, with some instances of more advanced forms and some instances of less advanced forms. Also, not all of the forms at earlier stages are incorrect (e.g., use of regular plural -*s);* rather, their continued use would be expected. This adds variability as children advance through stages of linguistic production. Ironically, minimal variability, as opposed to considerable variability, may be indicative of a problem in language production (Miller).

This expected variability does make the interpretation of the data difficult. For this reason, interpretation will be based on two stage assignments for each syntactic structure. First, a stage number will be assigned for each syntactic structure on the basis of the most frequently occurring stage for that structure. This means that the summary form will be examined and the number of instances of a particular stage for each

![Guide to Analysis of Language Transcripts]

Guide to Analysis of Language Transcripts

Production Characteristics Summary Form

Name of Child *Bridget*

	Stage	Grammatical Morphemes	Negation	Yes/No Questions	*Wh*-Questions	Noun Phrase Elaboration	Verb Phrase Elaboration	Complex Sentences
I	Early I							
I	Late I/ Early II							
II	II	1. — 2. *100%* 3. *100%*	/		////	𝍸 𝍸 𝍸 𝍸 /	𝍸 ////	
III	III	4. *0%* 5. *100%*		///	//	𝍸 𝍸 /	/	
III	Early IV						𝍸 𝍸 𝍸 //	/
	Late IV/ Early V		///			𝍸 𝍸 ////	/	
	Late V	6. *33%* 7. *43%* 8. *0%* 9. *35%* 10. *100%*			//		𝍸 𝍸 /	
	V+	11. *50%* 12. *50%* 13. — 14. —						
	V++							

structure will be counted. The stage with the greatest number of tallies is considered to be the most frequently occurring stage. This stage is considered to reflect the child's typical performance for that structure and is labeled the Most Typical Stage. Second, a stage number will be assigned for each structure on the basis of the Most Advanced Stage for that structure. The highest stage number for each structure will be identified regardless of the frequency of occurrence of that stage. This Most Advanced Stage reflects the forms the child is in the process of acquiring.

Finally, these two stage assignments for each structure (Most Typical Stage and Most Advanced Stage) are compared to each other, to the obtained MLU, and to the child's chronological age for interpretation. Like the variability expected for an individual structure, the stage assignments are expected to vary as much as two stages on either side of the MLU stage assignment (Miller, 1981). Again, since variability is expected, minimal variability may indicate a problem in syntactic aspects of language production.

Interpretation of data may be facilitated by transferring data obtained to the *Data Summary and Interpretation Form* from Appendix A (see page 245). First, record the MLU obtained from the morphemic analysis. An MLU of 2.00 morphemes was obtained for the 100-utterance sample transcript, so record 2.00 in the blank for MLU on the *Data Summary and Interpretation Form.* Next, by comparing this to Table 3.4 (see pages 111–112), it can be seen that this MLU is within the range of MLUs for Stage II (2.00–2.49 morphemes). Record Stage II in the next blank, indicating the stage assigned on the basis of MLU. This stage assignment is considered a pivot point to which other structures will be compared.

It is helpful also to complete the variability about the mean on the *Data Summary and Interpretation Form* using the formula from page 104 and the values from Table 3.2 (see page 107). The MLU for this child was 0.45 standard deviations below the expected mean.

Now record the upper and lower bound lengths obtained from the length distribution analysis. The upper bound length of 5 morphemes raises concerns about variations in utterance length for the obtained MLU.

Next, the Most Typical Stage and the Most Advanced Stage will be determined for each structure analyzed. The stage assignments for grammatical morphemes are the most difficult to make because these stage assignments are not based on the frequency of occurrence of a stage. These stage assignments are based on the percentages compiled for each grammatical morpheme. Consider the Most Typical Stage first. Looking at the *Production Characteristics Summary Form,* note that of the three grammatical morphemes in Stage II, this child used two at the mastery level. No data were obtained on the remaining grammatical morpheme for this stage. For Stage III grammatical morphemes, this child used one at the mastery level. The remaining grammatical morpheme for this stage was assigned a 0% use, which is different from no data, as previously discussed. For Late Stage V, percentages ranging from 0% to 100% use in obligatory contexts were obtained. In Stage V+, 50% use for two grammatical morphemes was obtained, and no data on the remaining two grammatical morphemes were available. To assign the Most Typical Stage, the stage that reflects consistent use of the grammatical morphemes of that stage at the mastery level must be determined. Because 0% use was obtained for the preposition *on,* grammatical morpheme #4 in Stage III, that stage cannot be assigned. Thus, record Stage II in the Grammatical Morphemes blank for the Most Typical

Structural Stage. If data on grammatical morpheme #4 had indicated greater than 90% correct use, Stage III would have been assigned as the Most Typical Stage.

To assign the Most Advanced Stage for grammatical morphemes, examine the *Production Characteristics Summary Form* for the stage that reflects more than 0% use for any of the grammatical morphemes in that stage. In the sample transcript, Bridget used grammatical morphemes #11 and #12 in 50% of the obligatory contexts. Thus, Stage V+ is assigned as the Most Advanced Stage. If no data or 0% use had been obtained for grammatical morphemes #11 and #12, Late Stage V would have been assigned as the Most Advanced Stage. But since this child is beginning to use the contractible auxiliary and the uncontractible copula (grammatical morphemes #11 and #12) in some of the obligatory contexts, Stage V+ can be considered the Most Advanced Stage for grammatical morphemes. Record this stage as the Most Advanced Stage for grammatical morphemes on the *Data Summary and Interpretation Form.*

Determination of the Most Typical Stage and the Most Advanced Stage for the remaining structures in the sample transcript is considerably easier than it was for grammatical morphemes. Beginning with negation, there were four negative structures tallied on the *Production Characterstics Summary Form:* one at the Late Stage I/Early Stage II–Stage II level and three at the Early Stage IV–Late Stage IV/Early V level. The stage with the greatest number of tallies is Early Stage IV–Late Stage IV/Early V. Record this stage number as the Most Typical Stage for negation. The Most Advanced Stage for negation is the same. Record Early Stage IV–Late Stage IV/Early V as the Most Advanced Stage for negation on the *Data Summary and Interpretation Form.*

Turning to yes/no questions, there were three yes/no questions tallied on the *Production Characteristics Summary Form* and all of them were typical of Early Stage I–Stage III. Thus, Early Stage I–Stage III is assigned as the Most Typical Stage and as the Most Advanced Stage. Record this in the appropriate blanks on the *Data Summary and Interpretation Form.*

For *wh-* questions, there were four questions tallied at Late Stage I/Early Stage II–II, two at Stage III, and two at Late Stage V. The Most Typical Stage is Late Stage I/Early Stage II–II and the Most Advanced Stage is Late Stage V. Record these in the appropriate blanks on the *Data Summary and Interpretation Form.*

For noun phrase elaboration, the *Production Characteristics Summary Form* reveals 21 utterances in which the noun phrase was typical of Stage I–Stage II, 11 utterances in which the noun phrase was typical of Stage III, and 14 utterances in which the noun phrase was typical of Late Stage IV/Early Stage V. The most frequently assigned stage was Stage I–Stage II, so record this under the Most Typical Stage. The Most Advanced Stage was Late Stage IV/Early Stage V, so record this in the blank for noun phrase elaboration on the *Data Summary and Interpretation Form.*

For verb phrase elaboration, there were 9 utterances in which the verb phrase was typical of Stage I–Stage II, 1 utterance in which the verb phrase was typical of Stage I–Stage III, 17 utterances in which the verb phrase was typical of Stage III, 1 utterance in which the verb phrase was typical of Late Stage IV/Early Stage V, and 11 utterances in which the verb phrase was typical of Late Stage V. The most frequently assigned stage was Stage III, of which there were 17 instances. Record Stage III as the Most Typical Stage for verb phrase elaboration on the *Data Summary and Interpretation Form.* The Most Advanced Stage for verb phrase elaboration was Late Stage V, with 11 instances, so record this as the Most Advanced Stage for verb phrase elaboration on the *Data Summary and Interpretation Form.*

Finally, examining complex sentences, note that only one complex sentence was in the sample transcript and it was an example of an Early Stage IV complex sentence. Thus, Early Stage IV is assigned as the Most Typical Stage and the Most Advanced Stage for complex sentences. Record this on the *Data Summary and Interpretation Form.*

Now check your stage assignments and your determination of Most Typical Stage and Most Advanced Stage for each of the syntactic structures with those in the sample provided on page 160. As previously mentioned, final interpretation is based on three comparisons: (1) the Most Typical Stage to MLU stage; (2) the Most Typical Stage to the Most Advanced Stage; and (3) MLU stage to the child's chronological age.

Comparison of Most Typical Stage to MLU Stage

When comparing the Most Typical Stage for each of the syntactic structures analyzed to the stage determined by the obtained MLU, considerable variability is evident. The MLU stage is the same as the stage assigned as the Most Typical Stage for grammatical morphemes. The Most Typical Stage for negation is two stages above the MLU stage. For yes/no questions, the MLU stage is the midpoint in the range of stages assigned as the Most Typical Stage. For *wh-* questions, the MLU Stage is within the range of stages assigned as the Most Typical Stage. For noun phrase elaboration, the MLU Stage is within the range of stages assigned as the Most Typical Stage. The Most Typical Stage for verb phrase elaboration is one stage higher than the MLU stage. Finally, the Most Typical Stage for complex sentences is two stages above the MLU stage.

So, what is the conclusion from this first set of comparisons? For five of the structures analyzed, the variability present would be expected on the basis of the obtained MLU. But the Most Typical Stage for two of the structures appears to be higher than would be expected on the basis of MLU: The Most Typical Stage for negation and complex sentences is two stages above the stage for MLU. One explanation could be that the sample is not representative and contains many elliptical utterances, resulting in an artificially low MLU. Another explanation could be that the child's MLU is lagging behind the child's abilities in formulating negative utterances and complex sentences, implying a length constraint. In other words, for some reason, physiological or cognitive, this child is unable to produce utterances as long as the complexity of those utterances would suggest. But the Most Typical Stage for negation and complex sentences was assigned on the basis of a total of four utterances. Concluding a length constraint on the basis of so few utterances would be inappropriate. Should a problem in terms of the length of utterance be suspected with this amount of data? Here is where the next set of comparisons enters the picture.

Comparison of Most Typical Stage to Most Advanced Stage

Results of the sample analysis revealed a difference of four stages between the Most Typical Stage and the Most Advanced Stage for grammatical morphemes. The Most Typical Stage for negation was the same as

Data Summary and Interpretation Form Name of Child Bridget

Mean Length of Utterance in Morphemes (MLU)

2.00 morphemes

Structural Stage by MLU: Stage II

Upper Bound Length: 5 morpheme(s)

Lower Bound Length: 1 morpheme(s)

CA = 28 mos.
use 27 mos. figures
$\frac{2.00 - 2.23}{.510} = -.45$

	Most Typical Stage	Most Advanced Stage
Grammatical Morphemes:	Stage II	Stage V+
Negation:	Stage EIV-LIV/EV	Stage EIV-LIV/EV
Yes/No Questions:	Stage EI-III	Stage EI-III
Wh- Questions:	Stage LI/EII-II	Stage LV
Noun Phrase Elaboration:	Stage I-II	Stage LIV/EV
Verb Phrase Elaboration:	Stage III	Stage LV
Complex Sentences:	Stage EIV	Stage EIV

Comments: Most Typical Stage assignments are consistent with or higher than the stage by MLU; largest gap is between MLU and stages of Negation and Complex Sentences. There are gaps between Most Typical Stage and Most Advanced Stage for all structures except Negation, Yes/No Questions, and Complex Sentences. Structural Stage by MLU is within normal limits for CA.

the Most Advanced Stage. For yes/no questions, the Most Typical Stage was the same as the Most Advanced Stage. For *wh-* questions, the Most Typical Stage was three stages lower than the Most Advanced Stage. The Most Typical Stage for noun phrase elaboration was two stages below the Most Advanced Stage. For verb phrase elaboration, the Most Typical Stage was also two stages below the Most Advanced Stage. Finally, the Most Typical Stage for complex sentences was the same as the Most Advanced Stage.

Returning to the question from the previous section, there is a reasonable gap between the Most Typical Stage and the Most Advanced Stage for four of the seven structures analyzed. This suggests that this child is exploring more sophisticated means of producing *wh-* questions, noun phrases, and verb phrases and exploring ways of consistently marking grammatical morphemes in obligatory contexts. For negation and yes/no questions, her production appears to have plateaued. Such plateaus are common in normal language acquisition (Miller, 1981). The variability observed is typical as the child works on more sophisticated accomplishments for some structures while she plateaus in her production in other areas. And with only one complex utterance in the sample, it is impossible to have anything other than no gap for complex sentences. The lack of a gap between the Most Typical Stage and the Most Advanced Stage for negation, yes/no questions, and complex sentences is not reason for concern for this particular child. The gap between the Most Typical Stage and the Most Advanced Stage is only one of the things examined in interpreting the summary information. If no gap is observed between the Most Typical Stage and the Most Advanced Stage for most of the structures analyzed, there may be reason for concern about the child's advancements in form for the production of some structures. This will be discussed in greater detail in the "Implications for Intervention" section, beginning on page 162.

Overall, it should be concluded that the transcript obtained from Bridget evidences a reasonable amount of variability in the developmental level of the structures analyzed. The Most Typical Stage for the seven structures analyzed are at levels appropriate for the MLU stage, and the relationship between the Most Typical Stage and the Most Advanced Stage reflects plateauing for some structures and acquisition of more sophisticated forms than typical performance for other structures. One final comparison is necessary.

Comparison of MLU Stage to Child's Chronological Age

Final interpretation of the analysis data requires comparison of the MLU stage to the child's chronological age. Regardless of the relationship between the Most Typical Stage and the MLU stage and the relationship between the Most Typical Stage and the Most Advanced Stage, this final comparison is crucial. When the child's age is higher than the age range for the MLU Stage as reported by Miller and Chapman (1981), it might be concluded that a delay in production exists. When the child's age falls within the age range for the MLU Stage, it can be assumed that the length of the child's utterances is appropriate for his age. And when the child's age is lower than the age range for the MLU Stage, the appropriate conclusion is that the child's production is advanced for his age. According to Miller and Chapman, these age ranges also can be translated into mental-age expectations.

For example, a 5-year-old child with cognitive abilities of a 2-year-old would be expected to produce utterances typical in length and complexity of Late Stage I/Early Stage II. Thus, the MLU stage assignment is pivotal in the interpretation of the child's age level and structural complexity.

The age of the child in the sample transcript is 28 months. On the basis of the predicted ages for Brown's stages (Miller and Chapman, 1981), this child falls within Stage II. And the MLU stage is Stage II. Thus, this child is producing utterances that are of an appropriate length for her age. And from the previous comparisons, it was concluded that she is producing utterances that reflect an appropriate amount of variability in developmental complexity. The sample transcript reflects normal development of this child's syntax.

Implications for Intervention

In review, the following are the results of comparison that are reason for concern. First, if the Most Typical Stage for some or all of the syntactic structures analyzed is lower than the MLU stage, it can be concluded that a delay in some aspect of syntax production exists. Second, if no gap is present between the Most Typical Stage and the Most Advanced Stage for most or all of the syntactic structures analyzed, it can be concluded that a delay in some aspect of syntax production exists. Third, if age (or cognitive level) is higher than the age range for the MLU stage, it can be concluded that a delay in language production exists.

As suggested by Fey (1986), factors in addition to MLU stage, Most Typical Stage, and Most Advanced Stage must be considered before concluding that the delay warrants intervention. These include no change versus dramatic change in language production during the past few months; negative versus positive reactions by parents and other caregivers to the child's communication attempts; history of middle ear problems in the child versus no such history; and nonstimulating versus stimulating linguistic environments. A child with a depressed MLU in combination with recent dramatic gains in language production and a stimulating linguistic environment may not be a candidate for intervention. On the other hand, a child with a low MLU, recurrent ear infections, and parents who are reacting negatively to the delay may need intervention.

How is the information from syntactic analysis procedures used in planning intervention of the observed delays? While this could be the topic of another extensive volume, the implication is obvious. Based on the sequence of accomplishments in normal language acquisition, forms that would appear next in the sequence to increase the length and complexity of the child's utterances can be taught. This may appear to oversimplify the process, but clinical experience has shown that from the detailed analysis of syntactic aspects of language production, the forms likely to emerge next are quite predictable. Advances are likely to be seen first in structures where a gap exists between the Most Typical Stage and the Most Advanced Stage. It also has been shown that the forms occurring next in the developmental sequence can be taught even when no gap exists between the Most Typical Stage and the Most Advanced Stage.

Consideration of as many structures as have been examined in this analysis has three purposes. First, variability in performance of each structure is assumed; therefore, data on as many structures as it is possible to obtain are necessary to capture both variability and consistency. Second, stage assignments for individual structures are considered estimates of overall production abilities; therefore, data on as many structures as it is possible to obtain are necessary to be confident of the estimates. Third, each structure provides the basis for a set of intervention goals and objectives; therefore, data on as many structures as it is possible to obtain are necessary for appropriate intervention. Only with such extensive analysis is documentation of the nature of the delay possible. The goals and objectives for intervention of the identified delay are the logical outgrowth of this extensive syntactic analysis.

PRAGMATIC ANALYSIS

Chapter 4

INTRODUCTION

Language as Communication

Language acquisition is not simply learning semantic rules and syntactic rules. Language acquisition is the process of learning to communicate with others. As Tomasello (1992) writes, "Language is social behavior. Its structures are social conventions. Its functions all derive in one way or another from communication. It can be acquired only through social interaction with human beings" (p. 67).

This view of language as social behavior illustrates its complexity, for language is not simply the use of the phonological, morphological, semantic, and syntactic aspects of language, "language is communication within a social context" (Duchan, 1984). The "meeting of meaning" between two or more persons in a social context results in communication. It is this meeting of meaning between young children and adults for purposes of communication that is the focus of this chapter.

The rules of language encompass social rules; thus an analysis of language abilities that does not document pragmatic structures and functions is incomplete. Documentation of the child's ability to appropriately use semantic and syntactic aspects of the language system within a communicative context is essential for full understanding of language production abilities. As a result, *Guide to Analysis of Language Transcripts* examines the child's pragmatic abilities within this communicative context, describing the child's abilities in relation to a conversational co-participant. Only within this exchange can we examine the conversational contingencies that impact the child's contributions.

The use of language for communication must be examined within the context of conversation. According to Hoskins (1987), "If pragmatics is the study of language in context, then that context is conversation" (p. 7). The ability to communicate within conversation is thought to develop from mutual focus and joint activity in which both participants engage in interaction (Bates, 1976; Bruner, 1975; Wells, 1981). It is the contention of these authors that the components and structures of language are not learned in isolation. The phonological, semantic, and syntactic/morphological components of language are acquired in social, communicative interactions. This is true for the pragmatic components of language as well: The child learns the pragmatic rules of language while engaged in conversation.

According to Hoskins (1996), to participate in conversation:

> A person must engage in mutual focus, take the perspective of another, and, thus, choose an appropriate topic. One must have an organized set of concepts from which to draw topics and the vocabulary to express those concepts. Moreover, one must be able to retrieve those words and formulate sentences and connected language to initiate and ultimately maintain conversation. (p. 4)

This description of conversation highlights how the components of language function together, and it explains why the examination of the pragmatic aspects of communication is critical. For children between the ages of 1 and 5 years, this examination must focus on conversation between children and familiar adults. This is the reason both participants within the conversations (i.e., the child and a familiar adult) will be examined in the analyses described in this chapter.

Larson and McKinley (1998) contend, conversations can be analyzed on at least three levels: (1) a macrolevel, which provides the conversational framework; (2) a midlevel, which specifies the pragmatic behaviors used; and (3) a microlevel, which examines the linguistic and paralinguistic behaviors employed. The procedures demonstrated in this chapter parallel the macro- and midlevels of analysis described by Larson and McKinley and the role of the conversational co-participants as described by Anderson-Wood Smith (1997) and Hoskins (1996) as the child engages in conversation, the components of language come together at the various levels of the conversation to result in mutual exchanges of meaning.

Pragmatic Language Disorders

While it appears that delays in pragmatic (i.e., conversational) abilities may co-occur with delays in semantic or syntactic abilities, it also appears that delays may occur in isolation (Craig, 1991). For the child whose semantic and/or syntactic delays have previously been identified, failure to examine pragmatic aspects of production results in an incomplete description of the language production disorder. This failure may result in overlooking factors contributing to the semantic and/or syntactic delays and stylistic variations of the conversational co-participant that may be hindering development. In addition, failure to examine the pragmatic aspects of the child's linguistic production system may result in overlooking the child with normal semantic and syntactic skills who has problems with some aspect of pragmatic production. This oversight may result in the child's language disorder persisting until the impact on academic performance becomes apparent. Either scenario can be avoided with a thorough examination of the pragmatic aspects of language production.

Procedures similar to those demonstrated in this chapter have been described in the literature as revealing developmental changes in pragmatic aspects of oral language and/or deviation from what is considered to be normal conversation (Damico, 1991; Larson and McKinley, 1998; Penn, 1988; Prutting and Kirchner, 1987; Roth and Spekman, 1984; Strong, 1998; Wetherby and Prizant, 1992). Numerous studies have described differences in pragmatic aspects of oral language for individuals with a language disorder. Table 4.1 summarizes potential difficulties of children with specific language impairment as compared to children with normal language development. The formats for identifying each of the characteristics described differ for each author. Some of the characteristics could be identified using the procedures described in this chapter.

TABLE 4.1
PRAGMATIC CHARACTERISTICS OF THE CHILD WITH SPECIFIC LANGUAGE IMPAIRMENT

Conversational Functions	Linguistic Forms	Investigations
Requesting	Few requests are grammatically complete	Prinz (1982)
Commenting	Comments may be stereotypic	Blank, Gessner, and Esposito (1979); Gallagher and Craig (1984)

Continued on next page

TABLE 4.1—Continued

Conversational Functions	Linguistic Forms	Investigations
Referencing Presuppositions	Presuppositions depend less on pronominals	Skarakis and Greenfield (1982)
Turn Taking	They relate to preceding discourse using more substitution devices and more inadequate forms	Liles (1985a, 1985b, 1987); van Kleeck and Frankel (1981)
	Turns involve less other-directed speech and are shorter in length	Craig and Evans (1989)
	Their utterances are less "adjacent," so they take longer to respond to a previous speaker with a turn of their own	Craig and Evans (1989)
	They do not use interruptions to gain the turn at speaking	Craig and Evans (1989)
Responding	Responses to requests for clarification are structurally diffuse	Brinton, Fujuki, Winkler, and Loeb (1986); Gallagher and Darnton (1978)
	Responses to other types of speech acts are likely to be unrelated, inappropriate,	Blank et al. (1979); Brinton and Fujuki
(1982);		
	and variable	Craig and Gallagher (1986); Leonard (1986); Leonard, Camarata, Rowan, and Chapman (1982)
Narratives	Their narratives are less complete and include different distributions of cohesive ties	Liles (1985a, 1985b, 1987); Merritt and Liles (1987)
Speech Adjustments	Their speech style modifications reflect fewer internal state questions and less adjustment of utterance length and complexity	Fey, Leonard, and Wilcox (1981)

From "Pragmatic Characteristics of the Child with Specific Language Impairment: An Interactionist Perspective," by H. Craig, 1991, in T. Gallagher (Ed.), *Pragmatics of Language: Clinical Practice Issues* (pp. 178–179), San Diego, CA: Singular Publishing Group.

Despite the attention given in recent years to the analysis of pragmatic aspects of conversation, no real normative data have emerged. According to Brinton (1990), the flurry of activity described as the pragmatic revolution has not yielded its primary goal: making clinical research and intervention easier. Specific typologies of conversational moves and variations in specificity, conciseness, and style have been identified as occurring in individuals with a language disorder (Brinton and Fujuki, 1984; Brinton, Fujuki, Loeb, and Winkler, 1986; Craig, 1991; Fey and Leonard, 1983; McTear, 1985; McTear and Conti-Ramsden, 1991; Prutting and Kirchner, 1987; Rice, Sell, and Hadley, 1990). However, the emergence of data implicating differences in typologies of conversational moves and/or variations in specificity, conciseness, or style still leaves us with many unanswered questions. The clinician is still "in the position of being able to identify problems, without being able to evaluate their significance" (Andersen-Wood and Smith, 1997, p. 28). Many of the pragmatic problems cited in Table 4.1 could be recognized using the procedures described in this chapter, including Speech Acts analysis (Dore, 1974), Conversational Acts analysis (Dore, 1978), Conversational Moves analysis (Martlew, 1980), and Appropriateness Judgments (Retherford, 1980). The prudent clinician should follow the procedures described in this chapter with the experimental techniques described in the studies cited in Table 4.1.

Narrative Analysis Procedures

Analysis of children's abilities to relate past events in storytelling frameworks has received considerable attention in recent years. Procedures for examining the structure of narratives have been based on loose guidelines of having children tell about their favorite book or summer vacation and/or tell versus retell versions of wordless picture books (e.g., Bishop and Edmundson's, 1987, use of Renfrew's, 1969, *Bus Story;* Stein and Glenn's, 1979, use of Mayer's, 1973, *Froggie on His Own).* Work in this area is promising in that various subgroups of children with language disorders may be distinguished on the basis of narrative analysis (Anderson-Wood and Smith, 1997; Carpenter, 1991; Griffith, Ripich, and Dastoli, 1986; Hughes, McGillivray, and Schmidek, 1997; Liles, 1985a, 1985b, 1987; Merritt and Liles, 1987; Roth, 1986; Smith and Leinonen, 1992; Strong, 1998). Collection and analysis of narrative samples are recommended for children who demonstrate difficulties with any aspect of pragmatic analysis described and/or analyzed in Chapter 4. However, it is not within the scope of *Guide* to present procedures for analyzing narratives and the normative data that exist; Hughes et al. and Strong provide detailed descriptions of a variety of descriptive analyses for narration.

Pragmatic Analysis Procedures

Chapter 4's pragmatic analysis procedures are compatible with the semantic and syntactic analysis procedures described in the preceding two chapters. It would be appropriate to analyze semantic, then syntactic, then pragmatic aspects of an obtained language transcript. While it is not necessary to complete the analyses in this order, following this order may be the most productive because it would provide a systematic organizational framework. Analysis information from Chapters 2, 3, and 4 should be combined to identify and diagnose language production problems and delays. The composite analysis information should also be combined with information obtained from narrative samples and from standardized tests to build a detailed picture of the child's communicative strengths and weaknesses, which should then be used to develop an intervention plan that includes specific goals and objectives to address any language production difficulties.

Analysis procedures described in this chapter are based on information provided by Dore (1974, 1978), Martlew (1980), and Retherford (1980) and on variables identified by Grice (1975), Keenan and Schieffelin (1976), and Shatz and Gelman (1973). The procedures are designed to be used with transcripts obtained from children at the one-word stage and beyond, including transcripts obtained from children functioning within Brown's stages of syntactic development. Not all analysis procedures described should be used for analysis of every transcript. Some procedures are appropriate for use with transcripts obtained from children at the one-word stage (Dore's Primitive Speech Acts, 1974), and other procedures are appropriate for use with transcripts obtained from children producing utterances longer than one word in length (Dore's Conversational Acts, 1978; Martlew's Conversational Moves, 1980; and Retherford's Appropriateness Judgments, 1980). Decisions about which procedure to use with a child can be made only after greater familiarity with each procedure.

Examining the pragmatic aspects of language production described in this chapter parallels two of the three major levels of distinction, described by Larson and McKinley (1998). The first distinction to be made is between the function of each utterance (i.e., its purpose or intent) and the role of each utterance in the development of the overall conversation—the macrolevel. This distinction between communicative functions and discourse relations has been recognized in the development of the procedures in this chapter. The first two procedures—Dore's Primitive Speech Acts and Dore's Conversational Acts—examine the communicative functions of utterances within children's conversation. The last two procedures—Martlew's Conversational Acts and Retherford's Appropriateness Judgments—investigate the discourse relations within children's conversation.

The second distinction necessary for a thorough consideration of pragmatic aspects of language transcripts is between quantitative and qualitative analyses—termed midlevel analysis by Larson and McKinley (1998). For many of the analysis procedures described in the previous two chapters, instances of each utterance type were tallied, subjected to analysis on the basis of the frequency of occurrence of each type, and then compared to frequency-of-occurrence normative data. This type of quantitative analysis ensures reasonably reliable conclusions about semantic and syntactic abilities. However, for some analysis procedures, particularly in the area of pragmatics, quantitative measurements are still not possible. Thus, qualitative analyses are employed. Although conclusions drawn from qualitative analyses may not be as reliable as those drawn from quantitative procedures, the importance of qualitative measures cannot be denied. In the case of the role that individual utterances play in ongoing discourse, it is not possible to say that a particular number of topic initiations is "normal." Judgments are made regarding the appropriateness of conversational moves, and the overall conclusion is based on individual judgments of appropriateness. These types of judgments may be more difficult for the beginning clinician to make, but with practice, clinicians become better at drawing conclusions from qualitative analyses.

The third and final distinction includes a description of the role the conversational co-participant plays in ongoing conversation. Analysis of conversational contributions of children without examining and describing what occurred linguistically before and after each child utterance would be incomplete (Anderson-Wood and Smith, 1997; Hoskins, 1996). However, are in no better position to judge the developmental adequacy or significance of the adult's contributions when conversing with a child than we are to judge the child's contributions. Therefore, the analysis procedures described for child utterances will also be used for adult contributions. However, adult utterance types and frequencies will not be compared to normative data, but rather to child utterance types and frequencies, to permit an examination of the conversation at large. According to Smith and Leinonen (as cited in Anderson-Wood and Smith), it is clear that each conversational co-participant "can do things that either help or hinder the process of communication" (p. 50). Thus, while it may not be possible to draw definitive conclusions from this description of the adult's utterance types and frequencies, such a description helps summarize the child's utterance types and frequencies more completely. It may also be possible to describe specific exchanges that are problematic for one or both of the participants. As a result, we will have a more thorough description of the child's participation in conversation than we would have without examining the conversational co-participant.

Documentation of pragmatic analysis as a diagnostic tool remains difficult. The research data are sketchy quantitatively and demonstrate extreme variability, thus preventing comparison of language samples to existing norms or making the comparison questionable. Perhaps at best:

> All a clinician can do is look at the range of normal behavior and make some educated guesses as to what normal behavior might be. Another possibility...is to look at the child's use of language content and form. Bottom of the range performance should be interpreted as normal if the child's language in other areas is [appropriate] (Fey, personal communication, September 1987).

Although pragmatic analysis is still in its infancy, this chapter attempts to present several pragmatic analysis procedures that can provide descriptive data and limited quantitative, albeit extremely variable, data.

Some procedures described in this chapter will be demonstrated on the sample transcript used in the preceding chapters (i.e., Bridget's) and some will be demonstrated using a transcript of a girl named Sara, from Appendix B. The reasons for this will become clear as each analysis procedure is considered. As always, blank forms for the analysis procedures described in this chapter are provided in Appendix A.

Dore's Primitive Speech Acts

The first procedure that will be used to analyze the pragmatic content of language transcripts is based on a set of categories developed by Dore (1974). The categories were used to code young children's utterances as they begin to acquire language and are based on Searle's (1969) speech acts, which Searle contends are those that adults perform when communicating. A *speech act* is a linguistic unit of communication consisting of conceptual information (i.e., a proposition) and an intention (i.e., the illocutionary force). The proposition and illocutionary force are expressed following conventional grammatical and pragmatic rules. A speaker's use of Searle's speech acts requires fairly complex language by the speaker, but Dore (1974) claims that the foundations for use of speech acts are laid in the early communicative attempts of the young child. In fact, Dore contends that children can perform what he calls "primitive speech acts" before they have acquired sentence structures. According to Dore, a *primitive speech act* is "an utterance, consisting formally of a single word or a single prosodic pattern which functions to convey the child's intentions before he acquires sentences" (p. 345). Table 4.2 lists and summarizes Dore's Primitive Speech Acts.

TABLE 4.2
PRIMITIVE SPEECH ACTS
(Adapted from Dore, 1974)

LABELING:	One or more words that function as a label produced while attending to an object. The child's word or words may label a part of the event or a situation as well. The child does not address the adult or wait for a response.
REPEATING:	One or more words or a prosodic pattern that repeats part of the adult utterance and is produced while attending to the adult utterance. The child does not address the adult or wait for a response.
ANSWERING:	One or more words that respond to an adult question or statement and are produced while attending to the adult utterance. The child addresses the adult but does not necessarily wait for a response.
REQUESTING ACTION:	One or more words or a prosodic pattern that functions as a request for an action and is produced while attending to an object or an event. The child addresses the adult and waits for a response. Often, the production is accompanied by a gesturing signal.
REQUESTING ANSWER:	One or more words that function as a request for an answer. The child addresses the adult and waits for a response. The child may gesture toward an object.
CALLING:	One or more words that are used to obtain another's attention. The child addresses the adult (or other participant) and waits for a response.
GREETING:	One or more words that are used to mark arrival or leave-taking and are produced while attending to the adult or an object. The child addresses the adult or object and does not necessarily wait for a response.
PROTESTING:	One or more words or a prosodic pattern that expresses disapproval of or dislike for an object or an action and is produced while attending to the adult. The child addresses the adult but does not necessarily wait for a response.
PRACTICING:	One or more words or a prosodic pattern that is not contingent upon preceding utterances and is produced while attending to an object or an event. The child does not address the adult and does not wait for a response. Dore suggests that this is a "catch-all" category that should be used whenever an utterance cannot be assigned clearly to another category.

A few utterances are provided for practice in assigning Dore's (1974) Primitive Speech Acts before attempting to categorize the utterances in the sample transcript. Some of the example utterances used for practice with Bloom's and Nelson's procedures in Chapter 2 are provided, along with a few others. Cover the right side of the page and categorize each example utterance using one of Dore's nine Primitive Speech Acts. Linguistic and nonlinguistic contexts are provided for each practice utterance, since this information is crucial for coding. When finished, check your results with those provided in the shaded section. Explanations are provided to help clarify discrepancies.

Practice Examples for Primitive Speech Acts

(C picks up toy horse) horsie/	LABELING The child produced this utterance while attending to the horse, and it is assumed that he is labeling the horse.
(C hears door opening) Dada/	LABELING, CALLING, or GREETING Without additional context information, it is impossible to differentiate these three categories; this underlines the necessity of noting complete contextual information.
(C picks up big toy horse) big/	LABELING The child says this while attending to the horse and is labeling a feature.
(C reaches for cup on table) cup/	REQUESTING ACTION The child appears to desire the cup, which is out of reach. He then labels the desired cup and by reaching, indicates the desire for the action of bringing it within reach.
(C reaches up to M, who has entered bedroom) up/	REQUESTING ACTION This utterance is also an example of a request for an action, but the child labels the action instead of the object of the action.
(dog barking in background) Dee Dee/	LABELING or CALLING The child appears to be either labeling the dog or calling the dog; additional context would need to be considered before coding the utterance.

Continued on next page

Practice Examples—*Continued*

(C takes a drink from cup) juice/	LABELING The child is labeling the substance.
(M says, "Where is that shoe?"; C points to chest of drawers and says) there/	ANSWERING The child is responding directly to the adult's question.
(C points to self in mirror) Baby/	LABELING The child is labeling himself. Recall from the practice examples for Bloom's and Nelson's analysis (pp. 36–37 and 43–45) that this child refers to himself as "Baby."
(C hands empty cup to M) drink/	REQUESTING ACTION The child is asking his mother to get him a drink.
(M attempts to wipe C's face) no/	PROTESTING The child is protesting his mother's attempt to wipe his face.
(C is holding box; M says, "What's in there?") /kiki/ [cookie]	ANSWERING The child is responding to his mother's question.
(C pulls block from bag) /bɑ/ [block]	LABELING The child is attending to the object retrieved from the bag and is labeling it.
(C holds up toy sheep and looks at M) moo↑/	REQUESTING ANSWER The child is asking his mother to confirm the label for the toy animal.
(C reaches arms up to M, who is standing by door) /ʌ/ [up]	REQUESTING ACTION The child is requesting that his mother pick him up.

Continued on next page

Practice Examples—*Continued*

(M places C in bed and turns to leave, saying, "Sleep tight, Megan") /naɪ naɪ/ [night-night]	GREETING Remember, this category is used both for arrivals and departures.
(C is playing in crib after nap and bats at mobile hanging above bed) /bwɪ/ [XXX]	PRACTICING The child is not addressing anyone, and therefore appears to be practicing some aspect of language.
(C is playing in crib after nap; M walks by the bedroom door) /mɑ/ [mom]	CALLING The child is calling for his mother. This utterance appears to be more clearly an example of CALLING instead of LABELING because the child uses more emphasis in saying /mɑ/.
(M stands up and says, "Let's have some cookies") /kiki/ [cookie]	REPEATING The child is repeating part of the mother's utterance without addressing her.
(M asks C, "Do you want some cookies?") ya/	ANSWERING The child is responding directly to the mother's question.

The above examples should be helpful as you code the utterances in Bridget's transcript. Using *Dore's Primitive Speech Acts* analysis sheet from Appendix A (page 246), progress through the sample transcript (pages 19–34) and examine each child utterance to determine the type of Primitive Speech Act it represents. Categorize each utterance, remembering that Dore supports the notion of using the PRACTICING category as a "catch-all" category. Record the utterance number next to the appropriate speech act on *Dore's Primitive Speech Acts* analysis sheet. (In the next section, you will learn about Dore's Conversational Acts, which will be used to code both the child's and the adult's utterances). When all child utterances have been coded, count the number of each speech act and enter them in each Total blank. Calculate the percent of total utterances (in this case 100 utterances) that accounts for each speech act and enter those percentages in each percent blank. Then compare your analysis sheet with the completed one provided on page 175.

Dore's Primitive Speech Acts

Name of Child Bridget

Act	Child Utterance Number	Total	%
Labeling	1, 8, 13, 17, 18, 20, 27, 32, 40, 41, 46, 61, 62, 65, 83, 84, 86, 94, 99	19	19
Repeating	50 (Not Labeling, because in the preceding turn, M asks about the stroller.)	1	1
Answering	2, 3, 4, 5, 9, 12, 21, 25, 30, 33, 34, 36, 37, 42, 43, 44, 45, 47, 48, 49, 51, 55, 56, 57, 58, 63, 64, 69, 75, 76, 77, 78, 79, 80, 81, 82, 85, 92, 93, 95, 97	41	41
Requesting Action	6, 10, 11, 14, 15, 22, 26, 28, 31, 38, 52, 53, 70, 72, 73, 87, 88, 89, 90, 100 (52: Directs adult to look at tail, not simply to answer.)	20	20
Requesting Answer	7, 16, 19, 23, 24, 29, 35, 59, 60, 66, 68, 74, 91, 96	14	14
Calling	71	1	1
Greeting	54, 98	2	2
Protesting	39	1	1
Practicing	67	1	1

The completed analysis sheet for the sample transcript shows that 19 of Bridget's utterances were examples of LABELING; 1 utterance was an example of REPEATING; 41 utterances were examples of ANSWERING; 20 utterances were examples of REQUESTING ACTION; 14 utterances were examples of REQUESTING ANSWER; 1 utterance was an example of CALLING; 2 utterances were examples of GREETING; 1 utterance was an example of PROTESTING; and 1 utterance was an example of PRACTICING.

As can be seen in Table 4.3, Bridget used the Primitive Speech Acts of LABELING and ANSWERING for 60% of her utterances. When the two requesting categories—REQUESTING ACTION and REQUESTING ANSWER—are added to this percentage, these four acts account for 94% of the child's utterances.

When these results are compared to results obtained by Dore (1974), substantial differences can be found. Table 4.4 summarizes the distribution of Primitive Speech Acts for two children, each 15 months of age, used in Dore's study. The analysis was based on 81 and 80 utterances respectively. While there are differences between the two children on whom Dore reported, there are more substantial differences between Dore's subjects and Bridget, the 28-month-old child in the sample transcript. For example, the Primitive Speech Act REPEATING accounted for 39.5% and 28.7% of utterances for Dore's subjects, but only 1% of utterances in Bridget's transcript. In addition, ANSWERING accounted for 14.8% and 10.0% of utterances for Dore's subjects, but 41% of utterances in Bridget's transcript. The observed differences could be the result of either the question-asking performance of the child's

TABLE 4.3
PERCENTAGE OF TOTAL UTTERANCES ACCOUNTED FOR BY PRIMITIVE SPEECH ACT TYPES FOR CHILD AGED TWO YEARS, FOUR MONTHS

	Bridget (% based on 100 utterances)
LABELING	19
REPEATING	1
ANSWERING	41
REQUESTING ACTION	20 } 34
REQUESTING ANSWER	14 }
CALLING	1
GREETING	2
PROTESTING	1
PRACTICING	1

TABLE 4.4
PERCENTAGE OF TOTAL UTTERANCES ACCOUNTED FOR BY PRIMITIVE SPEECH ACT TYPES FOR TWO CHILDREN AGED ONE YEAR, THREE MONTHS

(Recomputed from totals provided by Dore, 1974)

	Child M (% based on 81 utterances)	**Child J** (% based on 80 utterances)
LABELING	34.6	17.5
REPEATING	39.5	28.7
ANSWERING	14.8	10.0
REQUESTING (ACTION and ANSWER)	7.4	26.2
CALLING	0	11.2
GREETING	1.2	6.2
PROTESTING	2.5	0
PRACTICING	0	0

conversational partner or differences in the developmental level of the children (i.e., MLU or semantic or syntactic aspects reflecting a higher developmental level). Bridget appears to be using a more conversational interaction style while communicating, as evidenced by the high percentage of REQUESTING and ANSWERING speech acts. Dore's children used primarily LABELING and REPEATING, both decidedly less conversational in style, although Bridget's LABELING slightly exceeded Dore's Child J (see Table 4.4).

Other differences between Dore's (1974) subjects and Bridget were noted but do not appear to be as substantial as these differences, primarily because of the variability between Dore's two subjects. In fact, Dore considers the differences between his two subjects to be the result of different styles of language use. The child identified as M in Table 4.4 apparently used language at this stage of development to declare things about her environment. The child identified as J apparently used language to manipulate other people. These differences may be similar to, or the result of differences in, semantic use at the one-word stage, described in Chapter 2. For purposes of the present analysis, however, we are more concerned with the differences between Bridget's transcript and the results of Dore's analysis. These differences are the result of age differences between Bridget and the children studied by Dore. Dore's subjects were just into the one-word stage at 15 months. Bridget is beyond the one-word stage at the age of 28 months. The differences in frequency of use of various speech acts are obvious for these children. As a result, analysis of Dore's Primitive Speech Acts may not be the most revealing for children beyond the one-word stage. Such analysis, then, should be reserved for children at the one-word stage, where it can be used to identify differences in styles of language, differences that may be the result of a language delay and/or disorder, and differences in how the adult interacts with child.

Coggins and Carpenter (1981) have proposed a variation of Dore's (1974) system. Their *Communicative Intention Inventory* is based on the writings of Bates (1976), Greenfield and Smith (1976), and Halliday (1977). The *Communicative Intention Inventory* uses a criterion-referenced approach (i.e., determining how well a child has established a particular behavior) rather than a norm-referenced approach (i.e., comparing the behavior of one child with that of other children). Although Coggins and Carpenter published selected percentile ranks and a standard error of measurement for the frequency of each of eight categories of communicative intentions, the data were not intended as reference norms, but as a means "to provide the user with a perspective regarding the frequency of a set of intentional behaviors in a group of normal 16-month-old children who communicate primarily vocally and gesturally and are beginning to convey their intentions verbally" (p. 249). The inventory includes these eight intentional categories: Comment on Action, Comment on Object, Request for Action, Request for Object, Request for Information, Answering, Acknowledging, and Protesting. These eight categories were selected because they are likely communicative acts to occur in a clinical setting. Direct comparison with Coggins and Carpenter's frequency data is possible only if a 45-minute sample of the child and a familiar adult's interaction is videotaped in a clinical setting. Coggins and Carpenter note, "deviations from these guidelines [i.e., conditions under which the sample is obtained] may lead to erroneous estimates of what intentions a child is capable of communicating" (p. 239).

While Coggins and Carpenter's (1981) *Communicative Intention Inventory* has special merit for analyzing timed language samples obtained in a clinical setting, it is not appropriate to use with the 100-utterance samples in *Guide.* Coggins and Carpenter's system does not analyze the communicative intent of each utterance, but rather the intentional behaviors displayed (e.g., if the child repeats the word *drink* three times while drinking a glass of juice and looking toward the mother, those three utterances are tallied as one verbal comment on action, not three). Readers are urged to study Coggins and Carpenter's *Communicative Intention Inventory* and to apply it when appropriate, but its use will not be demonstrated with the language transcripts in *Guide.*

Perhaps more revealing than a comparison of the frequency of occurrence of specific speech acts used by Bridget to Dore's (1974) two subjects is a comparison of Bridget's use of specific speech acts to her mother's use of specific conversational acts. ANSWERING characterized 41% of Bridget's turns; thus this was her most frequently occurring conversational act. A quick look ahead reveals that the act of REQUEST characterized 61% of Bridget's mother's turns; thus this was her most frequently occurring conversational act. It appears that Bridget responded to more than half of her mother's requests and that these exchanges accounted for almost half of the interaction. Is this good? At the very least, it suggests that Bridget is participating in this conversation with her mother and is often responding when asked to respond.

Is Bridget's mother's use of REQUEST hindering Bridget's language development? We can't say for sure since Dore's (1978) REQUEST includes both yes/no and *wh-* questions. It would be important to follow this level of description of conversational act use with a more detailed examination of the nature of REQUEST by Bridget's mother.

In her summary of the literature on parent-child interaction comparing parents of children developing normally to parents of children with a language disorder, Cross (1984) found substantial differences in the sentence types used. Parents of children with a language disorder were more likely to use *wh-* questions than were parents of children developing normally. Parents of children with a language disorder were less likely to use yes/no questions that typically recast (i.e., rephrase) their own children's utterances. These recasts have a positive correlation with children's elaboration of the auxiliary verb system.

We must consider the concern raised earlier about the age differences between Dore's (1974) subjects and Bridget. Whereas an analysis of the use of Primitive Speech Acts by children at the one- and early two-word stage may be useful, Bridget is more than a year older than Dore's subjects. We may be able to clarify the interaction between Bridget and her mother more thoroughly by using Retherford's (1980) Appropriateness Judgments, discussed later in this chapter.

Dore's Conversational Acts

Another of Dore's analysis procedures (1978) may be more appropriate for the developmental level of the child in the sample transcript. This analysis procedure, like the preceding, examines the communicative functions of utterances based on the form of those utterances and their use in conversation. The procedure is based on what Dore defines as a *conversational act.* A conversational act consists of a proposition, a grammatical structure, and the illocutionary force. The proposition refers to the conceptual information in the utterances; that is, what the utterance means. The illocutionary force refers to how the speaker intends his utterance to be taken. Dore contends that the grammatical structure of the utterance alters the illocutionary force of the proposition. Therefore, all three components must be assumed to work together in communication.

Table 4.5 (on page 180) lists and defines Dore's (1978) Conversational Acts. Within each act's definition are subcategories to identify utterances that are examples of the act. Because the breakdown of subcategories within each Conversational Act is primarily the result of variations in form, semantic content, and/or minor shades of intention, only the major category distinctions are used in this analysis. The utterances of Bridget's conversational co-participant will also be coded in the sample transcript.

TABLE 4.5

CONVERSATIONAL ACTS

(Adapted from Dore, 1978)

REQUEST:	Utterance used to request information, action, or acknowledgment—including yes/no questions that seek true/false judgments; *wh-* questions that seek factual information; clarification questions about the content of a prior utterance; action requests in the form of questions or directives that seek action from the listener; permission requests; and rhetorical questions that seek acknowledgment from the listener permitting the speaker to continue.
RESPONSE TO REQUEST:	Utterance following a request that responds directly to the request—including yes/no answers that supply true/false judgments; *wh-* answers that supply solicited factual information; clarifications that supply relevant repetition; compliances that verbally express acceptance, denial, or acknowledgment of a prior action or permission request; qualifications that supply unexpected information in response to the soliciting question; and repetitions of part of prior utterances.
DESCRIPTION:	Utterance used to describe verifiable past and present facts—including identifications that label objects, events, etc.; descriptions of events, actions, propositions, etc.; descriptions of properties, traits, or conditions; expression of locations or directions; and reports of times.
STATEMENT:	Utterance used to state facts, rules, attitudes, feelings, or beliefs—including expressions of rules, procedures, definitions, etc.; evaluations that express attitudes, judgments, etc.; internal reports of emotions, sensations, and mental events, such as intents to perform future actions; attributions that report beliefs about others' internal states; and explanations that express reasons, causes, and predictions.
ACKNOWLEDGMENT:	Utterance used to indicate recognition of a response or nonrequest—including acceptances that neutrally recognize answers and nonrequests; approvals/agreements that positively recognize answers or nonrequests; disapprovals/disagreements that negatively evaluate answers or nonrequests; and returns that acknowledge rhetorical questions and some nonrequests.
ORGANIZATIONAL DEVICE:	Utterance used to regulate interaction and conversation—including boundary markers that indicate openings, closings, and other significant points in the conversation; calls that solicit attention; speaker selections that explicitly indicate the speaker of the next turn; politeness markers that indicate politeness; and accompaniments that maintain verbal contact.
PERFORMATIVE:	Utterance that is accomplished by being said—including protests that register complaints about the listener's behavior; jokes that display nonbelief toward a proposition for humorous effect; claims that establish rights; warnings that alert the listener of impending harm; and teases that taunt or playfully provoke the listener.
MISCELLANEOUS:	Utterance that is uninterpretable because it is unintelligible, incomplete, or anomalous or because it contains no propositional content, such as an exclamation.

Categorizing a few utterances for practice should be helpful before turning back to the sample transcript. Some of the same utterances used for practicing Dore's (1974) Primitive Speech Acts are provided, and then a few more examples are considered. Dore's (1978) Conversational Acts should be used for both adult and child utterances in transcripts with child utterances longer than one word. Adult examples have been interspersed for practice. As before, cover the right side of the page, categorize each utterance, and then check your results with those in the shaded section.

Practice Examples for Conversational Acts

(C picks up toy horse) horsie/	DESCRIPTION The child labels an object, the horse. Most utterances previously identified as LABELING will now be DESCRIPTION.
(C hears door opening) Dada/	DESCRIPTION or ORGANIZATIONAL DEVICE The problem previously encountered when differentiating Primitive Speech Acts exists here as well. Without additional contextual information, it is impossible to differentiate these two categories.
(C reaches for cup on table) cup/	REQUEST The child is requesting his cup. Dore (1978) does not differentiate types of requests for Conversational Acts analysis.
(M hands cup to child) Here's your cup/	DESCRIPTION The adult extends the child's topic by interpreting his request.
(C reaches up to M, who has entered bedroom) up/	REQUEST The child appears to be requesting to be picked up. Again, it is not necessary to differentiate types of requesting.
(dog barking in background) Dee Dee/	DESCRIPTION or ORGANIZATIONAL DEVICE If the child is labeling the dog, then it is coded DESCRIPTION. If the child is calling the dog, then it is coded ORGANIZATIONAL DEVICE. Analysis of additional context would determine which way to code it.
(C takes a drink from cup) juice/	DESCRIPTION This utterance identifies the substance as juice.

Continued on next page

Practice Examples—*Continued*

(M says, "Where is that shoe?"; C points to chest of drawers and says) there/	RESPONSE TO REQUEST Because the mother has asked a question, the child's utterance is considered to be a response to that question, rather than a DESCRIPTION of the object's location.
(C points to self in mirror) Baby/	DESCRIPTION Again, the child is labeling himself; therefore this utterance is considered to be a DESCRIPTION.
(C hands empty cup to M) drink/	REQUEST The child is requesting that his mother fill his empty cup.
(M attempts to wipe C's face) no/	PERFORMATIVE This type of Conversational Act refers to those utterances that are accomplished simply by being said. Perhaps one of the simplest forms of PERFORMATIVE is the protest, which this utterance is an example of.
(C is holding box; M says, "What's in there?") /kiki/ [cookie]	RESPONSE TO REQUEST The child is responding directly to the mother's request.
(C pulls block from bag) /bɑ/ [block]	DESCRIPTION The child is labeling the block he has pulled from the bag.
(C holds up toy sheep and looks at M) moo↑/	REQUEST The child is asking his mother to confirm his label for the toy animal.

Continued on next page

Practice Examples—*Continued*

(C reaches arms up to M, who is standing by door) /ʌ/ [up]	REQUEST The child is asking his mother to pick him up. All types of requests, including requests for labels and for action, are labeled REQUEST.
(M places C in bed and turns to leave, saying, "Sleep tight, Megan") /naɪ naɪ/ [night-night]	ORGANIZATIONAL DEVICE Types of greetings—including closings—are labeled in this manner, primarily because of the way in which they regulate conversation.
(C is playing in crib after nap and bats at mobile hanging above bed) /bwɪ/ [XXX]	MISCELLANEOUS This category is used for a variety of types of utterances. In this case, it is used to indicate that the propositional content of the utterance is unclear.
(C is playing in crib after nap; M walks by the bedroom door) /mɑ/ [mom]	ORGANIZATIONAL DEVICE The child is soliciting his mother's attention.
(M stands up and says, "Let's have some cookies") /kiki/ [cookie]	RESPONSE TO REQUEST The child's utterance indicates acceptance of the request and readiness for cookies.
(M asks C, "Do you want some cookies?") ya/	RESPONSE TO REQUEST Again, the child is responding directly to the request regarding his desire for cookies.
(C picks up toy sheep that's in corral with cows) that's not a cow/	DESCRIPTION This utterance describes a verifiable fact regarding the sheep.

Continued on next page

Practice Examples—*Continued*

(M looks at toy sheep) cows don't have wool/	STATEMENT This utterance states a fact about cows.
(C picks up two cylinder-shaped blocks) these are the ones what we need/	STATEMENT This utterance expresses a need statement that reports on an internal state. Because it is not verifiable, it is not a DESCRIPTION.
(C and M are playing with playground set; M puts boy doll on top of pavilion; C says) you're a silly mommy/	PERFORMATIVE The child is teasing his mother for her silly behavior. The utterance accomplishes the tease simply by being said.
(M responds) I am?	REQUEST This utterance rhetorically requests clarification of the child's utterance.
(C and M are playing with playground set; C takes doll off swing and says) he's not feeling very good/	STATEMENT This utterance reports the child's belief about the internal state of the doll. Thus, it is an example of a STATEMENT and not a DESCRIPTION.
(C pulls toy sandbox out of box and holds it up) wow!/	MISCELLANEOUS This utterance is an exclamation, which Dore considers to have no propositional content.
(M picks up table) I'm going to put the table in the shelter/	STATEMENT The mother states her intention to put a table in the shelter.
(C looks at table) okay/	ACKNOWLEDGMENT The child's utterance is indicating acceptance of the mother's utterance.

Continued on next page

Practice Examples—*Continued*

(M and C are playing with playground set; one of the dolls falls off swing; C picks it up and says) this one fell off 'cuz he weren't hanging on/	STATEMENT This utterance states the facts of the situation (the doll fell off the swing) but goes on to explain the reason for it ('cuz he weren't hanging on). Because of the inclusion of an explanation, this utterance is an example of a STATEMENT instead of a DESCRIPTION.

You may wish to use the CD-ROM at this time. Worksheets 1 to 7 in the CD-ROM use Dore's Primitive Speech Acts for the child and Dore's Conversational Acts for the adult. Worksheets 8–12 use Dore's Conversational Acts for both the child and the adult.

In many cases, Conversational Acts coding is easier for utterances longer than two or three words in length, because there is more language on which to base the category judgments. It also should be apparent that the major developmental change in use of Conversational Acts occurs when the child is able to produce STATEMENTS, which reflect the child's greater awareness of rules, internal states, attitudes, and feelings.

Now, code the sample transcript of Bridget using *Dore's Conversational Acts* analysis sheet from Appendix A (page 247). Progress through the transcript and determine the appropriate Conversational Act that characterizes each utterance. Record the utterance number next to the Conversational Act on the analysis sheet and calculate as you did for Dore's Primitive Speech Acts analysis. Do this for both conversational co-participants. When finished, check your results with those provided on page 186.

Because we used 100 of Bridget's utterances in our analysis, the following frequency counts can be considered percentages as well. Analysis of the Conversational Acts used by Bridget revealed use of 31 REQUESTS, 38 RESPONSES TO REQUESTS, 18 DESCRIPTIONS, 4 STATEMENTS, 2 ACKNOWLEDGMENTS, 5 ORGANIZATIONAL DEVICES, 1 PERFORMATIVE, and 1 MISCELLANEOUS.

Bridget's mother used 122 REQUESTS, or 61% of her utterances; 5 RESPONSES TO REQUESTS, or 2.5% of her utterances; 22 DESCRIPTIONS, or 11% of her utterances; 18 STATEMENTS, or 9% of her utterances; 11 ACKNOWLEDGMENTS, or 5.5% of her utterances; 8 ORGANIZATIONAL DEVICES, or 4% of her utterances; 3 PERFORMATIVES, or 1.5% of her utterances, and 11 MISCELLANEOUS, or 5.5% of her utterances.

Although Dore does not provide frequency-of-occurrence data for use of Conversational Acts, he does provide guidelines to aid in interpretation. However, before an attempt is made to interpret the results of this analysis, another transcript obtained from an older child (Sara) is provided for comparison. Using Sara's transcript from Appendix B (pages 257–268) and another blank *Dore's Conversational Acts* analysis sheet from Appendix A (page 247), categorize each mother and child utterance. This child's utterances are longer and may be easier to code than the utterances in Bridget's transcript, and the results obtained should be very different. Compare your results with those provided on page 187.

Dore's Conversational Acts

Name of Child *Bridget*

Total / %	Adult Utterance Number	Act	Child Utterance Number	Total / %
122 / 61	1, 2, 3, 4, 6, 8, 10, 11, 14, 15, 16, 17, 19, 20, 24, 26, 27, 28, 29, 30, 32, 33, 34, 36, 37, 38, 39, 41, 42, 44, 47, 50, 52, 53, 54, 55, 56, 58, 59, 60, 62, 63, 65, 68, 70, 71, 72, 73, 75, 76, 77, 78, 79, 80, 81, 82, 84, 85, 87, 89, 90, 91, 92, 93, 94, 96, 98, 99, 100, 105, 106, 107, 108, 110, 112, 115, 117, 119, 120, 121, 123, 126, 127, 128, 129, 130, 132, 135, 140, 141, 142, 143, 144, 145, 146, 147, 148, 149, 150, 152, 153, 158, 161, 162, 164, 167, 176, 177, 178, 179, 180, 181, 182, 183, 184, 186, 188, 189, 192, 196, 197, 198	Request	6, 7, 11, 15, 16, 19, 22, 23, 24, 26, 28, 29, 31, 35, 38, 52, 53, 59, 66, 68, 70, 72, 73, 74, 87, 88, 89, 90, 91, 96, 100	31 / 31
5 / 2.5	5, 23, 31, 133, 172 (The information before s/c is ignored.)	Response to Request	2, 3, 4, 5, 9, 12, 21, 25, 30, 33, 34, 36, 37, 42, 43, 44, 45, 47, 48, 49, 51, 55, 56, 57, 58, 64, 69, 75, 76, 77, 78, 79, 80, 81, 92, 93, 95, 97	38 / 38
22 / 11	13, 21, 22, 25, 43, 46, 48, 51, 86, 88, 102, 109, 111, 113, 124, 151, 155, 157, 165, 166, 193, 194	Description	8, 13, 14, 17, 20, 27, 32, 40, 41, 46, 50, 60, 61, 65, 83, 84, 86, 94	18 / 18
18 / 9	35, 57, 66, 95, 97, 103, 118, 131, 136, 137, 138, 139, 160, 169, 187, 190, 199, 200	Statement	18, 39, 62, 99	4 / 4
11 / 5.5	7, 9, 12, 40, 49, 61, 67, 69, 83, 104, 154 (M appears to be acknowledging B's choice of object.)	Acknow-ledgment	82, 85	2 / 2
8 / 4	114, 116, 122, 134, 159, 163, 185, 195	Organizational Device	10, 54, 63, 71, 98	5 / 5
3 / 1.5	74, 125, 191	Performative	1	1 / 1
11 / 5.5	18, 45, 64, 101, 156, 168, 170, 171, 173, 174, 175	Miscellaneous	67	1 / 1

Dore's Conversational Acts

Name of Child Sara

Total / %	Adult Utterance Number	Act	Child Utterance Number	Total / %
91 / 79.8	1, 2, 3, 4, 5, 6, 7, 8, 9, 10, 11, 12, 13, 14, 15, 16, 17, 18, 19, 21, 22, 24, 25, 26, 29, 30, 31, 33, 36, 37, 38, 39, 42, 43, 44, 45, 47, 50, 51, 52, 53, 55, 56, 58, 59, 60, 61, 62, 63, 65, 66, 67, 68, 69, 70, 71, 73, 74, 75, 76, 77, 78, 79, 80, 81, 82, 83, 86, 87, 88, 89, 90, 91, 92, 93, 94, 96, 98, 99, 100, 102, 104, 105, 107, 108, 109, 110, 111, 112, 113, 114	Request	30, 37, 39, 47, 58, 62, 98	7 / 7
4 / 3.5	48, 49, 57, 72	Response to Request	1, 2, 3, 4, 5, 7, 8, 9, 11, 12, 13, 16, 18, 19, 20, 21, 24, 25, 28, 29, 31, 33, 34, 35, 38, 40, 41, 42, 43, 45, 46, 48, 49, 51, 52, 54, 55, 56, 57, 59, 60, 61, 63, 64, 65, 66, 69, 70, 71, 72, 75, 77, 78, 79, 81, 82, 84, 85, 87, 88, 89, 93, 94, 95, 96, 99, 100	67 / 67
0 / 0		Description	6, 15, 17, 23, 44, 53, 73, 74, 76, 80, 91, 97	12 / 12
8 / 7	20, 23, 35, 41, 64, 85, 101, 106	Statement	10, 22, 26, 32, 36, 50, 67, 83, 86, 90, 92	11 / 11
9 / 7.9	27, 28, 34, 40, 54, 84, 95, 97, 103	Acknow-ledgment		0 / 0
1 / .9	46	Organizational Device		0 / 0
0 / 0		Performative	14, 68	2 / 2
1 / .9	32	Miscellaneous	27	1 / 1

Results of this analysis did, in fact, reveal differences: 7 of Sara's utterances were REQUESTS, 67 were RESPONSES TO REQUESTS, 12 were DESCRIPTIONS, 11 were STATEMENTS, none were ACKNOWLEDGMENTS or ORGANIZATIONAL DEVICES; 2 were PERFORMATIVES, and 1 was MISCELLANEOUS. The most obvious difference between the girls in these two transcripts is in their use of RESPONSES TO REQUESTS and REQUESTS: 67% of Sara's utterances were RESPONSES TO REQUESTS, whereas only 38% of Bridget's utterances were RESPONSES TO REQUESTS. REQUESTS characterized only 7% of Sara's utterances but 31% of Bridget's.

There are differences between the girls' mothers as well. Sara's mother produced 91 REQUESTS, or 79.8% of her 114 utterances; 4 RESPONSES TO REQUESTS (3.5%), no DESCRIPTIONS (0%), 8 STATEMENTS (7%), 9 ACKNOWLEDGMENTS (7.9%); 1 ORGANIZATIONAL DEVICE (.9%), no PERFORMATIVES (0%), and 1 MISCELLANEOUS (.9%). Thus, REQUESTS accounted for 61% of the utterances used by Bridget's mother and 79.8% of the utterances used by Sara's mother.

Dore (1978) and others (Bloom, Rocissano, and Hood, 1976; Brinton and Fujuki, 1984; Ervin-Tripp and Mitchell-Kernan, 1977; Garvey, 1975) have reported that the ability to appropriately initiate conversation increases as the child's developmental level increases. Using requests is one way of initiating conversation. Sara is older than Bridget, yet Bridget uses more than four times as many REQUESTS. So does this mean that Sara is pragmatically delayed? Not necessarily. There are other ways of initiating conversation besides asking questions. Dore contends that DESCRIPTIONS, STATEMENTS, and PERFORMATIVES also may function to initiate conversation and some researchers identify other conversation initiators. But if the totals for each of these categories are added to each child's total number of REQUESTS, the difference between the two children is even greater. A total of 54 of Bridget's utterances were Conversational Acts that could function to initiate conversation, but only 32 of Sara's utterances could function in that capacity. Still, this does not prove that Sara is pragmatically delayed. In fact, it may indicate a greater attention to the cohesiveness of ongoing conversation. Bloom et al. (1976) report a decrease in spontaneous, noncontingent speech in children 21–36 months of age and an increase in topically cohesive speech. With this in mind, should both Bridget and Sara be considered developmentally normal in their patterns of initiating and responding? Before any conclusion can be drawn, two other points must be considered.

First, Sara's tendency to respond is the result of a mother who asks a considerable number of questions. Of the 114 utterances that Sara's mother produced, 79.8% were REQUESTS, compared to only 61% of the 200 utterances of Bridget's mother. In fact, if Sara had responded to all of her mother's questions, her total number of responses would be even greater. To conclude that Sara is pragmatically delayed because the majority of her utterances were RESPONSES TO REQUESTS would be inappropriate, since her mother appears to be responsible for this high number of responses. It would be important to obtain another language sample, as suggested in Chapter 1, with Sara interacting with another familiar individual. Only then could it be determined if she is able to maintain a topic without questions to direct her.

The second point to consider before drawing a conclusion regarding the pragmatic abilities of these children is the setting in which the samples were obtained. While both were free-play situations, Sara's mother apparently felt a greater need to direct the interaction. As mentioned earlier in this chapter, Cross (1984) identified differences in the interaction patterns of parents and their children with language disorders compared to parents of children without language disorders. Of the differences noted, most relevant here are the increased use of *wh-* questions and the decreased use of declarative forms for the functions of commenting and stating. Sara's mother produced REQUESTS 79.8% of the time, produced STATEMENTS 7% of the time, and produced no DESCRIPTIONS. Compare these percentages to Bridget's mother, who produced REQUESTS 61% of the time, DESCRIPTIONS 11% of the time, and STATEMENTS 9% of the time. Whether the differences noted by Cross as well as those noted here implicate parents causally in a child's language disorder has not been documented. But the interaction style of Bridget conversing with her mother is very different from the interaction style of Sara conversing with her mother. Again, to determine whether Sara does not initiate conversation more frequently than the present sample indicates, it would be important to obtain another transcript in a different setting (in addition to the transcript obtained with another familiar individual, mentioned earlier).

Overall, Dore's (1974) Primitive Speech Acts analysis and Dore's (1978) Conversational Acts analysis provide information that, when taken together with data obtained from semantic and syntactic analyses, can be used to describe a child's language production. Identification of a pragmatic delay/disorder could not be made using Conversational Acts analysis and one language transcript. With Primitive Speech Acts analysis, only one transcript was necessary to draw conclusions. With Dore's Conversational Acts analysis, however, it would be necessary to obtain at least two additional samples of a particular child's language production abilities: one in a different setting and another with at least one other participant.

Martlew's Conversational Moves

The next analysis procedure that will be demonstrated is based on a set of discourse categories described by Martlew (1980). Her Conversational Moves categories were used to code utterances of children developing normally and their mothers at two points in time: When the children were approximately 3 years of age, and a year later when the children were approximately 4 years of age. Because Sara's age more closely matches Martlew's subjects, Sara's transcript will be analyzed.

Martlew's categories differentiate types of INITIATING MOVES and types of RESPONDING MOVES. While the subcategories of Martlew's Conversational Moves are not dissimilar to Dore's (1978) Conversational Acts, the focus in examining INITIATING MOVES versus RESPONDING MOVES is to document discourse abilities. The unit of analysis continues to be the utterance, but in examining the role utterances play in initiating and responding to topics, the results are closer to an account of the discourse relations of the conversation. This is particularly true when we examine both speakers participating in the conversation. Table 4.6 (on page 190) lists and describes the categories of Conversational Moves that Martlew posits. The names for many of the categories have been changed in *Guide* to aid in recall for coding.

Because coding of utterances is based primarily on the immediately preceding utterance of the conversational co-participant, but also at times on utterances several speaking turns prior to the utterance under consideration, it is impossible to present single-utterance examples for practice. The descriptions of Martlew's (1980) Conversational Moves in Table 4.6 should be sufficiently clear for successful coding of

TABLE 4.6

CONVERSATIONAL MOVES WITH LETTER IDENTIFICATION FOR CODING

(Adapted from Martlew, 1980)

INITIATING MOVES	
New Topic Introduction (N):	A new topic is introduced into the conversation.
Restarting Old Topic (R):	A previous topic is reintroduced into the conversation.
Eliciting Verbal Response (E):	The speaker invites the other participant to respond verbally, including questions.
Intruding (I):	The speaker intrudes into the conversation in an inappropriate manner or at an inappropriate time; topic may be irrelevant or a turn out of place.
RESPONDING MOVES	
Acknowledging (A):	The previous speaker's utterance is acknowledged through brief remarks.
Yes/No Responses (Y):	Simple affirmation or negation of previous speaker's turn.
One-Word Answers (O):	Brief responses contingent on previous speaker's utterance; "sit" and "sit down" would both be coded O in response to "What do you want him to do?"
Repeating (R):	The previous utterance is repeated partially or wholly, with or without additional information.
Sustaining Topic (S):	The topic is maintained by reformulating content without adding new information.
Extending Topic (E):	The topic is maintained but new information is added.
FALSE STARTS	An utterance is begun but is not completed; thus there is neither an INITIATING MOVE nor a RESPONDING MOVE. If utterances have been numbered according to the rules on page 18 no FALSE STARTS would appear numbered in a transcript.

utterances from the sample transcript, without the benefit of practice examples. In addition, final analysis of results will be based on the broad categories of INITIATING MOVES and RESPONDING MOVES; consequently, minimal variation in use of subcategories can be allowed. The CD-ROM does have practice worksheets for conversational moves and appropriateness judgments analysis.

Using Sara's transcript (pages 257–268) and a blank *Conversational Moves and Appropriateness Judgments Analysis Grid* in Appendix A (pages 248–252), code the Conversational Moves of Sara and her mother according to the modified Martlew (1980) categories. The first two columns on each half of the form are to be used to record the letter code given in Table 4.6 for the types of INITIATING MOVES and RESPONDING MOVES. For example, if Sara produced an utterance considered a New Topic Introduction, record an N under the Initiating Moves column on the Child portion of the sheet, next to the appropriate utterance number. Progress through the transcript and code each utterance, considering its role in relation to preceding utterances. When finished, check your results with those provided on pages 191–195. Then, count and record the resulting information on the *Conversational Moves and Appropriateness Judgments Summary Form,* found in Appendix A (page 253).

Conversational Moves and Appropriateness Judgments Analysis Grid

Name of Child Sara

Adult

UTT#	Conversational Moves: Initiating Moves	Conversational Moves: Responding Moves	Appropriateness Judgments: Referent Specificity	Appropriateness Judgments: Contributional Conciseness	Appropriateness Judgments: Communication Style
1	N				
2	E				
3	E				
4	E				
5	E				
6	E				
7	E				
8	E				
9	E				
10	E				
11	E				
12	E				
13	E				
14	E				
15		E			
16	E				
17	E				
18	E				
19	E				
20		E			
21	E				
22	E				
23		E			
24	E				
25	E				

Child

UTT#	Conversational Moves: Initiating Moves	Conversational Moves: Responding Moves	Appropriateness Judgments: Referent Specificity	Appropriateness Judgments: Contributional Conciseness	Appropriateness Judgments: Communication Style
1		O			
2		E			
3		R			
4		E			
5		E			
6		E			
7		E			
8		O			
9		E			
10		R			
11		E			
12		O			
13		O			
14		E			
15	N				
16		E			
17		E			
18		O			
19		E			
20		E			
21		E			
22		E			
23		E			
24		E			
25		R			

Conversational Moves and Appropriateness Judgments Analysis Grid

Name of Child Sara

Adult

UTT#	Conversational Moves: Initiating Moves	Conversational Moves: Responding Moves	Appropriateness Judgments: Referent Specificity	Appropriateness Judgments: Contributional Conciseness	Appropriateness Judgments: Communication Style
26	E				
27		R			
28		A			
29	E				
30	E				
31	E				
32		E			
33	E				
34		A			
35		E			
36	E				
37	E				
38	E				
39	E				
40		A			
41		A			
42	E				
43	E				
44	E				
45	E				
46	E				
47	E				
48		E			
49		Y			
50	E				

Child

UTT#	Conversational Moves: Initiating Moves	Conversational Moves: Responding Moves	Appropriateness Judgments: Referent Specificity	Appropriateness Judgments: Contributional Conciseness	Appropriateness Judgments: Communication Style
26		E			
27		R			
28		O			
29		E			
30	E				
31		O			
32		E			
33		O			
34		E			
35		O			
36	N				
37	N				
38		Y			
39	E				
40		O			
41		O			
42		Y			
43		O			
44		E			
45		O			
46		E			
47	E				
48		O			
49		O			
50		E			

Conversational Moves and Appropriateness Judgments Analysis Grid

Name of Child Sara

Adult

	Conversational Moves		Appropriateness Judgments		
UTT#	Initiating Moves	Responding Moves	Referent Specificity	Contributional Conciseness	Communication Style
51	E				
52	E				
53	E				
54		A			
55	E				
56	E				
57		E			
58	E				
59	E				
60	E				
61	E				
62	E				
63	E				
64		E			
65	E				
66	E				
67		S			
68	E				
69	E				
70	E				
71	E				
72		E			
73	E				
74	E				
75	E				

Child

	Conversational Moves		Appropriateness Judgments		
UTT#	Initiating Moves	Responding Moves	Referent Specificity	Contributional Conciseness	Communication Style
51		O			
52		E			
53	N				
54		E			
55		E			
56		S			
57		E			
58		E			
59		O			
60		E			
61		Y			
62	E				
63		E			
64		S			
65		Y			
66		E			
67		E			
68		E			
69		E			
70		E			
71		O			
72		E			
73		E			
74		R			
75		E			

Conversational Moves and Appropriateness Judgments Analysis Grid

Name of Child Sara

Adult

UTT#	Conversational Moves: Initiating Moves	Conversational Moves: Responding Moves	Appropriateness Judgments: Referent Specificity	Appropriateness Judgments: Contributional Conciseness	Appropriateness Judgments: Communication Style
76	E				
77	E				
78	E				
79	E				
80	E				
81	E				
82	E				
83	E				
84		R			
85		E			
86	E				
87	E				
88	E				
89	E				
90	E				
91	E				
92	E				
93	E				
94	E				
95		A			
96	E				
97		A			
98	E				
99	E				
100		E			

Child

UTT#	Conversational Moves: Initiating Moves	Conversational Moves: Responding Moves	Appropriateness Judgments: Referent Specificity	Appropriateness Judgments: Contributional Conciseness	Appropriateness Judgments: Communication Style
76		E			
77		E			
78		O			
79		E			
80	R				
81		E			
82		S			
83	N				
84		Y			
85		O			
86		E			
87		O			
88		Y			
89		E			
90		E			
91		E			
92		E			
93		E			
94		O			
95		O			
96		O			
97		E			
98	E				
99		E			
100		O			

Conversational Moves and Appropriateness Judgments Analysis Grid

Name of Child: Sara

Adult

UTT#	Conversational Moves: Initiating Moves	Conversational Moves: Responding Moves	Appropriateness Judgments: Referent Specificity	Appropriateness Judgments: Contributional Conciseness	Appropriateness Judgments: Communication Style
101		S			
102	E				
103		A			
104	E				
105	E				
106	N				
107	E				
108	E				
109	E				
110	E				
111	E				
112	E				
113	E				
114	E				

UTT#	Conversational Moves: Initiating Moves	Conversational Moves: Responding Moves	Appropriateness Judgments: Referent Specificity	Appropriateness Judgments: Contributional Conciseness	Appropriateness Judgments: Communication Style

Reviewing the summary form for Sara's transcript shows that 11 (11%) utterances were types of INITIATING MOVES and 89 (89%) utterances were types of RESPONDING MOVES. Sara's mother produced utterances that were types of INITIATING MOVES 78.9% of the time and utterances that were types of RESPONDING MOVES 21.1% of the time. When these results are compared to those obtained by Martlew (1980), there are differences. Table 4.7 summarizes the frequency of use of individual Conversational Moves as percentages of total utterances for eight mothers and their children at approximately 3 years of age, and then again at approximately 4 years of age, while engaged in free-play conversation.

As can be seen in Table 4.7, 28.2% of the children's utterances at approximately 3 years of age were types of INITIATING MOVES. One year later, 25.5% of

TABLE 4.7

PERCENTAGE OF TOTAL UTTERANCES ACCOUNTED FOR BY CONVERSATIONAL MOVES FOR EIGHT CHILDREN AT TWO POINTS IN TIME

(Adapted from Martlew, 1980)

	Time 1		Time 2	
	Mothers	**Children** (% at 3 years, 3 months)	**Mothers**	**Children** (% at 4 years, 3 months)
INITIATING MOVES				
New Topic Introduction	4.0	5.1	2.1	2.5
Restarting Old Topic	4.0	7.8	5.3	8.7
Eliciting Verbal Response	25.1	14.4	25.0	13.6
Intruding	0.7	0.9	0.8	0.7
TOTAL	**33.8**	**28.2**	**33.2**	**25.5**
RESPONDING MOVES				
Acknowledging	8.6	2.8	9.0	3.9
Yes/No Responses	4.0	10.3	5.8	15.1
One-Word Answers	1.8	10.3	1.4	8.9
Repeating	6.5	3.8	5.7	4.0
Sustaining Topic	15.4	9.4	15.7	9.2
Extending Topic	10.7	5.0	13.4	6.1
TOTAL*	**64.4**[1]	**66.7**[2]	**64.9**[3]	**68.2**[4]
FALSE STARTS		**4.8**		**6.4**

*The totals for Responding Moves include a subcategory called Comments, which Martlew does not define in her RESPONDING MOVES.

[1]This total includes 17.4% Comments.

[2]This total includes 25.1% Comments.

[3]This total includes 13.7% Comments.

[4]This total includes 21.0% Comments.

their utterances were types of INITIATING MOVES. At approximately 3 years of age, 66.7% of their utterances were types of RESPONDING MOVES; at approximately 4 years, 68.2% were types of RESPONDING MOVES. In fact, Martlew (1980) reports that for this group of mothers and children, INITIATING MOVES accounted for approximately 30% of utterances, and RESPONDING MOVES accounted for approximately 70% of utterances of the children and their mothers at both points in time. Changes that occurred were primarily in the use of individual categories. Overall distribution of utterances between INITIATING and RESPONDING MOVES remained relatively constant over time.

Sara used substantially fewer INITIATING MOVES and more RESPONDING MOVES than did Martlew's (1980) subjects. Should it be concluded that Sara is pragmatically delayed/disordered on the basis of this comparison? These concerns are similar to those that were raised as a result of Dore's (1978) Conversational Acts analysis. In that case, as now, it is important to consider the mother's role in these results. The distribution of INITIATING MOVES and RESPONDING MOVES for Sara's mother is even more dissimilar to Martlew's subjects than Sara's distribution was. In fact, Sara's mother produced utterances that reflected a reversal of the 30%/70% distribution that Martlew found: 78.9% of Sara's mother's utterances were INITIATING MOVES and 21.1% were RESPONDING MOVES. Martlew reported that the mothers in her study tended to ensure the maintenance of the conversation and the interchange between speakers. Clearly, Sara's mother appeared to be attempting to maintain the ongoing conversation and to promote an exchange of speaker/listener roles. However, her strategy for doing this included greater use of INITIATING MOVES than did the mothers in Martlew's study.

So are this mother and her child, as a pair, pragmatically delayed/disordered? The same conclusion that was drawn following Dore's (1978) Conversational Acts analysis holds here as well. A minimum of two additional transcripts are needed before a conclusion can be reached: one obtained from Sara and her mother while interacting under conditions other than free play, and one obtained from Sara while interacting with another familiar adult. If the distribution of INITIATING MOVES and RESPONDING MOVES is similar in the additional transcripts to the distribution obtained in the sample transcript, it would be appropriate to conclude that Sara has a limited repertoire of means available to her for initiating speaking turns. In other words, if changes in condition and/or conversational co-participant do not result in significant changes in the distribution of INITIATING MOVES and RESPONDING MOVES, the prudent conclusion would be that Sara's participation in conversation is restricted. This apparent pragmatic delay/disorder would warrant attention in intervention.

Perhaps a comparison of each conversational co-participant's use of the individual Conversational Moves making up the INITIATING MOVES and RESPONDING MOVES categories would be helpful. The percentages for use of individual INITIATING MOVES obtained for Sara were as follows: 5% (5 ÷ 100 total utterances) New Topic Introduction, 1% Restarting Old Topic, 5% Eliciting Verbal Response, and 0% Intruding. The percentages for use of individual RESPONDING MOVES were 0% Acknowledging, 6% Yes/No Responses, 25% One-Word Answers, 5% Repeating, 3% Sustaining Topic, and 50% Extending Topic. There were no instances of False Starts. The most striking differences between Sara's totals and totals for Martlew's (1980) subjects at either point in time are in the use of One-Word

Answers and Extending Topic. Sara used 25% One-Word Answers, and Martlew's subjects used 10.3% at approximately 3 years and 8.9% at approximately 4 years. In addition, Sara used 50% Extending Topic utterances, while Martlew's subjects used 5.0% at approximately 3 years and 6.1% at approximately 4 years.

The percentages for use of INITIATING MOVES for Sara's mother were as follows: 1.8% New Topic Introduction and 77.2% Eliciting Verbal Response. There were no instances of Restarting Old Topic or Intruding. The percentages for use of individual RESPONDING MOVES were 7.0% Acknowledging, .9% Yes/No Responses, 1.8% Repeating, 1.8% Sustaining, and 9.6% Extending Topic. There were no instances of One-Word Answers. The most striking difference between Sara's mother and the mothers in Martlew's (1980) study is in the use of the INITIATING MOVES category of Eliciting Verbal Response. While this was the most frequently occurring category of INITIATING MOVES for Martlew's mothers, their total use of 25.1% falls far short of the 77.2% that Sara's mother used.

So how is the disparity between our dyad and Martlew's (1980) dyads to be reconciled? Sara's mother, like the mothers in Martlew's study, facilitated the child's participation in the conversation. Her strategy for accomplishing this clearly differed from that of the mothers in Martlew's study. Nevertheless, can we conclude that her strategy for facilitating Sara's participation in conversation was, in fact, hindering Sara's pragmatic development or her overall language development? Clearly not. But these data support the contention that more transcripts must be obtained. Verification of the ability to control the conversation less, by using fewer INITIATING MOVES, and to respond to Sara more by using more RESPONDING MOVES, would be essential. It is crucial that definitive conclusions about child conversational abilities as well as adult conversational tendencies not be made on the basis of a single transcript.

Another point to consider is an ambiguity in Martlew's (1980) data. As noted in the footnote of Table 4.7, Martlew reports frequency-of-occurrence data for a Conversational Move that she does not define. This move, which she labels as Comments, occurred with the greatest frequency of either group of children for her RESPONDING MOVES. If the percentages obtained for Comments and Extending Topic utterances are added together, the resulting total approaches the total Extending Topic utterances obtained for Sara. Clearly, 30.1% and 27.1% are a long way from Sara's 50%, but it makes more sense than an Extending Topic of 5.0% and 6.1%. The inclusion of another category that reflects responding to the conversational co-participant may explain the differences between Sara and the children in Martlew's study. However, it does not explain the differences between Sara's mother and the mothers in Martlew's study.

It is obvious that additional transcripts must be obtained, including one with Sara participating in a conversation with another adult and one in another setting. In addition, the use of frequency-of-occurrence data on individual Conversational Moves may not be a valid tool to identify differences in pragmatic abilities. Judgments are best made on overall use of the broader categories of INITIATING MOVES versus RESPONDING MOVES. Use of individual moves may support overall conclusions but should not be considered diagnostic in and of themselves.

Retherford's Appropriateness Judgments

This next set of analysis procedures was developed by Retherford in 1980 for use in the first edition of *Guide to Analysis of Language Transcripts* (1987) and encompasses Appropriateness Judgments relative to three conversational variables: (1) referent specificity, (2) contributional conciseness, and (3) communication style. Although little support for the reliability of appropriateness judgments exists in the literature, the three analysis procedures described in the following sections are useful for descriptive purposes. The selection of these three variables from a variety of options discussed in the literature is an attempt to capture those aspects of conversation that may be problematic for children with a language delay and/or disorder. A lack of appropriateness in regard to these variables is fairly easy to identify. In addition, it appears that problems in each of these areas can be treated. Clinical experience has shown that behaviors to increase the level of appropriateness in each of these areas can be taught. Each of Retherford's (1980) Appropriateness Judgments will be considered individually as the sample transcript of Sara is analyzed.

Referent Specificity

In their discussion of discourse topic, Keenan and Schieffelin (1976) present a dynamic model that includes a sequence of steps for establishing a discourse topic in a conversation. This model is based on the assumption that speakers accomplish each step, and receive positive feedback from listeners that they have done so, before continuing the conversation. These four steps are (1) the speaker elicits the listener's attention; (2) the speaker speaks clearly enough for the listener to hear the utterance; (3) the speaker identifies the referent in the topic; and (4) the speaker identifies the surrounding semantic relations of the referent in the topic. Keenan and Schieffelin contend that all four steps may be accomplished in a single utterance or that it may take a separate utterance to accomplish each step. While all four steps are necessary to establish a discourse topic, each step could be applied to a successful single utterance.

It is the third step that will be used in the first judgment of appropriateness. Keenan and Schieffelin (1976) report that the process of identifying a topic's referent for the listener involves directing the listener to locate the referent in either "physical space" or "memory space." Young children initially rely on the listener's ability to locate the referent in physical space, and only later do they rely on the listener's ability to locate the referent in memory. In either case, young children presume the listener will do the locating with minimal assistance provided for the listener in the form of nonverbal behaviors, such as looking at, pointing to, and holding up the referent. Later, children begin to use verbal means to identify referents in physical space for their listeners, including the use of notice verbs (e. g., *look, see)*, deictic particles (e.g., *these, this)*, and interrogative forms (e.g., "What's this?").

Keenan and Schieffelin (1976) contend that children at the one-word stage can repair misunderstandings as a result of their attempts to specify referents located in physical space. Specifying the referent in memory space and/or repairing the situation when the listener fails to locate the referent in memory space is much more difficult for children. In fact, Keenan and Schieffelin report that before the age of 3 years, children experience enormous difficulty in specifying nonsituated referents, or referents that are not present in the immediate situation, and they provide a variety of semantic, syntactic, and pragmatic reasons for this. Semantically, children do not use the previously mentioned notice verbs to assist the listener in locating the referent in memory space. Also, the notice verbs for locating referents in memory space (e.g., *remember, recall)* are not yet available to young children. Syntactically, children are not yet using tense markers consistently. Use of these and other syntactic structures (e.g., anaphoric pronouns, definite articles) would indicate to the listener that the referent is not present in the immediate context. Pragmatically, children continue to rely on nonverbal cues to locate referents for listeners, and this strategy is not useful for referents located in memory space.

This discussion should be helpful in identifying instances in which children fail to specify the referent of the topic for the listener. In adult-child conversation, the adult typically indicates to the child that the referent is not clear. The adult may do this explicitly (e.g., "I don't know what you're talking about") or indirectly, through the use of repairs (e.g., "What?" or "Huh?"). As in Conversational Moves analysis, identifying instances of a lack of specificity requires examination of a sequence of utterances. It would be very difficult to provide a series of examples for practice; so, the example below should suffice.

Example Coding for Referent Specificity

(M and C are reading books;
C points to picture of cow and says)

C: baby cow/	
M: That's not a baby cow/	(referent not identified)
C: no! a baby cow/	(repair attempted)
M: But that's not a baby calf/	(referent not identified)
C: calf/	(repair attempted)
M: Let's find a baby calf/	
C: no! Grandma baby/	(repair attempted)
M: Grandma baby? Oh Grandma has a baby calf?/	(referent identified)
C: yeah baby calf/	(referent confirmed)

In this exchange, it would be important to indicate on the *Conversational Moves and Appropriateness Judgments Analysis Grid* under the Referent Specificity column that a sequence of four child utterances lacked sufficient specificity. This would be indicated on the grid by putting a minus sign (–) in the Referent Specificity column in the rows corresponding to the utterance numbers. The fifth child utterance in this example would be marked with a check mark (✓) because the referent was specific enough to be identified.

Obviously, it is impossible to consider each utterance in isolation. The most effective method is to examine a sequence of utterances while looking for clues from the other speaker that an utterance has not been specific enough; then, backtrack and identify the child utterance that is the source of the problem. The child utterance that has caused the breakdown can then be marked with a minus sign, as would the utterances subsequent to the problem utterance. Once shared content is re-established, check marks can be used again.

N/A = Not Applicable; this would be used when the child repeats part or all of the preceding adult utterances. Judgments about specificity and conciseness are not applicable in that case. NK = Not Known; this would be used when there is not follow-up adult utterance or action.

Turn to Sara's transcript (pages 257–268) and examine mother and child utterances for a lack of specificity. Keep in mind that an adult may choose to ignore child utterances that lack specificity; however, adults typically do attempt to repair the situation. Progress through the transcript, indicating on the *Conversational Moves and Appropriateness Judgments Analysis Grid* used earlier (for Conversational Moves analysis) whether each utterance is sufficiently specific to allow the listener to identify the referent (✓) or whether an utterance lacks specificity (–). When the analysis is complete, compare your results with those provided on pages 202–206.

As a result of the analysis of referent specificity, 12 utterance sequences should have been identified in which Sara was not specific enough in identifying the referent of her utterance so that her mother could locate it in either physical space or memory space. Five of the 12 instances will be explained further to help you understand the type of exchange that would warrant such codings. The first exchange in which Sara's utterance lacks specificity begins at utterance #37, when Sara refers to some girl with no apparent contextual support and her mother is not quite sure to whom Sara is referring. Sara's mother's query clarifies the situation. Another exchange lacking specificity begins at utterance #63, when Sara refers to "cow people." It takes three repairs from her mother to establish the referent. Another exchange lacking specificity begins at utterance #66. In spite of three repairs on the part of the mother, it is not clear whether the referent is eventually identified. Another exchange lacking specificity begins at utterance #83, when Sara comments on the resemblance of a scoop to a bunny ear. Sara's mother is not quite sure what Sara means and needs verification by examining the scoop herself. Once she does this, Sara's statement becomes clear. Another exchange lacking specificity begins at utterance #90, when Sara identifies a plate as a cover for the pot. Again, Sara's mother attempts to repair the lack of specificity, but Sara continues with her next utterance. No instances or utterance sequences lacking referent specificity were identified for Sara's mother.

What can be concluded from the analysis of referent specificity? Sara did not adequately specify her referent in every utterance to permit her mother to locate those referents without clarification. But should a child of Sara's age and/or language level be expected to be specific enough in every exchange to ensure listener comprehension? Probably not. Recall that Keenan and Schieffelin (1976) report that children 3 years of age have considerable difficulty specifying referents that are not present. But before it can be concluded that Sara's lack of specificity is within normal limits, her productions need to be analyzed under other conversational conditions. Two other language samples in another setting and with another familiar adult world need to be obtained to determine whether referent specificity is a persistent problem for Sara.

Conversational Moves and Appropriateness Judgments Analysis Grid

Name of Child Sara

Adult

UTT#	Conversational Moves: Initiating Moves	Conversational Moves: Responding Moves	Appropriateness Judgments: Referent Specificity	Appropriateness Judgments: Contributional Conciseness	Appropriateness Judgments: Communication Style
1	N		✓		
2	E		✓		
3	E		✓		
4	E		✓		
5	E		✓		
6	E		✓		
7	E		✓		
8	E		✓		
9	E		✓		
10	E		✓		
11	E		✓		
12	E		✓		
13	E		✓		
14	E		✓		
15		E	✓		
16	E		✓		
17	E		✓		
18	E		✓		
19	E		✓		
20		E	✓		
21	E		✓		
22	E		✓		
23		E	✓		
24	E		✓		
25	E		✓		

Child

UTT#	Conversational Moves: Initiating Moves	Conversational Moves: Responding Moves	Appropriateness Judgments: Referent Specificity	Appropriateness Judgments: Contributional Conciseness	Appropriateness Judgments: Communication Style
1		O	✓		
2		E	✓		
3		R	N/A		
4		E	✓		
5		E	✓		
6		E	✓		
7		E	✓		
8		O	✓		
9		E	✓		
10		R	N/A		
11		E	✓		
12		O	✓		
13		O	✓		
14		E	✓		
15	N		✓		
16		E	✓		
17		E	✓		
18		O	✓		
19		E	✓		
20		E	✓		
21		E	✓		
22		E	✓		
23		E	✓		
24		E	✓		
25		R	N/A		

Conversational Moves and Appropriateness Judgments Analysis Grid

Name of Child: Sara

Adult

UTT#	Conversational Moves: Initiating Moves	Conversational Moves: Responding Moves	Appropriateness Judgments: Referent Specificity	Appropriateness Judgments: Contributional Conciseness	Appropriateness Judgments: Communication Style
26	E		✓		
27		R	N/A		
28		A	✓		
29	E		✓		
30	E		✓		
31	E		✓		
32		E	✓		
33	E		✓		
34		A	✓		
35		E	✓		
36	E		✓		
37	E		✓		
38	E		✓		
39	E		✓		
40		A	✓		
41		A	✓		
42	E		✓		
43	E		✓		
44	E		✓		
45	E		✓		
46	E		✓		
47	E		✓		
48		E	✓		
49		Y	✓		
50	E		✓		

Child

UTT#	Conversational Moves: Initiating Moves	Conversational Moves: Responding Moves	Appropriateness Judgments: Referent Specificity	Appropriateness Judgments: Contributional Conciseness	Appropriateness Judgments: Communication Style
26		E	✓		
27		R	N/A		
28		O	✓		
29		E	✓		
30	E		✓		
31		O	✓		
32		E	✓		
33		O	✓		
34		E	✓		
35		O	✓		
36	N		✓		
37	N		—		
38		Y	✓		
39	E		✓		
40		O	✓		
41		O	✓		
42		Y	✓		
43		O	✓		
44		E	✓		
45		O	✓		
46		E	✓		
47	E		✓		
48		O	✓		
49		O	✓		
50		E	✓		

Conversational Moves and Appropriateness Judgments Analysis Grid

Name of Child Sara

Adult

UTT#	Conversational Moves: Initiating Moves	Conversational Moves: Responding Moves	Appropriateness Judgments: Referent Specificity	Appropriateness Judgments: Contributional Conciseness	Appropriateness Judgments: Communication Style
51	E		✓		
52	E		✓		
53	E		✓		
54		A	✓		
55	E		✓		
56	E		✓		
57		E	✓		
58	E		✓		
59	E		✓		
60	E		✓		
61	E		✓		
62	E		✓		
63	E		✓		
64		E	✓		
65	E		✓		
66	E		✓		
67		S	✓		
68	E		✓		
69	E		✓		
70	E		✓		
71	E		✓		
72		E	✓		
73	E		✓		
74	E		✓		
75	E		✓		

Child

UTT#	Conversational Moves: Initiating Moves	Conversational Moves: Responding Moves	Appropriateness Judgments: Referent Specificity	Appropriateness Judgments: Contributional Conciseness	Appropriateness Judgments: Communication Style
51		O	✓		
52		E	✓		
53	N		—		
54		E	✓		
55		E	—		
56		S	—		
57		E	✓		
58		E	✓		
59		O	✓		
60		E	✓		
61		Y	✓		
62	E		✓		
63		E	—		
64		S	—		
65		Y	✓		
66		E	—		
67		E	✓		
68		E	—		
69		E	✓		
70		E	✓		
71		O	✓		
72		E	✓		
73		E	✓		
74		R	N/A		
75		E	✓		

Conversational Moves and Appropriateness Judgments Analysis Grid

Name of Child Sara

Adult

UTT#	Conversational Moves: Initiating Moves	Conversational Moves: Responding Moves	Appropriateness Judgments: Referent Specificity	Appropriateness Judgments: Contributional Conciseness	Appropriateness Judgments: Communication Style
76	E		✓		
77	E		✓		
78	E		✓		
79	E		✓		
80	E		✓		
81	E		✓		
82	E		✓		
83	E		✓		
84		R	N/A		
85		E	✓		
86	E		✓		
87	E		✓		
88	E		✓		
89	E		✓		
90	E		✓		
91	E		✓		
92	E		✓		
93	E		✓		
94	E		✓		
95		A	✓		
96	E		✓		
97		A	✓		
98	E		✓		
99	E		✓		
100		E	✓		

Child

UTT#	Conversational Moves: Initiating Moves	Conversational Moves: Responding Moves	Appropriateness Judgments: Referent Specificity	Appropriateness Judgments: Contributional Conciseness	Appropriateness Judgments: Communication Style
76		E	✓		
77		E	✓		
78		O	✓		
79		E	✓		
80	R		✓		
81		E	—		
82		S	✓		
83	N		—		
84		Y	✓		
85		O	✓		
86		E	✓		
87		O	—		
88		Y	✓		
89		E	✓		
90		E	—		
91		E	✓		
92		E	✓		
93		E	✓		
94		O	✓		
95		O	✓		
96		O	✓		
97		E	✓		
98	E		✓		
99		E	✓		
100		O	NK		

Conversational Moves and Appropriateness Judgments Analysis Grid

Name of Child Sara

Adult

UTT#	Conversational Moves: Initiating Moves	Conversational Moves: Responding Moves	Appropriateness Judgments: Referent Specificity	Appropriateness Judgments: Contributional Conciseness	Appropriateness Judgments: Communication Style
101		S	✓		
102	E		✓		
103		A	✓		
104	E		✓		
105	E		✓		
106	N		✓		
107	E		✓		
108	E		✓		
109	E		✓		
110	E		✓		
111	E		✓		
112	E		✓		
113	E		✓		
114	E		NK		

UTT#	Conversational Moves: Initiating Moves	Conversational Moves: Responding Moves	Appropriateness Judgments: Referent Specificity	Appropriateness Judgments: Contributional Conciseness	Appropriateness Judgments: Communication Style

Contributional Conciseness

The next variable that will be considered has to do with the amount of conversational space taken up by a single utterance and the appropriateness of the detail provided in a particular contribution. The examination of this variable is based on one of a set of four conversational principles proposed by Grice (1975); namely, the quantity of conversational contributions. Grice contends that speakers should make their contributions as informative as required but no more informative than required.

Young children typically have greater difficulty providing their listeners with enough information than they do with providing too much information. It is the former that is considered in Appropriateness Judgments of referent specificity; it is the latter that is considered in Appropriateness Judgments of contributional conciseness. Think of an adult who provides the listener with so much information that the listener becomes bored or annoyed or thinks, "So what?" Children violate this principle as well. In fact, children as young as 4 years of age provide the listener with too much information, as the following example indicates.

Example Coding for Contributional Conciseness

(M and C are sitting in clinic observation area, observing a therapy session)	
C: you know the teddy what Aaron had?/	(referent identified)
M: Yes/	(identification confirmed)
C: the one what talked?/	
M: Yes/	(identification reconfirmed)
C: Aaron's teddy bear?/	
M: I know which one you mean/	(identification reconfirmed)
C: well Jason gots one too/	
M: Oh I see/	

In Appropriateness Judgments regarding contributional conciseness, a judgment will be made, as Prutting and Kirchner (1983) suggest, whether or not violation of the conciseness principle is penalizing to the child. In other words, an attempt will be made to determine if providing too much information interferes with the continuation of conversation. In the preceding example, the mother is on the verge of being irritated with her child for failing to see that she has enough information to know the referent of the child's sequence of utterances. The conversation does continue though. Perhaps if this child had persisted in failing to be sufficiently concise, it would have had negative consequences. Without more of the conversation, we cannot be certain.

In analyzing Sara's transcript, sequences of utterances (as opposed to each utterance in isolation) will be considered in an attempt to find instances of a lack of conciseness. Progress through the transcript, examining mother and child utterances in sequence and indicating with a check mark (✓) when the utterance is appropriately concise (follow the same coding procedure for N/A and NK as described for referent specificity). If evidence is found of Sara providing so much information that her mother responds negatively, mark a minus sign (–) in the Contributional Conciseness column in the row corresponding to the appropriate utterance number on the *Conversational Moves and Appropriateness Moves Analysis Grid* used earlier for referent specificity. (The same procedure would be followed if Sara's mother provided so much information that Sara responded negatively.) Keep in mind that inappropriately providing too much information often occurs over more than one utterance. When the entire transcript has been examined, compare results with those provided in the sample on pages 209–213.

Analysis of Sara's transcript revealed no instances in which she provided so much information that it was penalizing to her as a speaker. There were several instances in which she seemed to provide irrelevant information (e.g., utterances #3 and #68), but they did not appear to penalize her as a speaker; thus, these instances were not judged as inappropriate. It could be concluded that for this listener, Sara's utterances were not judged as lacking conciseness. In addition, no utterances on the part of Sara's mother appeared to provide too much information.

Again, no normative data are available to which the results can be compared. Clinical judgment regarding a child's failure to be appropriately concise must be relied upon when considering an individual child who is interacting with a variety of speakers. If the failure to be concise is penalizing to the child, intervention would be warranted. Explicit feedback would be provided to the child to increase awareness of listeners' reactions to providing too much information. Only then could the child be expected to make use of specific strategies for increasing the conciseness of contributions in appropriate situations. As always, two other language samples in another setting and with another familiar adult would need to be obtained to determine whether contributional conciseness is a persistent problem for Sara.

Communication Style

The final variable that will be considered in making Appropriateness Judgments is that of communication style, or the ability to alter the style of a contribution based on characteristics of the listener. Shatz and Gelman (1973) were the first to provide evidence indicating that young children could alter the form of their contributions on the basis of language differences of their listeners. In their study, the language of 4-year-old children was compared when the children interacted with 2-year-old children and then with adults. Results indicated that by 4 years of age, children could adjust length, complexity, and use of attention-holders in their language depending on the age and/or language abilities of conversational partners. Since this study, others have followed, indicating that children as young as 3 years of age can use various styles of interacting depending on whether they are assuming a role (as of a baby or a daddy), talking with a younger child, talking with a familiar adult, or talking with an unfamiliar adult (Berko Gleason, 1973; Sachs and Devin, 1976).

Conversational Moves and Appropriateness Judgments Analysis Grid

Name of Child Sara

Adult

UTT#	Conversational Moves: Initiating Moves	Conversational Moves: Responding Moves	Appropriateness Judgments: Referent Specificity	Appropriateness Judgments: Contributional Conciseness	Appropriateness Judgments: Communication Style
1	N		✓	✓	
2	E		✓	✓	
3	E		✓	✓	
4	E		✓	✓	
5	E		✓	✓	
6	E		✓	✓	
7	E		✓	✓	
8	E		✓	✓	
9	E		✓	✓	
10	E		✓	✓	
11	E		✓	✓	
12	E		✓	✓	
13	E		✓	✓	
14	E		✓	✓	
15		E	✓	✓	
16	E		✓	✓	
17	E		✓	✓	
18	E		✓	✓	
19	E		✓	✓	
20		E	✓	✓	
21	E		✓	✓	
22	E		✓	✓	
23		E	✓	✓	
24	E		✓	✓	
25	E		✓	✓	

Child

UTT#	Conversational Moves: Initiating Moves	Conversational Moves: Responding Moves	Appropriateness Judgments: Referent Specificity	Appropriateness Judgments: Contributional Conciseness	Appropriateness Judgments: Communication Style
1		O	✓	✓	
2		E	✓	✓	
3		R	N/A	N/A	
4		E	✓	✓	
5		E	✓	✓	
6		E	✓	✓	
7		E	✓	✓	
8		O	✓	✓	
9		E	✓	✓	
10		R	N/A	N/A	
11		E	✓	✓	
12		O	✓	✓	
13		O	✓	✓	
14		E	✓	✓	
15	N		✓	✓	
16		E	✓	✓	
17		E	✓	✓	
18		O	✓	✓	
19		E	✓	✓	
20		E	✓	✓	
21		E	✓	✓	
22		E	✓	✓	
23		E	✓	✓	
24		E	✓	✓	
25		R	N/A	N/A	

Conversational Moves and Appropriateness Judgments Analysis Grid

Name of Child Sara

Adult

UTT#	Conversational Moves: Initiating Moves	Conversational Moves: Responding Moves	Appropriateness Judgments: Referent Specificity	Appropriateness Judgments: Contributional Conciseness	Appropriateness Judgments: Communication Style
26	E		✓	✓	
27		R	N/A	N/A	
28		A	✓	✓	
29	E		✓	✓	
30	E		✓	✓	
31	E		✓	✓	
32		E	✓	✓	
33	E		✓	✓	
34		A	✓	✓	
35		E	✓	✓	
36	E		✓	✓	
37	E		✓	✓	
38	E		✓	✓	
39	E		✓	✓	
40		A	✓	✓	
41		A	✓	✓	
42	E		✓	✓	
43	E		✓	✓	
44	E		✓	✓	
45	E		✓	✓	
46	E		✓	✓	
47	E		✓	✓	
48		E	✓	✓	
49		Y	✓	✓	
50	E		✓	✓	

Child

UTT#	Conversational Moves: Initiating Moves	Conversational Moves: Responding Moves	Appropriateness Judgments: Referent Specificity	Appropriateness Judgments: Contributional Conciseness	Appropriateness Judgments: Communication Style
26		E	✓	✓	
27		R	N/A	N/A	
28		O	✓	✓	
29		E	✓	✓	
30	E		✓	✓	
31		O	✓	✓	
32		E	✓	✓	
33		O	✓	✓	
34		E	✓	✓	
35		O	✓	✓	
36	N		✓	✓	
37	N		—	✓	
38		Y	✓	✓	
39	E		✓	✓	
40		O	✓	✓	
41		O	✓	✓	
42		Y	✓	✓	
43		O	✓	✓	
44		E	✓	✓	
45		O	✓	✓	
46		E	✓	✓	
47	E		✓	✓	
48		O	✓	✓	
49		O	✓	✓	
50		E	✓	✓	

Conversational Moves and Appropriateness Judgments Analysis Grid

Name of Child Sara

Adult

UTT#	Conversational Moves: Initiating Moves	Conversational Moves: Responding Moves	Appropriateness Judgments: Referent Specificity	Appropriateness Judgments: Contributional Conciseness	Appropriateness Judgments: Communication Style
51	E		✓	✓	
52	E		✓	✓	
53	E		✓	✓	
54		A	✓	✓	
55	E		✓	✓	
56	E		✓	✓	
57		E	✓	✓	
58	E		✓	✓	
59	E		✓	✓	
60	E		✓	✓	
61	E		✓	✓	
62	E		✓	✓	
63	E		✓	✓	
64		E	✓	✓	
65	E		✓	✓	
66	E		✓	✓	
67		S	✓	✓	
68	E		✓	✓	
69	E		✓	✓	
70	E		✓	✓	
71	E		✓	✓	
72		E	✓	✓	
73	E		✓	✓	
74	E		✓	✓	
75	E		✓	✓	

Child

UTT#	Conversational Moves: Initiating Moves	Conversational Moves: Responding Moves	Appropriateness Judgments: Referent Specificity	Appropriateness Judgments: Contributional Conciseness	Appropriateness Judgments: Communication Style
51		O	✓	✓	
52		E	✓	✓	
53	N		—	✓	
54		E	✓	✓	
55		E	—	✓	
56		S	—	✓	
57		E	✓	✓	
58		E	✓	✓	
59		O	✓	✓	
60		E	✓	✓	
61		Y	✓	✓	
62	E		✓	✓	
63		E	—	✓	
64		S	—	✓	
65		Y	✓	✓	
66		E	—	✓	
67		E	✓	✓	
68		E	—	✓	
69		E	✓	✓	
70		E	✓	✓	
71		O	✓	✓	
72		E	✓	✓	
73		E	✓	✓	
74		R	N/A	N/A	
75		E	✓	✓	

Conversational Moves and Appropriateness Judgments Analysis Grid

Name of Child Sara

Adult

UTT#	Conversational Moves: Initiating Moves	Conversational Moves: Responding Moves	Appropriateness Judgments: Referent Specificity	Appropriateness Judgments: Contributional Conciseness	Appropriateness Judgments: Communication Style
76	E		✓	✓	
77	E		✓	✓	
78	E		✓	✓	
79	E		✓	✓	
80	E		✓	✓	
81	E		✓	✓	
82	E		✓	✓	
83	E		✓	✓	
84		R	N/A	N/A	
85		E	✓	✓	
86	E		✓	✓	
87	E		✓	✓	
88	E		✓	✓	
89	E		✓	✓	
90	E		✓	✓	
91	E		✓	✓	
92	E		✓	✓	
93	E		✓	✓	
94	E		✓	✓	
95		A	✓	✓	
96	E		✓	✓	
97		A	✓	✓	
98	E		✓	✓	
99	E		✓	✓	
100		E	✓	✓	

Child

UTT#	Conversational Moves: Initiating Moves	Conversational Moves: Responding Moves	Appropriateness Judgments: Referent Specificity	Appropriateness Judgments: Contributional Conciseness	Appropriateness Judgments: Communication Style
76		E	✓	✓	
77		E	✓	✓	
78		O	✓	✓	
79		E	✓	✓	
80	R		✓	✓	
81		E	—	✓	
82		S	✓	✓	
83	N		—	✓	
84		Y	✓	✓	
85		O	✓	✓	
86		E	✓	✓	
87		O	—	✓	
88		Y	✓	✓	
89		E	✓	✓	
90		E	—	✓	
91		E	✓	✓	
92		E	✓	✓	
93		E	✓	✓	
94		O	✓	✓	
95		O	✓	✓	
96		O	✓	✓	
97		E	✓	✓	
98	E		✓	✓	
99		E	✓	✓	
100		O	NK	NK	

Conversational Moves and Appropriateness Judgments Analysis Grid

Name of Child Sara

Adult

UTT#	Conversational Moves: Initiating Moves	Conversational Moves: Responding Moves	Appropriateness Judgments: Referent Specificity	Appropriateness Judgments: Contributional Conciseness	Appropriateness Judgments: Communication Style
101		S	✓	✓	
102	E		✓	✓	
103		A	✓	✓	
104	E		✓	✓	
105	E		✓	✓	
106	N		✓	✓	
107	E		✓	✓	
108	E		✓	✓	
109	E		✓	✓	
110	E		✓	✓	
111	E		✓	✓	
112	E		✓	✓	
113	E		✓	✓	
114	E		NK	NK	

UTT#	Conversational Moves: Initiating Moves	Conversational Moves: Responding Moves	Appropriateness Judgments: Referent Specificity	Appropriateness Judgments: Contributional Conciseness	Appropriateness Judgments: Communication Style

The analysis of the ability to use stylistic variations in communication is based on two assumptions. The first assumption is that the child's ability to make adjustments reflects an abstract knowledge of the appropriateness of speech to the listener (Sachs and Devin, 1976). This assumption implies an integration of the cognitive system and the linguistic system. The second assumption is that a child who does not make adjustments will be penalized in some way as a speaker. Prutting and Kirchner (1983) suggest that a failure to adjust even loudness level can have a negative impact on the reactions of strangers, classmates, and/or teachers regarding the child's communicative abilities. Both of these assumptions serve to justify the examination of a pragmatic variable that may occur infrequently.

In the example below, the child uses a style of communication that is too informal for a school situation when adults are present. The mother reminds the child of the need to use a more polite form when addressing the teacher and the child immediately modifies the form of his request. The more polite form is a stylistic modification that would be noted when analyzing a transcript for appropriate or inappropriate use of communication style.

In making Appropriateness Judgments regarding communication style, identify the child's failure to make syntactic modifications, vocal quality modifications, and vocal intensity modifications as demanded by the situation. For example, if the child is interacting with a younger child and fails to shorten the length and/or reduce the complexity of his utterances, enter a minus sign (–) in the Communication Style column (on the *Conversational Moves and Appropriateness Judgments Analysis Grid* used earlier for contributional conciseness) corresponding to the utterances where those modifications would have been appropriate. If the child is role-playing and fails to make vocal quality changes (e.g., lower voice for the daddy, higher voice for the baby) and/or syntactic changes (e.g., more imperatives for the daddy, babbling and/or one-word utterances for the baby) as a result of his role, enter a minus sign in the Communication Style column corresponding to the utterances where those modifications would have been appropriate. Or if the child fails to use politeness markers when interacting with unfamiliar adults and/or uses aggressive vocal intensity when interacting with peers or adults, put a minus sign in the Communication Style column. If either speaker made appropriate adjustments, put a

Example Coding for Communication Style

(M, C, and teacher are at table; C reaches for crayon near teacher) C: gimme that/	Child fails to modify language to include polite forms.
M: Excuse me?	
C: can I have that crayon please?/	When prompted by mother, child uses more appropriate style.

Conversational Moves and Appropriateness Judgments Analysis Grid

Name of Child Sara

Adult

UTT#	Conversational Moves: Initiating Moves	Conversational Moves: Responding Moves	Appropriateness Judgments: Referent Specificity	Appropriateness Judgments: Contributional Conciseness	Appropriateness Judgments: Communication Style
1	N		✓	✓	
2	E		✓	✓	
3	E		✓	✓	
4	E		✓	✓	
5	E		✓	✓	
6	E		✓	✓	
7	E		✓	✓	
8	E		✓	✓	
9	E		✓	✓	
10	E		✓	✓	
11	E		✓	✓	
12	E		✓	✓	
13	E		✓	✓	
14	E		✓	✓	
15		E	✓	✓	
16	E		✓	✓	
17	E		✓	✓	
18	E		✓	✓	
19	E		✓	✓	
20		E	✓	✓	
21	E		✓	✓	
22	E		✓	✓	
23		E	✓	✓	
24	E		✓	✓	
25	E		✓	✓	

Child

UTT#	Conversational Moves: Initiating Moves	Conversational Moves: Responding Moves	Appropriateness Judgments: Referent Specificity	Appropriateness Judgments: Contributional Conciseness	Appropriateness Judgments: Communication Style
1		O	✓	✓	
2		E	✓	✓	
3		R	N/A	N/A	
4		E	✓	✓	
5		E	✓	✓	
6		E	✓	✓	
7		E	✓	✓	
8		O	✓	✓	
9		E	✓	✓	
10		R	N/A	N/A	
11		E	✓	✓	
12		O	✓	✓	
13		O	✓	✓	
14		E	✓	✓	
15	N		✓	✓	
16		E	✓	✓	
17		E	✓	✓	
18		O	✓	✓	
19		E	✓	✓	
20		E	✓	✓	
21		E	✓	✓	
22		E	✓	✓	
23		E	✓	✓	
24		E	✓	✓	
25		R	N/A	N/A	

Conversational Moves and Appropriateness Judgments Analysis Grid

Name of Child: Sara

Adult

UTT#	Conversational Moves: Initiating Moves	Conversational Moves: Responding Moves	Appropriateness Judgments: Referent Specificity	Appropriateness Judgments: Contributional Conciseness	Appropriateness Judgments: Communication Style
26	E		✓	✓	
27		R	N/A	N/A	
28		A	✓	✓	
29	E		✓	✓	
30	E		✓	✓	
31	E		✓	✓	
32		E	✓	✓	
33	E		✓	✓	
34		A	✓	✓	
35		E	✓	✓	
36	E		✓	✓	
37	E		✓	✓	
38	E		✓	✓	
39	E		✓	✓	
40		A	✓	✓	
41		A	✓	✓	
42	E		✓	✓	
43	E		✓	✓	
44	E		✓	✓	
45	E		✓	✓	
46	E		✓	✓	
47	E		✓	✓	
48		E	✓	✓	
49		Y	✓	✓	
50	E		✓	✓	

Child

UTT#	Conversational Moves: Initiating Moves	Conversational Moves: Responding Moves	Appropriateness Judgments: Referent Specificity	Appropriateness Judgments: Contributional Conciseness	Appropriateness Judgments: Communication Style
26		E	✓	✓	
27		R	N/A	N/A	
28		O	✓	✓	
29		E	✓	✓	
30	E		✓	✓	
31		O	✓	✓	
32		E	✓	✓	
33		O	✓	✓	
34		E	✓	✓	
35		O	✓	✓	
36	N		✓	✓	
37	N		—	✓	
38		Y	✓	✓	
39	E		✓	✓	
40		O	✓	✓	
41		O	✓	✓	
42		Y	✓	✓	
43		O	✓	✓	
44		E	✓	✓	
45		O	✓	✓	
46		E	✓	✓	
47	E		✓	✓	
48		O	✓	✓	
49		O	✓	✓	
50		E	✓	✓	

Conversational Moves and Appropriateness Judgments Analysis Grid

Name of Child Sara

Adult

	Conversational Moves		Appropriateness Judgments		
UTT#	Initiating Moves	Responding Moves	Referent Specificity	Contributional Conciseness	Communication Style
51	E		✓	✓	
52	E		✓	✓	
53	E		✓	✓	
54		A	✓	✓	
55	E		✓	✓	
56	E		✓	✓	
57		E	✓	✓	
58	E		✓	✓	
59	E		✓	✓	
60	E		✓	✓	
61	E		✓	✓	
62	E		✓	✓	
63	E		✓	✓	
64		E	✓	✓	
65	E		✓	✓	
66	E		✓	✓	
67		S	✓	✓	
68	E		✓	✓	
69	E		✓	✓	
70	E		✓	✓	
71	E		✓	✓	
72		E	✓	✓	
73	E		✓	✓	
74	E		✓	✓	
75	E		✓	✓	

Child

	Conversational Moves		Appropriateness Judgments		
UTT#	Initiating Moves	Responding Moves	Referent Specificity	Contributional Conciseness	Communication Style
51		O	✓	✓	
52		E	✓	✓	
53	N		—	✓	
54		E	✓	✓	
55		E	—	✓	
56		S	—	✓	
57		E	✓	✓	
58		E	✓	✓	
59		O	✓	✓	
60		E	✓	✓	
61		Y	✓	✓	
62	E		✓	✓	
63		E	—	✓	
64		S	—	✓	
65		Y	✓	✓	
66		E	—	✓	
67		E	✓	✓	
68		E	—	✓	
69		E	✓	✓	
70		E	✓	✓	
71		O	✓	✓	
72		E	✓	✓	
73		E	✓	✓	
74		R	N/A	N/A	
75		E	✓	✓	

Conversational Moves and Appropriateness Judgments Analysis Grid

Name of Child Sara

Adult

UTT#	Conversational Moves: Initiating Moves	Conversational Moves: Responding Moves	Appropriateness Judgments: Referent Specificity	Appropriateness Judgments: Contributional Conciseness	Appropriateness Judgments: Communication Style
76	E		✓	✓	
77	E		✓	✓	
78	E		✓	✓	
79	E		✓	✓	
80	E		✓	✓	
81	E		✓	✓	
82	E		✓	✓	
83	E		✓	✓	
84		R	N/A	N/A	
85		E	✓	✓	
86	E		✓	✓	
87	E		✓	✓	
88	E		✓	✓	
89	E		✓	✓	
90	E		✓	✓	
91	E		✓	✓	
92	E		✓	✓	
93	E		✓	✓	
94	E		✓	✓	
95		A	✓	✓	
96	E		✓	✓	
97		A	✓	✓	
98	E		✓	✓	
99	E		✓	✓	
100		E	✓	✓	

Child

UTT#	Conversational Moves: Initiating Moves	Conversational Moves: Responding Moves	Appropriateness Judgments: Referent Specificity	Appropriateness Judgments: Contributional Conciseness	Appropriateness Judgments: Communication Style
76		E	✓	✓	
77		E	✓	✓	
78		O	✓	✓	
79		E	✓	✓	
80	R		✓	✓	
81		E	—	✓	
82		S	✓	✓	
83	N		—	✓	
84		Y	✓	✓	
85		O	✓	✓	
86		E	✓	✓	
87		O	—	✓	
88		Y	✓	✓	
89		E	✓	✓	
90		E	—	✓	
91		E	✓	✓	
92		E	✓	✓	
93		E	✓	✓	
94		O	✓	✓	
95		O	✓	✓	
96		O	✓	✓	
97		E	✓	✓	
98	E		✓	✓	
99		E	✓	✓	
100		O	NK	NK	NK

Conversational Moves and Appropriateness Judgments Analysis Grid

Name of Child: Sara

Adult

	Conversational Moves		Appropriateness Judgments		
UTT#	Initiating Moves	Responding Moves	Referent Specificity	Contributional Conciseness	Communication Style
101		S	✓	✓	
102	E		✓	✓	
103		A	✓	✓	
104	E		✓	✓	
105	E		✓	✓	
106	N		✓	✓	
107	E		✓	✓	
108	E		✓	✓	
109	E		✓	✓	
110	E		✓	✓	
111	E		✓	✓	
112	E		✓	✓	
113	E		✓	✓	
114	E		NK	NK	NK

	Conversational Moves		Appropriateness Judgments		
UTT#	Initiating Moves	Responding Moves	Referent Specificity	Contributional Conciseness	Communication Style

plus sign (+) in the Communication Style column corresponding to the utterances where the adjustments were made. Use the NK coding feature as described earlier. All other boxes in the Communication Style column should be left blank.

Now turn to Sara's transcript and review sequences of utterances to determine whether there was a need for Sara or her mother to alter her communication style and whether the appropriate adjustments were made. The same procedure should be followed for the utterances of both Sara and Sara's mother. When the entire transcript has been examined, compare your results with those in the sample on pages 215–219.

Analysis of Sara's transcript revealed no instances in which she should have made adjustments in her communication style and did not make them. In fact, there were no instances in which she should have made adjustments and did. In addition, there were no instances in which Sara's mother should have made adjustments in her communication style and did not make them, nor were there instances in which she should not have made adjustments and did. This clearly points out the need to have samples of communicative interaction under a variety of conditions and with a variety of partners. Only then can it be concluded that a child does or does not make adjustments in his communication style.

And what should be done if a child does not make adjustments in communication style as situations demand? It is possible to teach the child to make the appropriate syntactic and vocal adjustments and to recognize when these adjustments are necessary. Because the ability to vary communication style is a reflection of the integration of the child's cognitive, semantic, syntactic, and pragmatic systems, this appropriateness variable is important in determining the overall communicative abilities of a child. Two other language samples in another setting and with another familiar adult would need to be obtained to determine whether communication style is a persistent problem for Sara.

Implications for Intervention

Completion of each of the appropriate pragmatic analyses should be followed by a synthesis of results. The *Conversational Moves and Appropriateness Judgments Summary Form* (page 253) can be used for this synthesis. A completed summary form for Sara's transcript appears on page 221.

While problems with any one of the areas analyzed may not be related to problems in another area, results of each analysis procedure completed must be reviewed to develop comprehensive goals and objectives for intervention. The sequence of normal development is not as detailed for pragmatic milestones as it is for semantic and syntactic behaviors; however, judgments about what to target in treatment for identified pragmatic problems continue to be based on what is known about normal language acquisition. Norms are not readily available, but knowledgeable judgments can be made. As in previous chapters, the suggestions provided here should be considered general guidelines, not hard-and-fast rules, for developing intervention goals and objectives.

Data obtained from frequency-of-occurrence analysis of various pragmatic categories (i.e., Dore's Primitive Speech Acts, 1974; Dore's Conversational Acts, 1978; or Martlew's Conversational Moves, 1980) that indicate a limited range of categories used can provide the foundation for developing objectives that target use of a wider variety of categories. For

Conversational Moves and Appropriateness Judgments Summary Form

Name of Child: Sara

CHILD'S TOTAL UTTERANCES 100

CONVERSATIONAL MOVES					
INITIATING MOVES	5	New Topic Introduction	=	5	% of Total Utterances
	1	Restarting Old Topic	=	1	% of Total Utterances
	5	Eliciting Verbal Response	=	5	% of Total Utterances
	0	Intruding	=	0	% of Total Utterances
RESPONDING MOVES	0	Acknowledging	=	0	% of Total Utterances
	6	Yes/No Responses	=	6	% of Total Utterances
	25	One-Word Answers	=	25	% of Total Utterances
	5	Repeating	=	5	% of Total Utterances
	3	Sustaining Topic	=	3	% of Total Utterances
	50	Extending Topic	=	50	% of Total Utterances
FALSE STARTS	0		=	-	% of Total Utterances
APPROPRIATENESS JUDGMENTS					
Referent Specificity	12	Lacked Specificity	=	12	% of Total Utterances
Contributional Conciseness	0	Lacked Conciseness	=	-	% of Total Utterances
Communication Style	0	Lacked Stylistic Variation	=	-	% of Total Utterances

ADULT'S TOTAL UTTERANCES 114

CONVERSATIONAL MOVES					
INITIATING MOVES	2	New Topic Introduction	=	1.8	% of Total Utterances
	0	Restarting Old Topic	=	-	% of Total Utterances
	88	Eliciting Verbal Response	=	77.2	% of Total Utterances
	0	Intruding	=	-	% of Total Utterances
RESPONDING MOVES	8	Acknowledging	=	7	% of Total Utterances
	1	Yes/No Responses	=	.9	% of Total Utterances
	0	One-Word Answers	=	-	% of Total Utterances
	2	Repeating	=	1.8	% of Total Utterances
	2	Sustaining Topic	=	1.8	% of Total Utterances
	11	Extending Topic	=	9.6	% of Total Utterances
FALSE STARTS	0		=	-	% of Total Utterances
APPROPRIATENESS JUDGMENTS					
Referent Specificity	0	Lacked Specificity	=	-	% of Total Utterances
Contributional Conciseness	0	Lacked Conciseness	=	-	% of Total Utterances
Communication Style	0	Lacked Stylistic Variation	=	-	% of Total Utterances

example, if a child's language abilities are at a one-word level overall and he is using a limited number of types of Primitive Speech Acts, it would be appropriate to provide the child with opportunities to use a broader range of Primitive Speech Acts. If the child's language abilities are typical of children with normal language skills between 2 and 5 years of age and he is using a limited number of Conversational Acts, it would be appropriate to provide the child with opportunities to use additional Conversational Acts. In either case, it would be crucial to consider the role that the conversational co-participant may play in the opportunities for expressing a variety of communicative functions, such as those specified in Dore's Primitive Speech Acts and Conversational Acts analysis.

Examination of the roles expressed by Sara's mother raised questions regarding the opportunities Sara may have had for expressing various conversational roles. In addition, Dore (1978) concludes that variations in setting (e.g., preschool classroom vs. supermarket) and in situation or condition (e.g., group vs. dyad; question asking vs. free play) may result in different distributions of types of conversational acts. Consequently, targeting an increase in use of particular functions or acts in an intervention goal can only be accomplished by varying the child's opportunity to engage in conversation with different partners, in different settings, and under different conditions. Results of analysis using Martlew's (1980) Conversational Moves revealing a distribution of INITIATING MOVES and RESPONDING MOVES substantially different from results obtained by Martlew may indicate a need to teach the child additional means of initiating or responding. In other words, for a child whose INITIATING MOVES constitute substantially less than 30% of his speaking turns, Martlew's types of INITIATING MOVES could be taught in the context of a variety of conversational settings and situations with a variety of conversational partners. For a child whose INITIATING MOVES constitute substantially more than 30% of his speaking turns, it would be productive to teach the child to use various types of RESPONDING MOVES by paying attention to the contributions of his conversational co-participant and by using more diverse types of Martlew's RESPONDING MOVES. In addition, it may be necessary to provide the parent with suggestions for using fewer INITIATING MOVES and/or controlling moves so that a child may have the opportunity to use more INITIATING MOVES or more types of RESPONDING MOVES.

Again, attention to the setting, situation, and partner is very important when attempting to target discourse aspects of communication. Various accounts of proposed intervention formats targeting turn taking, conversational contributions, and other discourse variables are beginning to appear in the literature (Anderson-Wood and Smith, 1997; Bedrosian, 1985; Beveridge and Conti-Ramsden, 1987; Brinton and Fujuki, 1989; Cross, 1984; Fey, 1986; Gallagher, 1991; Leinonen and Smith, 1994; Leonard and Fey, 1991; McTear, 1985; McTear and Conti-Ramsden, 1991; Norris and Damico, 1990; Owens, 1991; Smedley, 1989; Smith and Leinonen, 1992). Consideration of each of these discourse variables will be helpful in developing intervention goals, objectives, and techniques.

Data obtained from analysis of discourse variables that result in Appropriateness Judgments can be used to target behaviors that would increase the appropriateness of each variable. For example, if a child lacks specificity in referent identification, he can be taught to respond to explicit feedback from the conversational co-participant in order to be more specific. While the child's ability to respond to decreasing explicitness in requests for revision increases with age, children as young as 2 years of age can respond to requests for revision. In addition, the types of revisions that children make change developmentally. Therefore, the expectations for adding specificity must be developmentally appropriate and based on what is known about normal language acquisition. These guidelines also hold for the child who is too informative. This child can be taught to respond to feedback from the conversational co-participant, indicating that the amount of information provided is inappropriately high, resulting in the judgment of a lack of conciseness. The child can be taught various syntactic conventions for increasing conciseness (e.g., use of pronouns, ellipsis), and he can be taught to decrease the number of speaking turns used to establish his referent. Again, behaviors targeted must be developmentally appropriate and based on normal language acquisition information. In addition, like all preceding pragmatic variables, it is crucial to consider the impact that setting, situation, and conversational co-participant will have on the child's ability to make modifications that could lead to judgments of appropriate referent specificity and contributional conciseness.

Finally, the child who does not vary his communication style depending on the setting and/or conversational co-participant can be taught to recognize such a need and then to vary his style. The ability to recognize a need to vary communication style will change developmentally, as will the conventions available to vary that style. Judgments about what behaviors to target must be based on what is known about normal language development in relation to the child's overall language production.

In general, analysis of communicative functions and discourse relations yields quantitative and qualitative data that can be used to identify children with problems in the pragmatic area of language production. These data also can be used to develop intervention goals and objectives. The suggestions and the information on the normal language acquisition sequence provided in this chapter (e.g., Primitive versus Conversational Acts) can lead to the appropriate development of productive goals and objectives. In addition, the variables to consider in developing goals and objectives can be used in diagnostic therapy to ensure accurate judgments of pragmatic performance.

Blank Forms

Appendix A

The form on p. 252 without utterance #s or speaker headings can be used to capture sequential turn-taking exchanges for an entire transcript or can be used for additional adult utterances beyond 100.

Name of Child ______________________________ Chronological Age ____________

Type of Situation ______________________________ Date ____________

Length of Tape ____________ Length of Transcript ____________ Time of Day ____________

Materials Present ____

People Present ____

ADULT	CONTEXT	CHILD

ADULT	CONTEXT	CHILD

Bloom's One-Word Utterance Types

Name of Child ________________

Substantive Words	Naming Words	Function Words

__________ Substantive Words = __________% of Total One-Word Utterances

__________ Naming Words = __________% of Total One-Word Utterances

__________ Function Words = __________% of Total One-Word Utterances

TOTAL NUMBER OF ONE-WORD UTTERANCES __________

TOTAL NUMBER OF UTTERANCES __________

__________% OF TOTAL UTTERANCES

Nelson's One-Word Utterance Types

Name of Child ____________

Specific Nominals	General Nominals	Action Words	Modifiers	Personal-Social Words	Function Words

_______ Specific Nominals = ___________% of Total One-Word Utterances

_______ General Nominals = ___________% of Total One-Word Utterances

_______ Action Words = ___________% of Total One-Word Utterances

_______ Modifiers = ___________% of Total One-Word Utterances

_______ Personal-Social Words= ___________% of Total One-Word Utterances

_______ Function Words = ___________% of Total One-Word Utterances

TOTAL NUMBER OF ONE-WORD UTTERANCES ___________

TOTAL NUMBER OF UTTERANCES ___________

___________**% OF TOTAL UTTERANCES**

Semantic Roles Coding Sheet

Name of Child ____________________

Utterance Number	Semantic Coding	Question

Guide to Analysis of Language Transcripts

Total Use of 20 Semantic Roles

Name of Child ____________________

ROLES	TALLY	#	%	ROLES	TALLY	#	%
Action				Beneficiary			
Locative				Comitative			
Agent				Created Object			
Object				Instrument			
Demonstrative				State			
Recurrence				Entity (one-term)			
Possessor				Entity (multiterm)			
Quantifier				Negation			
Experiencer				Attribute			
Recipient				Adverbial			
				TOTAL			

Meaning Relationships in One-Word and Multiword Utterances

Name of Child ______________

Utterance Number	One-Term	Two-Term	Three-Term	Four-Term Plus	Conversational Device	Communication Routine	Complex	Other
1								
2								
3								
4								
5								
6								
7								
8								
9								
10								
11								
12								
13								
14								
15								
16								
17								
18								
19								
20								
21								
22								
23								
24								
25								

Utterance Number	One-Term	Two-Term	Three-Term	Four-Term Plus	Conversational Device	Communication Routine	Complex	Other
26								
27								
28								
29								
30								
31								
32								
33								
34								
35								
36								
37								
38								
39								
40								
41								
42								
43								
44								
45								
46								
47								
48								
49								
50								

Meaning Relationships in One-Word and Multiword Utterances

Name of Child ______________

Utterance Number	One-Term	Two-Term	Three-Term	Four-Term Plus	Conversational Device	Communication Routine	Complex	Other
51								
52								
53								
54								
55								
56								
57								
58								
59								
60								
61								
62								
63								
64								
65								
66								
67								
68								
69								
70								
71								
72								
73								
74								
75								

Utterance Number	One-Term	Two-Term	Three-Term	Four-Term Plus	Conversational Device	Communication Routine	Complex	Other
76								
77								
78								
79								
80								
81								
82								
83								
84								
85								
86								
87								
88								
89								
90								
91								
92								
93								
94								
95								
96								
97								
98								
99								
100								
Total								

Semantic Roles Summary Form

Name of Child ____________

Total Number of Semantically Coded Utterances _______=______% of Total Utterances

Percentage of Total Semantic Roles Accounted For by each Semantic Role:

ACTION	=	__________	%
LOCATIVE	=	__________	%
AGENT	=	__________	%
OBJECT	=	__________	%
DEMONSTRATIVE	=	__________	%
RECURRENCE	=	__________	%
POSSESSOR	=	__________	%
QUANTIFIER	=	__________	%
EXPERIENCER	=	__________	%
RECIPIENT	=	__________	%
BENEFICIARY	=	__________	%
COMITATIVE	=	__________	%
CREATED OBJECT	=	__________	%
INSTRUMENT	=	__________	%
STATE	=	__________	%
ENTITY (one-term)	=	__________	%
ENTITY (multiterm)	=	__________	%
NEGATION	=	__________	%
ATTRIBUTE	=	__________	%
ADVERBIAL	=	__________	%

Total Number of Utterances Coded **Conversational Device**	________	=	__________	%	of Total Utterances
Total Number of Utterances Coded **Communication Routine**	________	=	__________	%	of Total Utterances
Total Number of Utterances Coded **Complex**	________	=	__________	%	of Total Utterances
Total Number of Utterances Coded **Other**	________	=	__________	%	of Total Utterances

Guide to Analysis of Language Transcripts

Brown's Prevalent Semantic Relations

Name of Child ________________

		Utterance Number	Demonstrative	Attributive	Possessive
Two-Term	Agent-Action				
	Action-Object				
	Agent-Object				
	Demonstrative-Entity				
	Entity-Locative				
	Action-Locative				
	(-Entity)* Possessor-Possession				
	(Recurrence-)* Attribute-Entity				
Three-Term	Agent-Action-Object				
	Agent-Action-Locative				
	Action-Object-Locative				

*Per Retherford et al. (1981)

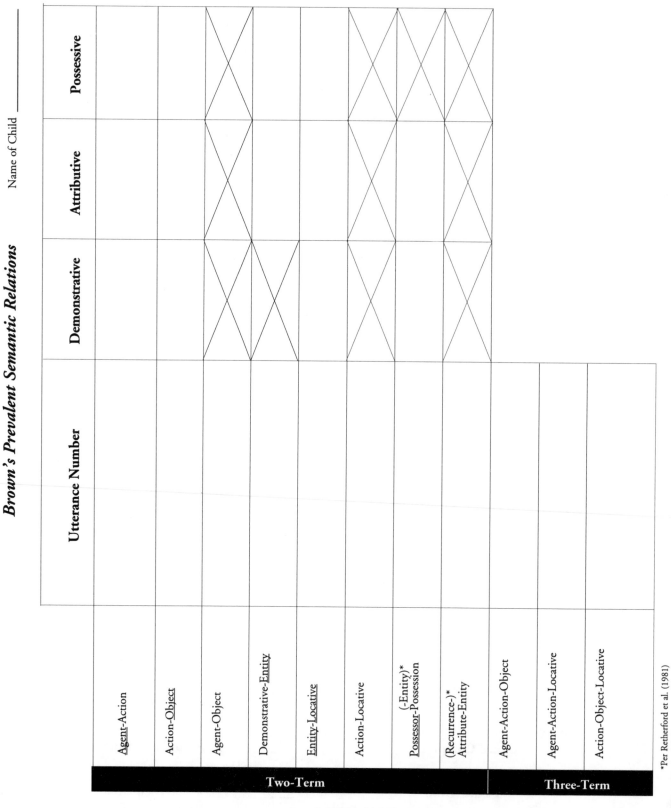

Brown's Prevalent Semantic Relations Summary Form Name of Child ________

TWO-TERM PREVALENT SEMANTIC RELATIONS		EXPANSIONS			
______ Agent-Action	______ Dem	______ Att	______ Poss	= ______	
______ Action-Object	______ Dem	______ Att	______ Poss	= ______	
______ Agent-Object					
______ Demonstrative-Entity		______ Att	______ Poss	= ______	
______ Entity-Locative	______ Dem	______ Att	______ Poss	= ______	
______ Action-Locative					
______ Possessor-Possession	______ Dem	______ Att		= ______	
______ Attribute-Entity				______	**Total Expansions**
______ **Total Two-Term Utterances**					

THREE-TERM PREVALENT SEMANTIC RELATIONS

______ Agent-Action-Object

______ Agent-Action-Locative

______ Action-Object-Locative

______ **Total Three-Term Utterances**

______ Two-Term Utterances ÷ ______ Multiterm Utterances = ______ % of Multiterm Utterances Accounted For by Brown's Two-Term Semantic Relations

______ Two-Term Utterances ÷ ______ Semantically Coded Utterances = ______ % of Semantically Coded Utterances Accounted For by Brown's Two-Term Semantic Relations

______ Total Expansions ÷ ______ Multiterm Utterances = ______ % SemanticallyCoded Utterances Accounted For by Expansions of Brown's Prevalent Semantic Relations

______ Three-Term Utterances ÷ ______ Multiterm Utterances = ______ % of Multiterm Utterances Accounted For by Brown's Three-Term Semantic Relations

______ Three-Term Utterances ÷ ______ Semantically Coded Utterances = ______ % of Semantically Coded Utterances Accounted For by Brown's Three-Term Relations

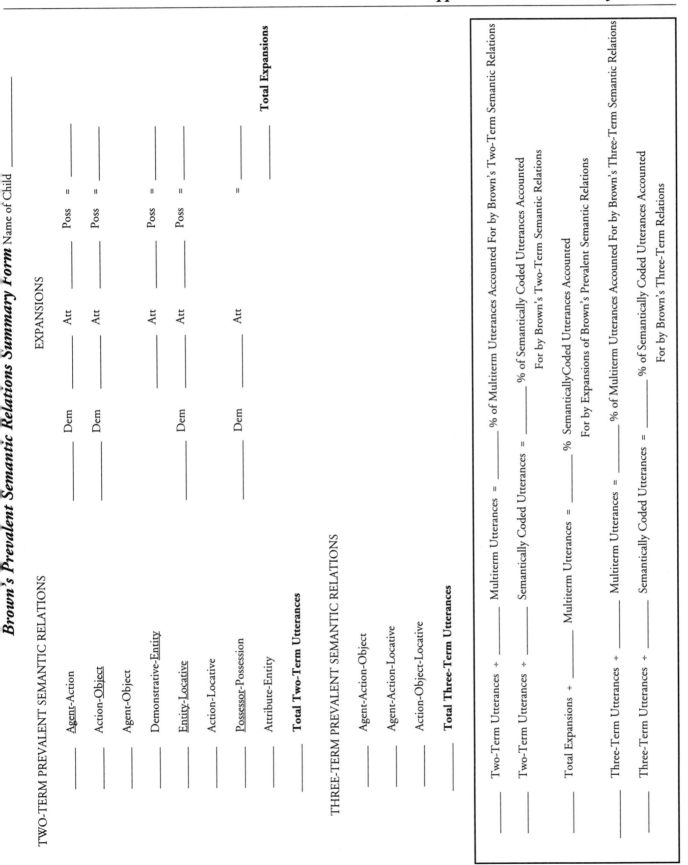

Templin's Type-Token Ratio

Name of Child ______________

50 Utterances # ______________

Nouns	Verbs	Adjectives	Adverbs	Prepositions
				Others

Pronouns	**Conjunctions**	**Negatives/Affirmatives**	**Articles**	***Wh*- Words**

Total Number of Different:

Nouns ____________

Verbs ____________

Adjectives ____________

Adverbs ____________

Prepositions ____________

Others ____________

Pronouns ____________

Conjunctions ____________

Negatives/Affirmatives ____________

Articles ____________

Wh- Words ____________

TOTAL NUMBER OF DIFFERENT WORDS ____________

Total Number of:

Nouns ____________

Verbs ____________

Adjectives ____________

Adverbs ____________

Prepositions ____________

Others ____________

Pronouns ____________

Conjunctions ____________

Negatives/Affirmatives ____________

Articles ____________

Wh- Words ____________

TOTAL NUMBER OF WORDS ____________

$$\frac{\text{Total Number of Different Words}}{\text{Total Number of Words}}$$ ____ = = ______ = ____ Type-Token Ratio (TTR)

Structural Stage Analysis Grid

Name of Child ______________

Utterance Number	Number of Morphemes	Negation	Yes/No Question	*Wh*-Question	Noun Phrase Elaboration	Verb Phrase Elaboration	Complex Sentence
1							
2							
3							
4							
5							
6							
7							
8							
9							
10							
11							
12							
13							
14							
15							
16							
17							
18							
19							
20							
21							
22							
23							
24							
25							

Utterance Number	Number of Morphemes	Negation	Yes/No Question	*Wh*-Question	Noun Phrase Elaboration	Verb Phrase Elaboration	Complex Sentence
26							
27							
28							
29							
30							
31							
32							
33							
34							
35							
36							
37							
38							
39							
40							
41							
42							
43							
44							
45							
46							
47							
48							
49							
50							
Subtotal 1							

Structural Stage Analysis Grid

Name of Child ____________

Utterance Number	Number of Morphemes	Negation	Yes/No Question	*Wh*-Question	Noun Phrase Elaboration	Verb Phrase Elaboration	Complex Sentence
51							
52							
53							
54							
55							
56							
57							
58							
59							
60							
61							
62							
63							
64							
65							
66							
67							
68							
69							
70							
71							
72							
73							
74							
75							

Utterance Number	Number of Morphemes	Negation	Yes/No Question	*Wh*-Question	Noun Phrase Elaboration	Verb Phrase Elaboration	Complex Sentence
76							
77							
78							
79							
80							
81							
82							
83							
84							
85							
86							
87							
88							
89							
90							
91							
92							
93							
94							
95							
96							
97							
98							
99							
100							
Subtotal 2							

[ ] No. of Morphemes (Subtotal 1) + [ ] No. of Morphemes (Subtotal 2) = ____ Total Number of Morphemes

Total Number of Morphemes / Total Number of Utterances = [ ] / [ ] = ____ MLU

Length Distribution

Name of Child ___________

Length in Morphemes	Tally	Total
1		
2		
3		
4		
5		
6		
7		
8		
9		
10		
11		
12		
13		
14		
15		

Upper Bound Length = ___________ morpheme(s)

Lower Bound Length = ___________ morpheme(s)

Grammatical Morphemes

Name of Child ___________

Grammatical Morpheme	Obligatory Context	Use	% Use
1. *-ing*			
2. plural_*-s*			
3. *in*			
4. *on*			
5. possessive *-s*			
6. regular past_*-ed*			
7. irregular past			
8. regular third person singular			
9. articles *a, an, the*			
10. contractible copula			
11. contractible auxiliary			
12. uncontractible copula			
13. uncontractible auxiliary			
14. irregular third person singular			

Guide to Analysis of Language Transcripts

Production Characteristics Summary Form

Name of Child_______________

	Stage	Grammatical Morphemes	Negation	Yes/No Questions	*Wh*-Questions	Noun Phrase Elaboration	Verb Phrase Elaboration	Complex Sentences
I	Early I							
I	Late I/ Early II							
II	II	1. 2. 3.						
III	III	4. 5.						
III	Early IV							
	Late IV/ Early V							
	Late V	6. 7. 8. 9. 10.						
	V+	11. 12. 13. 14.						
	V++							

Data Summary and Interpretation Form

Name of Child ____________

Mean Length of Utterance in Morphemes (MLU)

____________________ morphemes

Structural Stage by MLU: Stage ______________

Upper Bound Length: ____________________ morphemes

Lower Bound Length: ____________________ morphemes

	Most Typical Stage	Most Advanced Stage
Grammatical Morphemes:	Stage ____________________	Stage ____________________
Negation:	Stage ____________________	Stage ____________________
Yes/No Questions:	Stage ____________________	Stage ____________________
Wh- Questions:	Stage ____________________	Stage ____________________
Noun Phrase Elaboration:	Stage ____________________	Stage ____________________
Verb Phrase Elaboration:	Stage ____________________	Stage ____________________
Complex Sentences:	Stage ____________________	Stage ____________________

Comments: ____

____

____

____

____

____

Dore's Primitive Speech Acts

Name of Child ______________

Act	Child Utterance Number	Total / %
Labeling		
Repeating		
Answering		
Requesting Action		
Requesting Answer		
Calling		
Greeting		
Protesting		
Practicing		

Dore's Conversational Acts

Name of Child ____________

Total / %	Adult Utterance Number	Act	Child Utterance Number	Total / %
		Request		
		Response to Request		
		Description		
		Statement		
		Acknow-ledgment		
		Organizational Device		
		Performative		
		Miscellaneous		

Conversational Moves and Appropriateness Judgments Analysis Grid

Name of Child ____________________

Adult

	Conversational Moves		Appropriateness Judgments		
UTT#	Initiating Moves	Responding Moves	Referent Specificity	Contributional Conciseness	Communication Style
1					
2					
3					
4					
5					
6					
7					
8					
9					
10					
11					
12					
13					
14					
15					
16					
17					
18					
19					
20					
21					
22					
23					
24					
25					

Child

	Conversational Moves		Appropriateness Judgments		
UTT#	Initiating Moves	Responding Moves	Referent Specificity	Contributional Conciseness	Communication Style
1					
2					
3					
4					
5					
6					
7					
8					
9					
10					
11					
12					
13					
14					
15					
16					
17					
18					
19					
20					
21					
22					
23					
24					
25					

Conversational Moves and Appropriateness Judgments Analysis Grid

Name of Child ____________

Adult

UTT#	Conversational Moves: Initiating Moves	Conversational Moves: Responding Moves	Appropriateness Judgments: Referent Specificity	Appropriateness Judgments: Contributional Conciseness	Appropriateness Judgments: Communication Style
26					
27					
28					
29					
30					
31					
32					
33					
34					
35					
36					
37					
38					
39					
40					
41					
42					
43					
44					
45					
46					
47					
48					
49					
50					

Child

UTT#	Conversational Moves: Initiating Moves	Conversational Moves: Responding Moves	Appropriateness Judgments: Referent Specificity	Appropriateness Judgments: Contributional Conciseness	Appropriateness Judgments: Communication Style
26					
27					
28					
29					
30					
31					
32					
33					
34					
35					
36					
37					
38					
39					
40					
41					
42					
43					
44					
45					
46					
47					
48					
49					
50					

Conversational Moves and Appropriateness Judgments Analysis Grid

Name of Child ______________________

Adult

	Conversational Moves		Appropriateness Judgments		
UTT#	Initiating Moves	Responding Moves	Referent Specificity	Contributional Conciseness	Communication Style
51					
52					
53					
54					
55					
56					
57					
58					
59					
60					
61					
62					
63					
64					
65					
66					
67					
68					
69					
70					
71					
72					
73					
74					
75					

Child

	Conversational Moves		Appropriateness Judgments		
UTT#	Initiating Moves	Responding Moves	Referent Specificity	Contributional Conciseness	Communication Style
51					
52					
53					
54					
55					
56					
57					
58					
59					
60					
61					
62					
63					
64					
65					
66					
67					
68					
69					
70					
71					
72					
73					
74					
75					

Conversational Moves and Appropriateness Judgments Analysis Grid

Name of Child ______________

Adult

UTT#	Conversational Moves		Appropriateness Judgments		
	Initiating Moves	Responding Moves	Referent Specificity	Contributional Conciseness	Communication Style
76					
77					
78					
79					
80					
81					
82					
83					
84					
85					
86					
87					
88					
89					
90					
91					
92					
93					
94					
95					
96					
97					
98					
99					
100					

Child

UTT#	Conversational Moves		Appropriateness Judgments		
	Initiating Moves	Responding Moves	Referent Specificity	Contributional Conciseness	Communication Style
76					
77					
78					
79					
80					
81					
82					
83					
84					
85					
86					
87					
88					
89					
90					
91					
92					
93					
94					
95					
96					
97					
98					
99					
100					

Guide to Analysis of Language Transcripts

Conversational Moves and Appropriateness Judgments Analysis Grid

Name of Child ______________________

	Conversational Moves		Appropriateness Judgments		
UTT#	Initiating Moves	Responding Moves	Referent Specificity	Contributional Conciseness	Communication Style

	Conversational Moves		Appropriateness Judgments		
UTT#	Initiating Moves	Responding Moves	Referent Specificity	Contributional Conciseness	Communication Style

Conversational Moves and Appropriateness Judgments Summary Form

Name of Child ____________

CHILD'S TOTAL UTTERANCES _______

CONVERSATIONAL MOVES

INITIATING MOVES	____________	New Topic Introduction	=	____________	% of Total Utterances
	____________	Restarting Old Topic	=	____________	% of Total Utterances
	____________	Eliciting Verbal Response	=	____________	% of Total Utterances
	____________	Intruding	=	____________	% of Total Utterances
RESPONDING MOVES	____________	Acknowledging	=	____________	% of Total Utterances
	____________	Yes/No Responses	=	____________	% of Total Utterances
	____________	One-Word Answers	=	____________	% of Total Utterances
	____________	Repeating	=	____________	% of Total Utterances
	____________	Sustaining Topic	=	____________	% of Total Utterances
	____________	Extending Topic	=	____________	% of Total Utterances
FALSE STARTS	____________		=	____________	% of Total Utterances

APPROPRIATENESS JUDGMENTS

Referent Specificity	____________	Lacked Specificity	=	____________	% of Total Utterances
Contributional Conciseness	____________	Lacked Conciseness	=	____________	% of Total Utterances
Communication Style	____________	Lacked Stylistic Variation	=	____________	% of Total Utterances

ADULT'S TOTAL UTTERANCES _______

CONVERSATIONAL MOVES

INITIATING MOVES	____________	New Topic Introduction	=	____________	% of Total Utterances
	____________	Restarting Old Topic	=	____________	% of Total Utterances
	____________	Eliciting Verbal Response	=	____________	% of Total Utterances
	____________	Intruding	=	____________	% of Total Utterances
RESPONDING MOVES	____________	Acknowledging	=	____________	% of Total Utterances
	____________	Yes/No Responses	=	____________	% of Total Utterances
	____________	One-Word Answers	=	____________	% of Total Utterances
	____________	Repeating	=	____________	% of Total Utterances
	____________	Sustaining Topic	=	____________	% of Total Utterances
	____________	Extending Topic	=	____________	% of Total Utterances
FALSE STARTS	____________		=	____________	% of Total Utterances

APPROPRIATENESS JUDGMENTS

Referent Specificity	____________	Lacked Specificity	=	____________	% of Total Utterances
Contributional Conciseness	____________	Lacked Conciseness	=	____________	% of Total Utterances
Communication Style	____________	Lacked Stylistic Variation	=	____________	% of Total Utterances

ANALYZED TRANSCRIPT

Appendix B

The following analyses were performed on Sara's transcript and appear on the pages indicated. Her transcript was not subjected to Bloom's (1973) One-Word Utterance Types, Nelson's (1973) One-Word Utterance Types, or Dore's (1974) Primitive Speech Acts analyses, because Sara's utterances were too long and complex for such analyses.

Name of Child *Sara* Chronological Age *4;10*

Type of Situation *free play in playroom of preschool* Date *10-6*

Length of Tape *45 min* Length of Transcript *100 utterances* Time of Day *2 pm*

Materials Present *playground set, bendable people, toy dishes*

People Present *S = Sara; M = Mother*

ADULT	CONTEXT	CHILD
1 What do you have huh?		
		toys/ 1
2 Toys?		
3 What is that?	(M pointing to swing set)	
4 What does it look like to you?		
	(S shrugs shoulders)	
5 What is it?		
6 What does it look like?		
7 Where would you go to play		
with toys like this?		
		XXX/
8 If we said we were going		
somewhere · to play with toys like this		
where would you play with these?		
		at the park!/ 2
9 It looks like a park doesn't it?		
		a park/ 3
10 What's that?		
	(S touches slide)	
		it's a swing set/ 4
	(M touches slide)	

ADULT	CONTEXT	CHILD
11 This is?		
		no that a slide/ 5
	(S pointing to swing set)	there's the swing set/ 6
12 What do you do with it?		
	(S climbs slide with fingers)	
	(S using finger to slide down)	climb up and wee/ 7
13 Why don't you take one of the		
people and show me what you do?		
	(S picks up doll)	
14 Who's that?		
		Mama/ 8
15 Show me how she does it/		
	(S slides doll down slide)	
		she can't go/ 9
		she can't go down/ 10
16 How come?		
		'cuz she's stuck there/ 11
	(M points to sandbox)	
17 What's that?		
		sandbox/ 12
18 What do you do with a sandbox?		
	(S picks up cup and puts it up	
	to her mouth)	
19 What are you doing?		
		drinking/ 13
	(S picks up sand spilled on floor)	

ADULT	CONTEXT	CHILD
		uh-oh/ 14
	(S puts cup in sandbox)	
		I make coffee/ 15
20 Okay we'll make coffee/		
	(M pulls picnic table toward herself)	
21 What's this?		
		that's a picnic table/ 16
		and that's a swing set/ 17
22 What do you do on a swing set?		
		swing/ 18
	(S pours sand into cup)	
23 Let's hold it over here/		
	(S stirs sand in cup with spoon)	
24 Now what are you doing?		
		um I mix it up/ 19
25 Then what?		
	(S covers top of cup with hand)	
		then you · shake it/ 20
	(S shakes cup)	
26 Who should we pretend that we are?		
		not done yet/ 21
27 Oh not done yet/		
		now it's done/ 22
	(S pours into another cup)	
28 Okay/		
	(S picking up spoon and stirring in cup)	I use a spoon/ 23

ADULT	CONTEXT	CHILD
29 What are you doing?		
		I mixing/ 24
30 Mixing it up?		
		mixing it up/ 25
		now put it in the cup/ 26
31 What's that?	(M pointing to picnic table)	
		XXX/
	(S drops cup in sandbox, which	
	spills sand)	
32 Oops/		
		oops/ 27
33 What is that over there?		
		table/ 28
34 Okay/		
35 That looks like a picnic table/		
36 What do you do at a picnic table?		
		sit on it/ 29
	(S picks up girl doll)	
37 Put them over there?		
38 Can you put them over there?		
	(S tries to bend doll's legs)	
		how do you do this?/ 30
39 What do you want her to do?		
		sit down/ 31
40 Okay/		
	(S looks at M)	

ADULT	CONTEXT	CHILD
		also she lays down/ 32
41 She can/		
	(S sits dolls at picnic table)	
42 What are they doing?		
		sitting/ 33
43 What are they gonna do now?		
		they are um gonna eat/ 34
44 They are?		
45 What are they gonna eat?		
		pancakes/ 35
	(S takes another doll off	
	swing set and puts it at table)	
		it's time to go/ 36
46 Oh?		
	(S looking at camera)	where's that um girl?/ 37
47 Beret?		
		yeah Beret/ 38
48 She's in the other room/		
		'cuz she isn't playing↑/ 39
49 Um-hmm/		
50 Now what are the people eating?		
		pancakes/ 40
51 And what else?		
	(S straightens doll)	
		milk/ 41
52 That's all they need?		

ADULT	CONTEXT	CHILD	
		yeah/	42
53 Who made the meal · who made the pancakes?			
		Mama/	43
	(S picks up man doll)		
		and this is the daddy/	44
54 Okay/			
55 Who are these two?	(M pointing to dolls at table)		
		children/	45
56 Do you want to give them names?			
		Mark · Kristen · Pete/	46
	(S picks up woman doll)		
		who's this?/	47
57 That's the mommy/			
	(M points to swing set)		
58 What's this thing?			
		swing set/	48
59 And what do you do on a swing set?			
		swing/	49
	(S puts woman doll down and picks up man doll)		
		now he's gonna go on/	50
60 What's this?	(M pointing to teeter-totter)		
	(S shrugs shoulders)		
61 What is this one?			
		teetotter/	51

ADULT	CONTEXT	CHILD
62 What do you do on it?		
	(S puts doll on one end and	
	goes up and down)	
		teetot · teetot/ (sg) 52
	(S sifts "sand" in sandbox)	
		this is birdseed/ 53
63 It is?		
		yeah but it also's sand/ 54
64 Um-hmm · we're pretending it's		
sand though/		
65 Now how does a teeter-totter work?		
	(M and S each hold doll on the	
	ends of teeter-totter)	
		teetot · teetot/ (sg) 55
66 Tell me how it works/		
		teetot · teetot/ (sg) 56
67 Tell me/		
		I don't know/ 57
68 Well can it put $_{s/c}$ can one		
person do the teeter-totter?		
	(S slides doll down teeter-totter)	
		put it down here/ 58
69 How many does it take?		
		two · two · two/ 59
	(M points to shelter)	
70 What's this for?		

ADULT	CONTEXT	CHILD
		that's a house/ 60
71 Do you know what this is called?		
		no/ 61
		what?/ 62
72 This is called a shelter/		
73 What do you think they would		
use that for?		
		for cow people/ 63
74 Cow people?		
		for cow people/ 64
75 What does that mean?		
	(S shrugs shoulders)	
		that means _______ /
76 Cowboys?		
		yeah/ 65
77 What if you saw one of these at		
the park?		
78 What do you think it's for?		
	(S picks up doll)	
		for he-mans/ 66
79 He-mans?		
	(S dances doll on roof of shelter)	
		this goes like this/ 67
		he-mans · he-mans · he-mans/ (sg) 68
80 Where did you learn about that?		
		at Kristi's house/ 69

	ADULT	CONTEXT	CHILD	
81	At Kristi's house?			
82	What would happen if it			
	started to rain?			
		(S shrugging shoulders)	go in the house/	70
83	What's this called?	(M pointing to shelter)		
			shelter house/	71
84	Shelter house/			
85	Let's pretend it's raining/			
86	What would you do?			
			play with kids inside the shelter/	72
		(S singing and dancing dolls	inside we go go go go/ (sg)	73
		into house)		
		(S picks up another doll)		
			inside we go/	74
87	What if they want to eat lunch now?			
			they can/	75
			it stopped raining/	76
88	Okay what should they do now?			
		(S taking doll out of house)	go outside/	77
89	What do you think they would			
	like to play on?			
		(S pointing to trapeze)	that/	78
90	Okay what is that?			
		(S shrugs shoulders)		
91	It looks like a trapeze doesn't it?			
		(S puts doll's feet through		

ADULT	CONTEXT	CHILD
	trapeze rings)	
92 Now what are they gonna play with?		
		in the sandbox/ 79
	(S makes doll fly to sandbox)	
	(S getting dishes out of box)	I fixed supper already/ 80
93 Can you put the dishes on the table?		
	(S spoons sand into cups)	
94 What are you doing?		
		making popcorn/ 81
95 Okay/		
96 What are you fixing for supper		
tonight?		
		I said popcorn/ 82
97 Oh okay/		
98 What else?		
	(S picking up scoop)	hey this looks like a bunny ear/ 83
99 A bunny ear?		
		yeah/ 84
100 Let me see/	(M reaching for scoop)	
101 Oh it does look like a bunny's ear/		
102 How many ears does a bunny have?		
		two/ 85
	(S turns scoop over)	
		and it almost like a ear/ 86
103 Um-hmm/		
	(M picks up another scoop	

ADULT	CONTEXT	CHILD	
	and turns it over)		
104 What does this one look like?			
	(S leaning over)	a shell/	87
105 A shell?			
	(S takes scoop)		
		um-hmm/	88
	(cup of sand falls off picnic table)		
106 Oop · I'll clean it up ·			
107 You set the rest of the table okay?			
	(M brushes sand into hand;		
	S puts plates on table)		
108 What are you doing?			
		putting the plates on/	89
	(S turns plate over in hand)		
		this is the cover for the pot/	90
109 The cover for the pot?			
	(S puts spoons in cups)		
		in the cups/	91
		that goes on there/	92
	(S puts knife on table)		
110 What are those?			
		knife and spoon/	93
		knife and spoon/	
111 How many plates are there?			
	(S pointing to each plate)	one↗/	94
		two↗/	95

ADULT	CONTEXT	CHILD	
		three↗/	96
		there's not enough/	97
	(S looks in box)		
		how 'bout for the children?/	98
112 How 'bout for the children?			
113 Oh I think there's s/c how many			
do we need?			99
114	(S pointing to each plate)	one two three/	
How many people are there?			
	(S points to each doll)		100
		four/	

Semantic Roles Coding Sheet

Name of Child *Sara*

Utterance Number	Semantic Coding	Question
1	One-Term Entity	
2	Locative	
3	One-Term Entity	
4	Experiencer—State—Multiterm Entity	
5	(CD Yes/No Response) Demonstrative—Multiterm Entity	
6	Demonstrative—State—Multiterm Entity	
7	COMPLEX	
8	One-Term Entity	
9	Agent—Negation—Action	
10	Agent—Negation—Action—Locative	
11	COMPLEX	
12	One-Term Entity	
13	Action	
14	CR (Sounds Accompanying)	
15	Agent—Action—Created Object	
16	Demonstrative—State—Attribute—Multiterm Entity	
17	COMPLEX	
18	Action	
19	(CD Interjection) Agent—Action—Object	
20	COMPLEX	
21	Negation—State—Adverbial	
22	Adverbial—Experiencer—State—Adverbial	
23	Agent—Action—Instrument	
24	Agent—Action	
25	Action—Object	

"No"

"Swing set" is considered one word.

In "go down," "down" distinctly refers to location.

Semantic Roles Coding Sheet

Name of Child *Sara*

Utterance Number	Semantic Coding	Question
26	Adverbial—Action—Object—Locative	
27	CR (Sounds Accompanying)	
28	One-Term Entity	
29	Action—Object	
30	Adverbial—Agent—Action—Object	✓
31	Action	
32	COMPLEX	
33	Action	
34	Agent (CD Interjection) Action	
35	One-Term Entity	
36	COMPLEX	
37	Locative—State—Demonstrative (CD Interjection) Experiencer	✓
38	(CD Yes/No Response) One-Term Entity	
39	COMPLEX	
40	One-Term Entity	
41	One-Term Entity	
42	CD (Yes/No Response)	
43	One-Term Entity	
44	COMPLEX	
45	One-Term Entity	
46	OTHER	
47	Multiterm Entity—State—Demonstrative	✓
48	One-Term Entity	
49	Action	
50	Adverbial—Agent—Action	

Although "this" is a demonstrative pronoun, it serves as the object of the action, and thus that semantic role takes precedence over the demonstrative role.

Semantic Roles Coding Sheet

Name of Child Sara

Utterance Number	Semantic Coding	Question
51	One-Term Entity	
52	CR (Sounds Accompanying)	
53	Demonstrative—State—Multiterm Entity	
54	COMPLEX	
55	CR (Sounds Accompanying)	
56	CR (Sounds Accompanying)	
57	Agent—Negation—Action	
58	Action—Object—Locative	
59	Quantifier	
60	Demonstrative—State—Multiterm Entity	
61	Negation	
62	One-Term Entity	✓
63	Beneficiary	
64	Beneficiary	
65	CD (Yes/No Response)	
66	Beneficiary	
67	Agent—Action—Adverbial	
68	CR (Sounds Accompanying)	
69	Locative	
70	Action—Locative	
71	Attribute—Multiterm Entity	
72	Action—Comitative—Locative	
73	Locative—Agent—Action CR (Sounds Accompanying)	
74	Locative—Agent—Action	
75	Agent—Action	

Although this a demonstrative pronoun, because of the action verb, it's clear that the pronoun serves as the agent of the action.

Semantic Roles Coding Sheet

Name of Child Sara

Utterance Number	Semantic Coding	Question
76	COMPLEX	
77	Action—Locative	
78	Demonstrative	
79	Locative	
80	Agent—Action—Created Object—Adverbial	
81	Action—Created Object	
82	Agent—Action—Object	
83	(CD Interjection) Demonstrative—State—Attribute—Multiterm Entity	
84	CD (Yes/No Response)	
85	Quantifier	
86	COMPLEX	
87	One-Term Entity	
88	CD (Yes/No Response)	
89	Action—Object ("Put on" is considered a two-part verb.)	
90	Demonstrative—State—Multiterm Entity—Possessor	
91	Locative	
92	Demonstrative—State—Locative	
93	COMPLEX	
94	One-Term Entity	
95	One-Term Entity	
96	One-Term Entity	
97	Demonstrative—State—Negation—Quantifier	
98	Adverbial—Beneficiary	✓
99	One-Term Entity	
100	One-Term Entity	

Total Use of 20 Semantic Roles

Name of Child *Sara*

ROLES	TALLY	#	%	ROLES	TALLY	#	%
Action	𝍸 𝍸 𝍸 𝍸 𝍸 𝍸	30	19.1	Beneficiary	////	4	2.5
Locative	𝍸 𝍸 ////	14	8.9	Comitative	/	1	0.6
Agent	𝍸 𝍸 𝍸 /	16	10.2	Created Object	///	3	2.0
Object	𝍸 ///	8	5.1	Instrument	/	1	0.6
Demonstrative	𝍸 𝍸 //	12	7.6	State	𝍸 𝍸 ///	13	8.3
Recurrence		0	—	Entity (one-term)	𝍸 𝍸 𝍸 𝍸	20	12.7
Possessor	/	1	0.6	Entity (multiterm)	𝍸 𝍸	10	6.4
Quantifier	///	3	2.0	Negation	𝍸 /	6	3.8
Experiencer	///	3	2.0	Attribute	///	3	2.0
Recipient		0	—	Adverbial	𝍸 ////	9	5.7
				TOTAL		157	100.1

Meaning Relationships in One-Word and Multiword Utterances

Name of Child Sara

Utterance Number	One-Term	Two-Term	Three-Term	Four-Term Plus	Conver-sational Device	Commu-nication Routine	Complex	Other
1	✓							
2	✓							
3	✓							
4			✓					
5		✓						
6			✓					
7							✓	
8	✓							
9			✓					
10				✓				
11							✓	
12	✓							
13	✓							
14						✓		
15			✓					
16				✓				
17							✓	
18	✓							
19			✓					
20							✓	
21			✓					
22				✓				
23			✓					
24		✓						
25		✓						

Utterance Number	One-Term	Two-Term	Three-Term	Four-Term Plus	Conver-sational Device	Commu-nication Routine	Complex	Other
26				✓				
27						✓		
28	✓							
29		✓						
30				✓				
31	✓							
32							✓	
33	✓							
34		✓						
35	✓							
36							✓	
37				✓				
38	✓							
39							✓	
40	✓							
41	✓							
42					✓			
43	✓							
44							✓	
45	✓							
46								✓
47			✓					
48	✓							
49	✓							
50			✓					

Meaning Relationships in One-Word and Multiword Utterances

Name of Child Sara

Utterance Number	One-Term	Two-Term	Three-Term	Four-Term Plus	Conversational Device	Communication Routine	Complex	Other
51	✓							
52						✓		
53			✓					
54							✓	
55						✓		
56						✓		
57			✓					
58			✓					
59	✓							
60			✓					
61	✓							
62	✓							
63	✓							
64	✓							
65					✓			
66	✓							
67			✓					
68						✓		
69	✓							
70		✓						
71		✓						
72			✓					
73			✓					
74			✓					
75		✓						

Utterance Number	One-Term	Two-Term	Three-Term	Four-Term Plus	Conversational Device	Communication Routine	Complex	Other
76							✓	
77		✓						
78	✓							
79	✓							
80				✓				
81		✓						
82			✓					
83				✓				
84					✓			
85	✓							
86							✓	
87	✓							
88					✓			
89		✓						
90				✓				
91	✓							
92			✓					
93							✓	
94	✓							
95	✓							
96	✓							
97				✓				
98		✓						
99	✓							
100	✓							
Total	36	12	19	10	4	6	12	1

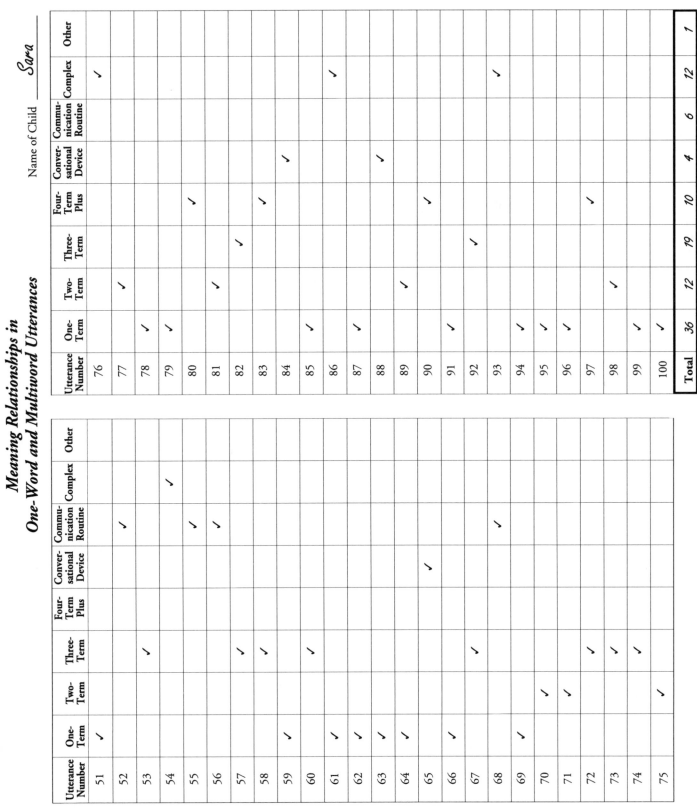

Guide to Analysis of Language Transcripts

Semantic Roles Summary Form

Name of Child Sara

Total Number of Semantically Coded Utterances 77 = 77.0 % of Total Utterances

Percentage of Total Semantic Roles Accounted for by each Semantic Role:

ACTION	=	19.1	%
LOCATIVE	=	8.9	%
AGENT	=	10.2	%
OBJECT	=	5.1	%
DEMONSTRATIVE	=	7.6	%
RECURRENCE	=	—	%
POSSESSOR	=	0.6	%
QUANTIFIER	=	2.0	%
EXPERIENCER	=	2.0	%
RECIPIENT	=	—	%
BENEFICIARY	=	2.5	%
COMITATIVE	=	0.6	%
CREATED OBJECT	=	2.0	%
INSTRUMENT	=	0.6	%
STATE	=	8.3	%
ENTITY (one-term)	=	12.7	%
ENTITY (multiterm)	=	6.4	%
NEGATION	=	3.8	%
ATTRIBUTE	=	2.0	%
ADVERBIAL	=	5.7	%

Total Number of Utterances Coded **Conversational Device**	4	=	4.0	%	of Total Utterances
Total Number of Utterances Coded **Communication Routine**	6	=	6.0	%	of Total Utterances
Total Number of Utterances Coded **Complex**	12	=	12.0	%	of Total Utterances
Total Number of Utterances Coded **Other**	1	=	1.0	%	of Total Utterances

Brown's Prevalent Semantic Relations

Name of Child Sara

		Utterance Number	Demonstrative	Attributive	Possessive
Two-Term	Agent-Action	24, 34, 75			
	Action-Object	25, 29, 89			
	Agent-Object		X	X	X
	Demonstrative-Entity	5	X		
	Entity-Locative				
	Action-Locative	70, 77	X	X	X
	(-Entity)* Possessor-Possession				X
	(Recurrence-)* Attribute-Entity	71	X	X	X
Three-Term	Agent-Action-Object	19, 82			
	Agent-Action-Locative	73, 74			
	Action-Object-Locative	58			

*Per Retherford et al. (1981)

Brown's Prevalent Semantic Relations Summary Form Name of Child Sara

Guide to Analysis of Language Transcripts

TWO-TERM PREVALENT SEMANTIC RELATIONS		EXPANSIONS: Dem	Att	Poss	=
3	Agent-Action	0	0	0	0
3	Action-Object	0	0	0	0
0	Agent-Object				
1	Demonstrative-Entity		0	0	0
0	Entity-Locative	0	0	0	0
2	Action-Locative				
0	Possessor-Possession	0	0		0
1	Attribute-Entity				0 **Total Expansions**
10	**Total Two-Term Utterances**				

THREE-TERM PREVALENT SEMANTIC RELATIONS

2	Agent-Action-Object
2	Agent-Action-Locative
1	Action-Object-Locative
5	**Total Three-Term Utterances**

10 Two-Term Utterances ÷ 41 Multiterm Utterances = 24.4 % of Multiterm Utterances Accounted For by Brown's Two-Term Semantic Relations

10 Two-Term Utterances ÷ 77 Semantically Coded Utterances = 13.0 % of Semantically Coded Utterances Accounted For by Brown's Two-Term Semantic Relations

0 Total Expansions ÷ 41 Multiterm Utterances = 0 % Semantically Coded Utterances Accounted For by Expansions of Brown's Prevalent Semantic Relations

5 Three-Term Utterances ÷ 41 Multiterm Utterances = 12.2 % of Multiterm Utterances Accounted For by Brown's Three-Term Semantic Relations

5 Three-Term Utterances ÷ 77 Semantically Coded Utterances = 6.5 % of Semantically Coded Utterances Accounted For by Brown's Three-Term Relations

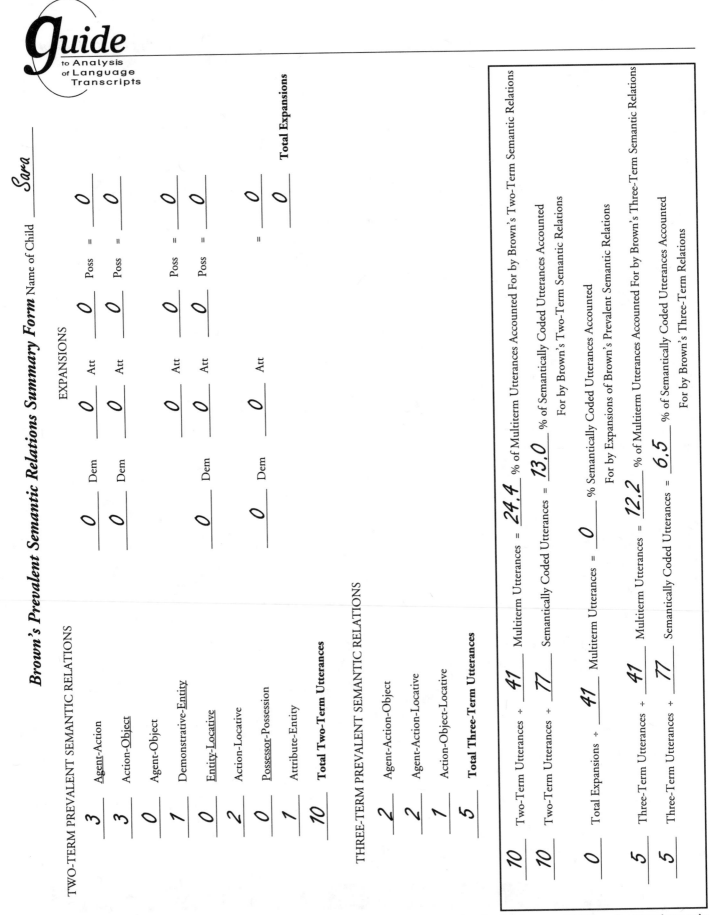

Templin's Type-Token Ratio

Name of Child Sara

50 Utterances # 26–75

Nouns	Verbs	Adjectives	Adverbs	Prepositions
cup	put /	swing /	now /	in /
table	sit /	two	down //	on /
pancakes /	do /	shelter /	time	to
girl	lays		here	for //
Beret	sitting		like	at
milk	are		inside //	with
Mama	gonna /			
daddy	eat			
children	's ~~////~~			
Mark	go ////			
Kristen	isn't			
Pete	playing			
set	is /			
teetotter	don't			
teetot //	know			6 10
birdseed	goes			**Others**
sand	play			
house ///	can			oops
cow /				um /
people /				
he-mans /				
Kristi's				
kids				
23 32	18 32	3 5	6 11	2 3

"Swing set" is counted as two words in this analysis per Templin's rules.

Pronouns	Conjunctions	Negatives/Affirmatives	Articles	*Wh-* Words
it ////	'cuz	yeah ///	the ///	how
you	and	no	a	where
this ~~////~~	but			who
she /	also /			what
they /				
that /				
he /				
we /				
9 22	4 5	2 5	2 5	4 4

Total Number of Different:	
Nouns	23
Verbs	18
Adjectives	3
Adverbs	6
Prepositions	6
Others	2
Pronouns	9
Conjunctions	4
Negatives/Affirmatives	2
Articles	2
Wh- Words	4
TOTAL NUMBER OF DIFFERENT WORDS	79

$$\frac{79 - 120.4}{27.6} = -1.5$$

Total Number of:	
Nouns	32
Verbs	32
Adjectives	5
Adverbs	11
Prepositions	10
Others	3
Pronouns	22
Conjunctions	5
Negatives/Affirmatives	5
Articles	5
Wh- Words	4
TOTAL NUMBER OF WORDS	134

$$\frac{134 - 268.8}{72.6} = -1.86$$

$$\frac{\text{Total Number of Different Words}}{\text{Total Number of Words}} = \frac{79}{134} = .5895 = .59$$ Type-Token Ratio (TTR)

Structural Stage Analysis Grid

Name of Child Sara

"Swing set" considered 1 morpheme (utterances 4 and 6)

Response to yes/no question (utterance 5, Negation)

Article in prep phrase (utterance 26, Noun Phrase Elaboration)

The dummy "do" does not make a complex sentence. (utterance 30, Complex Sentence)

This sentence contains "and," but it does not conjoin two sentences. (utterance 44, Complex Sentence)

Utterance Number	Number of Morphemes	Negation	Yes/No Question	Wh-Question	Noun Phrase Elaboration	Verb Phrase Elaboration	Complex Sentence
1	2	—	—	—	I-II	—	—
2	3	—	—	—	III	—	—
3	2	—	—	—	III	—	—
4	(4)	—	—	—	LIV/EV	LV	—
5	4	(—)	—	—	III	—	—
6	(4)	—	—	—	III	LV	—
7	4	—	—	—	—	III	EIV
8	1	—	—	—	I-II	—	—
9	4	EIV-LIV/EV	—	—	LIV/EV	III	—
10	5	EIV-LIV/EV	—	—	LIV/EV	III	—
11	5	—	—	—	LIV/EV	LV	V+
12	1	—	—	—	I-II	—	—
13	2	—	—	—	—	I-II	—
14	1	—	—	—	—	—	—
15	3	—	—	—	LIV/EV	III	—
16	5	—	—	—	III	LV	—
17	5	—	—	—	III	LV	EIV
18	1	—	—	—	—	I-II	—
19	4	—	—	—	LIV/EV	III	—
20	4	—	—	—	LIV/EV	III	—
21	3	LI/EII—II	—	—	—	—	—
22	4	—	—	—	III	LV	—
23	4	—	—	—	LIV/EV	III	—
24	3	—	—	—	LIV/EV	I-II	—
25	4	—	—	—	I-II	I-II	—

Utterance Number	Number of Morphemes	Negation	Yes/No Question	Wh-Question	Noun Phrase Elaboration	Verb Phrase Elaboration	Complex Sentence
26	6	—	—	—	(III)	I-II	—
27	1	—	—	—	—	—	—
28	1	—	—	—	I-II	—	—
29	3	—	—	—	I-II	I-II	—
30	5	—	—	EIV	LIV/EV	III	(—)
31	2	—	—	—	—	I-II	—
32	5	—	—	—	LIV/EV	LV	—
33	2	—	—	—	—	I-II	—
34	4	—	—	—	LIV/EV	V+	II
35	2	—	—	—	I-II	—	—
36	5	—	—	—	LIV/EV	LV	EIV
37	4	—	—	EIV	III	LV	—
38	2	—	—	—	I-II	—	—
39	6	EIV-LIV/EV	EI—III	—	LIV/EV	LIV/EV	V+
40	2	—	—	—	I-II	—	—
41	1	—	—	—	I-II	—	—
42	1	—	—	—	—	—	—
43	1	—	—	—	I-II	—	—
44	5	—	—	—	III	V+	(—)
45	1	—	—	—	I-II	—	—
46	3	—	—	—	I-II	—	—
47	3	—	—	III	III	LV	—
48	1	—	—	—	I-II	—	—
49	1	—	—	—	—	I-II	—
50	6	—	—	—	LIV/EV	V+	II
Subtotal 1	155						

Structural Stage Analysis Grid

Name of Child Sara

Singsong fillers

The elliptical "Yeah [it is]" is conjoined to the next sentence with "but."

Utterance Number	Number of Morphemes	Negation	Yes/No Question	Wh-Question	Noun Phrase Elaboration	Verb Phrase Elaboration	Complex Sentence
51	1	–	–	–	I-II	–	–
52	–	–	–	–	–	–	–
53	3	–	–	–	III	V+	–
54	6	–	–	–	LIV/EV	LV	LIV/EV
55	–	–	–	–	–	–	–
56	–	–	–	–	–	–	–
57	4	EIV-LIV/EV	–	–	LIV/EV	III	–
58	4	–	–	–	I-II	I-II	–
59	1	–	–	–	–	–	–
60	4	–	–	–	III	LV	–
61	1	–	–	–	–	–	–
62	1	–	–	–	–	–	–
63	3	–	–	–	I-II	–	–
64	3	–	–	–	I-II	–	–
65	1	–	–	–	–	–	–
66	3	–	–	–	I-II	–	–
67	5	–	–	–	III	LV	–
68	–	–	–	–	–	–	–
69	4	–	–	–	LIV/EV	–	–
70	4	–	–	–	III	I-II	–
71	2	–	–	–	I-II	–	–
72	7	–	–	–	III	III	–
73	3	–	–	–	LIV/EV	III	–
74	3	–	–	–	LIV/EV	III	–
75	2	–	–	–	LIV/EV	III	–

Utterance Number	Number of Morphemes	Negation	Yes/No Question	Wh-Question	Noun Phrase Elaboration	Verb Phrase Elaboration	Complex Sentence
76	5	–	–	–	LIV/EV	LV	V+
77	2	–	–	–	–	I-II	–
78	1	–	–	–	I-II	–	–
79	3	–	–	–	III	–	–
80	5	–	–	–	LIV/EV	LV	–
81	3	–	–	–	I-II	I-II	–
82	3	–	–	–	LIV/EV	LV	–
83	7	–	–	–	III	LV	–
84	1	–	–	–	–	–	–
85	1	–	–	–	–	–	–
86	6	–	–	–	LIV/EV	–	–
87	2	–	–	–	III	–	–
88	1	–	–	–	–	–	–
89	6	–	–	–	III	I-II	–
90	7	–	–	–	LIV/EV	V+	–
91	4	–	–	–	III	–	–
92	5	–	–	–	III	LV	–
93	3	–	–	–	I-II	–	–
94	1	–	–	–	–	–	–
95	1	–	–	–	–	–	–
96	1	–	–	–	–	–	–
97	4	EIV-LIV/EV	–	–	III	LV	–
98	5	–	–	EIV	III	–	–
99	3	–	–	–	–	–	–
100	1	–	–	–	–	–	–
Subtotal 2	146						

There is no verb, so the utterance cannot be complex.

[155] No. of Morphemes (Subtotal 1) + [146] No. of Morphemes (Subtotal 2) = 301 Total Number of Morphemes

Total Number of Morphemes / Total Number of Utterances = [301] / [96] = 3.14 MLU

4-0 morphemes (fillers)

Length Distribution

Name of Child Sara

Length in Morphemes	Tally	Total
1	~~||||~~ ~~||||~~ ~~||||~~ ~~||||~~ ~~||||~~	25
2	~~||||~~ ~~||||~~ //	12
3	~~||||~~ ~~||||~~ ~~||||~~ ///	18
4	~~||||~~ ~~||||~~ ~~||||~~ ////	19
5	~~||||~~ ~~||||~~ ///	13
6	~~||||~~ /	6
7	///	3
8		0
9		0
10		0
11		0
12		0
13		0
14		0
15		0

Upper Bound Length = 7 morpheme(s)

Lower Bound Length = 1 morpheme(s)

4-Ø morphemes (fillers)

Grammatical Morphemes

Name of Child Sara

Grammatical Morpheme	Obligatory Context	Use	% Use
1. *-ing*	13, 15, 19, 24, 25, 33, 39, 81, 89	13, 24, 25, 33, 39, 81, 89	78
2. plural *-s*	1, 35, 40, 72, 89, 91	1, 35, 40, 72, 89, 91	100
3. *in*	26, 70, 79, 91	26, 70, 79, 91	100
4. *on*	29, 50, 89, 92	29, 50, 89, 92	100
5. possessive *-s*	69	69	100
6. regular past *-ed*	76, 80	76, 80	100
7. irregular past	82	82	100
8. regular third person singular	32, 67, 83, 92	32, 67, 83, 92	100
9. articles *a, an, the*	2, 3, 4, 5, 6, 16, 17, 23, 26, 44, 60, 70, 72, 79, 83, 86, 87, 89, 90, 90, 91, 98	2, 3, 4, 5, 6, 16, 17, 23, 26, 44, 60, 70, 72, 79, 83, 86, 87, 89, 90, 90, 91, 98	100
10. contractible copula	4, 5, 6, 11, 16, 17, 22, 36, 37, 47, 54, 60, 86, 97	4, 6, 11, 16, 17, 22, 36, 37, 47, 54, 60, 97	86
11. contractible auxiliary	15, 19, 24, 34, 50	34, 50	40
12. uncontractible copula	44, 53, 90	44, 53, 90	100
13. uncontractible auxiliary	39	39	100
14. irregular third person singular			—

Production Characteristics Summary Form

Name of Child Sara

	Stage	Grammatical Morphemes	Negation	Yes/No Questions	*Wh*-Questions	Noun Phrase Elaboration	Verb Phrase Elaboration	Complex Sentences
I	Early I							
I	Late I/ Early II							
II	II	1. 78% 2. 100% 3. 100%	/			𝍸 𝍸 𝍸 𝍸 ///	𝍸 𝍸 ////	//
III	III	4. 100% 5. 100%		/	/	𝍸 𝍸 𝍸 𝍸 ////	𝍸 𝍸 ///	
III	Early IV				///			///
	Late IV/ Early V		𝍸			𝍸 𝍸 𝍸 𝍸 𝍸 /	/	/
	Late V	6. 100% 7. 100% 8. 100% 9. 100% 10. 86%					𝍸 𝍸 𝍸 ////	
	V+	11. 40% 12. 100% 13. 100% 14. —					𝍸	///
	V++							

Guide to Analysis of Language Transcripts

Data Summary and Interpretation Form

Name of Child: Sara

Mean Length of Utterance in Morphemes (MLU)

3.14 morphemes

CA = 58 mos.
use 57 mos. figures

$\frac{3.14 - 5.32}{1.125} = -1.94$

Structural Stage by MLU:	Stage E/V	
Upper Bound Length:	7	morpheme(s)
Lower Bound Length:	1	morpheme(s)

	Most Typical Stage	Most Advanced Stage
Grammatical Morphemes:	Stage L/V	Stage V+
Negation:	Stage E/V-L/V/EV	Stage E/V-L/V/EV
Yes/No Questions:	Stage E/-///	Stage E/-///
Wh- Questions:	Stage E/V	Stage E/V
Noun Phrase Elaboration:	Stage L/V/EV	Stage L/V/EV
Verb Phrase Elaboration:	Stage LV	Stage V+
Complex Sentences:	Stage E/V, V+	Stage V+

Comments: MLU stage is higher than Most Typical Stage for Yes/No Questions, commensurate with Negation and Wh- Questions, lower than Grammatical Morphemes, Noun Phrase and Verb Phrase, and split for Complex Sentences. Gaps between the Most Typical and the Most Advanced Stage for Grammatical Morphemes and Verb Phrases. No gap for all others. MLU almost 2 standard deviations below mean.

Dore's Conversational Acts

Name of Child: Sara

Total / %	Adult Utterance Number	Act	Child Utterance Number	Total / %
91 / 79.8	1, 2, 3, 4, 5, 6, 7, 8, 9, 10, 11, 12, 13, 14, 15, 16, 17, 18, 19, 21, 22, 24, 25, 26, 29, 30, 31, 33, 36, 37, 38, 39, 42, 43, 44, 45, 47, 50, 51, 52, 53, 55, 56, 58, 59, 60, 61, 62, 63, 65, 66, 67, 68, 69, 70, 71, 73, 74, 75, 76, 77, 78, 79, 80, 81, 82, 83, 86, 87, 88, 89, 90, 91, 92, 93, 94, 96, 98, 99, 100, 102, 104, 105, 107, 108, 109, 110, 111, 112, 113, 114	Request	30, 37, 39, 47, 58, 62, 98	7 / 7
4 / 3.5	48, 49, 57, 72	Response to Request	1, 2, 3, 4, 5, 7, 8, 9, 11, 12, 13, 16, 18, 19, 20, 21, 24, 25, 28, 29, 31, 33, 34, 35, 38, 40, 41, 42, 43, 45, 46, 48, 49, 51, 52, 54, 55, 56, 57, 59, 60, 61, 63, 64, 65, 66, 69, 70, 71, 72, 75, 77, 78, 79, 81, 82, 84, 85, 87, 88, 89, 93, 94, 95, 96, 99, 100	67 / 67
0 / 0		Description	6, 15, 17, 23, 44, 53, 73, 74, 76, 80, 91, 97	12 / 12
8 / 7	20, 23, 35, 41, 64, 85, 101, 106	Statement	10, 22, 26, 32, 36, 50, 67, 83, 86, 90, 92	11 / 11
9 / 7.9	27, 28, 34, 40, 54, 84, 95, 97, 103	Acknow-ledgment		0 / 0
1 / .9	46	Organizational Device		0 / 0
0 / 0		Performative	14, 68	2 / 2
1 / .9	32	Miscellaneous	27	1 / 1

Conversational Moves and Appropriateness Judgments Analysis Grid

Name of Child Sara

Adult

UTT#	Conversational Moves: Initiating Moves	Conversational Moves: Responding Moves	Appropriateness Judgments: Referent Specificity	Appropriateness Judgments: Contributional Conciseness	Appropriateness Judgments: Communication Style
1	N		✓	✓	
2	E		✓	✓	
3	E		✓	✓	
4	E		✓	✓	
5	E		✓	✓	
6	E		✓	✓	
7	E		✓	✓	
8	E		✓	✓	
9	E		✓	✓	
10	E		✓	✓	
11	E		✓	✓	
12	E		✓	✓	
13	E		✓	✓	
14	E		✓	✓	
15		E	✓	✓	
16	E		✓	✓	
17	E		✓	✓	
18	E		✓	✓	
19	E		✓	✓	
20		E	✓	✓	
21	E		✓	✓	
22	E		✓	✓	
23		E	✓	✓	
24	E		✓	✓	
25	E		✓	✓	

Child

UTT#	Conversational Moves: Initiating Moves	Conversational Moves: Responding Moves	Appropriateness Judgments: Referent Specificity	Appropriateness Judgments: Contributional Conciseness	Appropriateness Judgments: Communication Style
1		O	✓	✓	
2		E	✓	✓	
3		R	N/A	N/A	
4		E	✓	✓	
5		E	✓	✓	
6		E	✓	✓	
7		E	✓	✓	
8		O	✓	✓	
9		E	✓	✓	
10		R	N/A	N/A	
11		E	✓	✓	
12		O	✓	✓	
13		O	✓	✓	
14		E	✓	✓	
15	N		✓	✓	
16		E	✓	✓	
17		E	✓	✓	
18		O	✓	✓	
19		E	✓	✓	
20		E	✓	✓	
21		E	✓	✓	
22		E	✓	✓	
23		E	✓	✓	
24		E	✓	✓	
25		R	N/A	N/A	

Conversational Moves and Appropriateness Judgments Analysis Grid

Name of Child Sara

Adult

UTT#	Conversational Moves: Initiating Moves	Conversational Moves: Responding Moves	Appropriateness Judgments: Referent Specificity	Appropriateness Judgments: Contributional Conciseness	Appropriateness Judgments: Communication Style
26	E		✓	✓	
27		R	N/A	N/A	
28		A	✓	✓	
29	E		✓	✓	
30	E		✓	✓	
31	E		✓	✓	
32		E	✓	✓	
33	E		✓	✓	
34		A	✓	✓	
35		E	✓	✓	
36	E		✓	✓	
37	E		✓	✓	
38	E		✓	✓	
39	E		✓	✓	
40		A	✓	✓	
41		A	✓	✓	
42	E		✓	✓	
43	E		✓	✓	
44	E		✓	✓	
45	E		✓	✓	
46	E		✓	✓	
47	E		✓	✓	
48		E	✓	✓	
49		Y	✓	✓	
50	E		✓	✓	

Child

UTT#	Conversational Moves: Initiating Moves	Conversational Moves: Responding Moves	Appropriateness Judgments: Referent Specificity	Appropriateness Judgments: Contributional Conciseness	Appropriateness Judgments: Communication Style
26		E	✓	✓	
27		R	N/A	N/A	
28		O	✓	✓	
29		E	✓	✓	
30	E		✓	✓	
31		O	✓	✓	
32		E	✓	✓	
33		O	✓	✓	
34		E	✓	✓	
35		O	✓	✓	
36	N		✓	✓	
37	N		—	✓	
38		Y	✓	✓	
39	E		✓	✓	
40		O	✓	✓	
41		O	✓	✓	
42		Y	✓	✓	
43		O	✓	✓	
44		E	✓	✓	
45		O	✓	✓	
46		E	✓	✓	
47	E		✓	✓	
48		O	✓	✓	
49		O	✓	✓	
50		E	✓	✓	

Conversational Moves and Appropriateness Judgments Analysis Grid

Name of Child Sara

Adult

UTT#	Conversational Moves: Initiating Moves	Conversational Moves: Responding Moves	Appropriateness Judgments: Referent Specificity	Appropriateness Judgments: Contributional Conciseness	Appropriateness Judgments: Communication Style
51	E		✓	✓	
52	E		✓	✓	
53	E		✓	✓	
54		A	✓	✓	
55	E		✓	✓	
56	E		✓	✓	
57		E	✓	✓	
58	E		✓	✓	
59	E		✓	✓	
60	E		✓	✓	
61	E		✓	✓	
62	E		✓	✓	
63	E		✓	✓	
64		E	✓	✓	
65	E		✓	✓	
66	E		✓	✓	
67		S	✓	✓	
68	E		✓	✓	
69	E		✓	✓	
70	E		✓	✓	
71	E		✓	✓	
72		E	✓	✓	
73	E		✓	✓	
74	E		✓	✓	
75	E		✓	✓	

Child

UTT#	Conversational Moves: Initiating Moves	Conversational Moves: Responding Moves	Appropriateness Judgments: Referent Specificity	Appropriateness Judgments: Contributional Conciseness	Appropriateness Judgments: Communication Style
51		O	✓	✓	
52		E	✓	✓	
53	N		—	✓	
54		E	✓	✓	
55		E	—	✓	
56		S	—	✓	
57		E	✓	✓	
58		E	✓	✓	
59		O	✓	✓	
60		E	✓	✓	
61		Y	✓	✓	
62	E		✓	✓	
63		E	—	✓	
64		S	—	✓	
65		Y	✓	✓	
66		E	—	✓	
67		E	✓	✓	
68		E	—	✓	
69		E	✓	✓	
70		E	✓	✓	
71		O	✓	✓	
72		E	✓	✓	
73		E	✓	✓	
74		R	N/A	N/A	
75		E	✓	✓	

Conversational Moves and Appropriateness Judgments Analysis Grid

Name of Child Sara

Adult

UTT#	Conversational Moves: Initiating Moves	Conversational Moves: Responding Moves	Appropriateness Judgments: Referent Specificity	Appropriateness Judgments: Contributional Conciseness	Appropriateness Judgments: Communication Style
76	E		✓	✓	
77	E		✓	✓	
78	E		✓	✓	
79	E		✓	✓	
80	E		✓	✓	
81	E		✓	✓	
82	E		✓	✓	
83	E		✓	✓	
84		R	N/A	N/A	
85		E	✓	✓	
86	E		✓	✓	
87	E		✓	✓	
88	E		✓	✓	
89	E		✓	✓	
90	E		✓	✓	
91	E		✓	✓	
92	E		✓	✓	
93	E		✓	✓	
94	E		✓	✓	
95		A	✓	✓	
96	E		✓	✓	
97		A	✓	✓	
98	E		✓	✓	
99	E		✓	✓	
100		E	✓	✓	

Child

UTT#	Conversational Moves: Initiating Moves	Conversational Moves: Responding Moves	Appropriateness Judgments: Referent Specificity	Appropriateness Judgments: Contributional Conciseness	Appropriateness Judgments: Communication Style
76		E	✓	✓	
77		E	✓	✓	
78		O	✓	✓	
79		E	✓	✓	
80	R		✓	✓	
81		E	—	✓	
82		S	✓	✓	
83	N		—	✓	
84		Y	✓	✓	
85		O	✓	✓	
86		E	✓	✓	
87		O	—	✓	
88		Y	✓	✓	
89		E	✓	✓	
90		E	—	✓	
91		E	✓	✓	
92		E	✓	✓	
93		E	✓	✓	
94		O	✓	✓	
95		O	✓	✓	
96		O	✓	✓	
97		E	✓	✓	
98	E		✓	✓	
99		E	✓	✓	
100		O	NK	NK	NK

Guide to Analysis of Language Transcripts

Conversational Moves and Appropriateness Judgments Analysis Grid

Name of Child Sara

Adult

	Conversational Moves		Appropriateness Judgments		
UTT#	Initiating Moves	Responding Moves	Referent Specificity	Contributional Conciseness	Communication Style
101		S	✓	✓	
102	E		✓	✓	
103		A	✓	✓	
104	E		✓	✓	
105	E		✓	✓	
106	N		✓	✓	
107	E		✓	✓	
108	E		✓	✓	
109	E		✓	✓	
110	E		✓	✓	
111	E		✓	✓	
112	E		✓	✓	
113	E		✓	✓	
114	E		NK	NK	NK

	Conversational Moves		Appropriateness Judgments		
UTT#	Initiating Moves	Responding Moves	Referent Specificity	Contributional Conciseness	Communication Style

Conversational Moves and Appropriateness Judgments Summary Form

Name of Child Sara

CHILD'S TOTAL UTTERANCES 100

CONVERSATIONAL MOVES					
INITIATING MOVES	5	New Topic Introduction	=	5	% of Total Utterances
	1	Restarting Old Topic	=	1	% of Total Utterances
	5	Eliciting Verbal Response	=	5	% of Total Utterances
	0	Intruding	=	-	% of Total Utterances
RESPONDING MOVES	0	Acknowledging	=	-	% of Total Utterances
	6	Yes/No Responses	=	6	% of Total Utterances
	25	One-Word Answers	=	25	% of Total Utterances
	5	Repeating	=	5	% of Total Utterances
	3	Sustaining Topic	=	3	% of Total Utterances
	50	Extending Topic	=	50	% of Total Utterances
FALSE STARTS	0		=	-	% of Total Utterances
APPROPRIATENESS JUDGMENTS					
Referent Specificity	12	Lacked Specificity	=	12	% of Total Utterances
Contributional Conciseness	0	Lacked Conciseness	=	-	% of Total Utterances
Communication Style	0	Lacked Stylistic Variation	=	-	% of Total Utterances

ADULT'S TOTAL UTTERANCES 114

CONVERSATIONAL MOVES					
INITIATING MOVES	2	New Topic Introduction	=	1.8	% of Total Utterances
	0	Restarting Old Topic	=	-	% of Total Utterances
	88	Eliciting Verbal Response	=	77.2	% of Total Utterances
	0	Intruding	=	-	% of Total Utterances
RESPONDING MOVES	8	Acknowledging	=	7	% of Total Utterances
	1	Yes/No Responses	=	.9	% of Total Utterances
	0	One-Word Answers	=	-	% of Total Utterances
	2	Repeating	=	1.8	% of Total Utterances
	2	Sustaining Topic	=	1.8	% of Total Utterances
	11	Extending Topic	=	9.6	% of Total Utterances
FALSE STARTS	0		=	-	% of Total Utterances
APPROPRIATENESS JUDGMENTS					
Referent Specificity	0	Lacked Specificity	=	-	% of Total Utterances
Contributional Conciseness	0	Lacked Conciseness	=	-	% of Total Utterances
Communication Style	0	Lacked Stylistic Variation	=	-	% of Total Utterances

Unanalyzed Transcripts

Appendix C

Name of Child *Gretchen*

Chronological Age *2;5*

Type of Situation *clinic kitchen playroom*

Date *4-13*

Length of Tape *50 min*

Length of Transcript

Time of Day *1:45 pm*

Materials Present *kitchen items*

People Present *G = Gretchen; M = Mother; C = Clinician*

ADULT	CONTEXT	CHILD
You wanna play kitchen?	(M and G moving toward play kitchen)	
		yeah/
Oh what a nice kitchen/		
They have many nice things/		
	(G picks up yellow chair)	
		/gɛtən jɛo/ [Gretchen's yellow]
Gretchen's yellow chair/		
		uh-huh/
	(G points to self)	
		/ʌ gɛtən/ [I'm Gretchen]
	(G points to M)	
		/ʌ/ Mama/ [you're Mama]
And I'm Mama/		
And we're in the play kitchen/		
	(G picks up pink cup)	
		/ʌ pi/ [that's pink]
Yes that's a pink one/		
Are there more in the cupboard?		
	(G opens cupboard)	
		/kiki/ [cookies]
Are there cookies in there?		

ADULT	CONTEXT	CHILD
		uh-huh/
	(G opens refrigerator)	
		/wʌzæ/?/ [what's that?]
	(G pulls out egg carton with	
	Ping-Pong balls inside)	
What are those?		
		/aɪ/ [eggs]
You're right/		
You could make scrambled eggs/		
	(G carrying eggs to stove)	yeah/
	(G starts to put eggs down	
	and turns to M)	
		/ʌ/ hot/ [that's hot]
Oh the stove is hot/		
		uh-huh/
	(G looks at her finger)	
		a owie/
Yes you have an owie/		
How did you get that owie?		
		/ʌ/ hot/ [it was hot]
Yes on the hot stove/		
	(G opens the oven and finds comb)	
		/ʌ hɑr/ [for hair]
A comb!/		
That's a silly thing to be in the oven/		
	(G pointing to M's hair)	/ʌ hɑr/ [your hair]

ADULT	CONTEXT	CHILD
My hair?		
	(G reaches for M's hair)	
You wanna comb my hair?		
		yeah/
	(G combs M's hair and turns	
	back to cupboard)	
What color is that comb?		
	(G pulls on cupboard door)	
		/win/ [green]
Pull hard/		
Can you get it?		
		uh-huh/
	(G gets door open)	
What's in there?		
		/kiki/ [cookies]
	(G picks up cup and turns to M)	
		more /dus/ [more juice]
You want more juice?		
Well let's see/		
Here's the juice/		
	(M pours "juice" from carton)	
	(M hanging cup to G)	/ʌ dʌ/ [thank you]
	(G opens cookie box)	
		Mama!/
What?/		
		poopie/

ADULT	CONTEXT	CHILD
		I poopie/
	(G and M exit)	
	•	
	•	
	•	
	(G and M return)	
What should we do now?		
	(G points to telephone)	
Oh should we play telephone?		
		uh-huh/
		/ʌ/ home/ [at home]
Yes we have one like that at home/		
	(G moves to cupboard and	
	points to wooden milk bottles)	
		/ʌ mok/ [that's milk]
um-hmm/		
	(G putting dishes on table)	/taɪ i/ [time to eat]
Is it time to eat?		
		yeah/
What are we having?		
		/kik/ [cake]
We're having cake?		
		/æn kiki/ [and cookies]
That's my favorite meal/		
	(G picks up box of cookies)	
		/mʌ kiki↑/ [more cookies?]

ADULT	CONTEXT	CHILD
Oh yes/		
I like cookies/		
		no /kiki/ [no cookies]
	(G sets box down)	
		/aʊ dʌn/ [alldone]
Are we all done eating?		
	(G turns to stove)	
		/ʌ/ hot/ [it's hot]
Yes/		
What's in the oven?		
	(G opens oven)	
		no more/
Nothing?		
Is that oven empty?		
		/ʌ/ no more/ [there's no more]
	(G turns back to table and	
	pours tea in her cup)	
		/ʌ gɛtən/ [this is Gretchen's]
Um-hmm/		
Do you like milk in your tea?		
		uh-huh/
	(G picks up milk and hands it to M)	
		here Mom/
Should I pour?		
		yeah/
Which one's yours?		

ADULT	CONTEXT	CHILD
		/gɛtən/ tea/ [Gretchen's tea]
	(G gets up and goes to refrigerator)	
		/i · i/ [eat, eat]
Are you gonna come and eat too?		
		uh-huh/
		more juice/
	(G gets pitcher out of refrigerator)	
		here Mom/
	(G hands pitcher to M and picks	
	up cup)	
Oh thank you/		
		/aʊ doti/ [all dirty]
Is that cup dirty?		
You could wash it/		
		uh-huh/
	(G carries cup to sink then turns	
	as camera moves)	
		/wʌ zæ/?/ [what's that?]
That's the camera/		
It's taking a picture of you/		
	(C enters room and talks with M)	
	(M leaves and C stays)	
Are you playing house?		
		uh-huh/
	(G brings pan from oven to table)	
		/ʌ/ hot/ [that's hot]

ADULT	CONTEXT	CHILD
Is that cake hot?		
		uh-huh/
Gretchen what's this?	(C showing teacup)	
		/ʌ/ home/
You have one at home?		
But what is this?		
		/ʌp/ [cup]
		/gɛtən/ [Gretchen's]
That's Gretchen's cup/		
You're right/		
	(C picks up bag of cars)	
What are these?		
		/ʌ/ home/ [at home]
You have these at home?		
What are they?		
You tell me/		
		/ɑrz/ [cars]
You're right/		
They're cars/		
Can you come sit down?	(C pulling out chair)	
Come sit down/		
	(G walks toward table)	
		okay/
	(G points to chair)	
		/jɛo/ [yellow]
Yellow/		

ADULT	CONTEXT	CHILD
The chair is yellow/		
Do you have a yellow chair like		
that at home?		
		yeah/
		/ʌ/ home/ [at home]
You have a yellow chair at home?		
		uh-huh/
Can you sit down?		
	(G turns back to refrigerator)	
		a cake/
	(G brings cake to table)	
Oh you need the cake/		
	(G points to table)	
		Mama there/
Is that Mama's place?		
		um-hmm/
Do you help your mom at home?		
		home cake/
	(G picks up container of	
	raisins and looks at C)	
Those are raisins/		
		eat/
Sure you can eat them/		
	(G opens container and takes	
	out raisin)	
		eat/

ADULT	CONTEXT	CHILD
You can eat it/		
	(G puts raisin in mouth)	
		mmm/
Is that good?		
	(G turns back to cupboard)	
Now what are you making?		
		/kiki æn/ juice/ [cookies and juice]
Cookies and juice?		
Oh boy/		
	(G walks back to table)	
		/mɑ b√ aɪ/ back/ [Mom be right back]
Yup/		
Your mom will be right back/		
		/bʌ kiki/ [bake cookies]
Oh you're going to make cookies?		
		no /mɑ/ [no Mom]
Oh/		
Your mom is going to bake cookies?		
When she comes back in?		
		no home/
Oh I see/		
Gretchen what's this?	(C holding up blue cup)	
		/bu/ [blue]
That's what color it is/		
	(G points to pink cup)	
		/æ pi/ [that's pink]

ADULT	CONTEXT	CHILD
You're right!/		
That one is pink/		
Do you know what color this is?	(C holding up white fork)	
		/ɪ ʌ aɪt/ [it is white]
Very good!/		
	(G turns to stove and picks up	
	teapot)	
Careful you don't burn yourself/		
		a owie/
Yes you'd get an owie/		
	(G shows C empty cookie box)	
		no more /kiki/ [no more cookies]
Oh are the cookies all gone?		
		uh-huh/
No more cookies/		
	(G turns on "water" in sink)	
		/ʌ duti/ [all dirty]
Are your hands all dirty?		
	(G nods head)	
You washed your hands/		
	(G comes back to table)	
Can I eat your mom's food?		
		/ʌ/ Mama/ [that's Mama's]
Oh that's your mother's food?		
		/ʌ/ Mama eat/ [my mama eat]
Okay/		

ADULT	CONTEXT	CHILD
I'll leave it so Mama can eat it/		
	(C starts putting cars back in bag)	
		no/
		mine/
Oh don't put those away?/		
Oh they're yours/		
But we need to put them in the bag/		
	(G reaches for bag)	
		/ʌ aut/ [take out]
Do you want them out?		
Okay/		
Let's put 'em on the table/		
	(G and C take cars out of bag	
	and line them up on the table)	
There!/		
	(C picks up box of buttons)	
What are these?		
		/bʌʔən/ [buttons]
Buttons good/		
That's right/		
		/ʌ/ home/ [at home]
Oh you have those at home too?		
	(G looking at door)	Mama/
Gretchen/		
Where is your mom?		
		be /aɪ/ back/ [be right back]

ADULT	CONTEXT	CHILD
You're right/		
She'll be right back/		
Gretchen?		
Where's the sink?		
	(G turns to sink)	
		/ʌvɚ/ there/ [over there]
You're right/	(G walking to sink)	
It's over there/		
	(G turns on "water")	
What's Gretchen doing?		
		/ʌ duti/ [all dirty]
I see/		
Your hands are all dirty?		
	(G starts stirring in pan on stove)	
		/ʌ/ Mama/ [for Mama]
Mama?		
Are you being a mama?		
		/ʌ/ Mama/ [for Mama]
You making something for Mama?		
	(G carries pan over to table)	
		Mama /dɪ/ [Mama sit]
Oh your mama _____ /		
	(G walks around chair and falls down)	
		oop/
		/ɔ/ down/ [fall down]
	(C reaches for G)	

ADULT	CONTEXT	CHILD
Whoops/		
Are you okay?		
	(G gets up)	
You fell down/		
	(G looks toward door)	
		Mama be /aɪt/ back/ [Mama be right back]
	(camera moves)	
You're right/		
		/wʌz æt/?/ [what's that?]

Guide to Analysis of Language Transcripts

Name of Child *Matthew* Chronological Age *6;2*

Type of Situation *playing with play dough and cars* Date *9-24*

Length of Tape *50 min* Length of Transcript ______ Time of Day *4 pm*

Materials Present *play dough; car mat and cars*

People Present *M = Matthew; C = Clinician*

ADULT	CONTEXT	CHILD
	(M and C playing with	I want the other color/
	play dough at table)	
What other color would you like?		
The blue?		
		I need a color/
	(M tries to open tub with teeth)	
Oh can I help you please?		
	(M hands her the tub)	
		can I have part of your dough↑/
Are they the same color?		
		are they↑/
No they're not/		
You can have all of mine though/		
		I want all of your/
	(M pointing to Cookie Monster	I will make it/
	cookie cutter)	
Okay/		
I am making a smiley face/		
		what a smiley face?/
I'll show you/		
	(M picking up a cutter)	oh is it this↑/

ADULT	CONTEXT	CHILD
Kind of/		
She has a smiley face/	(C pointing to M's cookie cutter)	
		okay/
I'm going to make it on my own/		
	(M holding up cookie cutter)	how 'bout this?/
How about that?		
	(M pointing to another color)	you will use this↑/
No I'm going to use my hands/		
		oh you will use your fingers to
		make that I think/
Yep I sure will/		
	(M makes a Cookie Monster)	
Look at that!/		
	(play dough crumbles)	
		oh this icky!/
		hey my Cookie Monster break!/
Oh no!/		
It broke/		
	(Cookie Monster falls apart)	
		hey!/
What?		
	(M pointing to yellow dough mixed in)	that play dough s/c
		it is not your dough↑/
Nope/		
It's not my dough/		
I don't know whose it is/		

ADULT	CONTEXT	CHILD
		what other color there is?/
What other color is there?		
Well there's blue/		
	(M sees white play dough)	
		white!/
	(M shaking head)	no not white/
Okay not white/		
	(M sees C's play dough)	
	(M pointing to C's play dough)	oh that the smiley face↑/
Yep that's the smiley face/		
		I think I will/
You think you will what?		
		do something else/
What are you going to do?		
	(M looks at blue play dough)	
	(M pointing to C's play dough)	I need that/
	(M gets play dough but it crumbles)	
		not that/
Not that?		
Is that too crumbly?		
	(M drops chunk of play	
	dough on the floor)	
		oh no!/
What happened?		
		there play dough on the floor!/
Yep/		

ADULT	CONTEXT	CHILD
There is some play dough on the floor/		
		you don't matter that↑/
No that's okay/		
		I need hard dough/
You need hard dough?		
		yep/
	(M finds some hard play dough)	
		oh this!/
Can I help you squish it together?		
Then it won't crumble/		
		allright/
		how 'bout rolling it up?/
Would that help?		
		yeah/
	(M and C stick play dough together)	
		now we will roll it up/
Okay/		
	(play dough sticks together)	
		cool/
	(M makes noise with play dough)	
I'm playing with red now/	(C picking up red play dough)	
	(M cutting play dough with knife)	cutting it/
You're cutting the witch out/		
	(M cuts out witch with knife)	
Cool/		
I like your witch/		

ADULT	CONTEXT	CHILD
		and you like me cutting it out↑/
I do/		
	(play dough falls off table)	
Uh-oh/		
It fell/		
That's okay/		
		do you have a vacuum cleaner here↑/
I think so but I don't know where/		
		why . you ever vacuum?/
I've never vacuumed here/		
		but you vacuum at home↑/
Yeah I vacuum a lot at home/		
		oh the witch is done/
Awesome witch Matt/		
		now I'm going to make all
		different color dough/
All different colored dough?		
Just remember you can't mix the		
dough together remember/		
		yep/
Do you want to use my red?		
		yippee/
	(C smiles at "yippee")	
		what you so funny about?/
I'm happy you're happy/		
	(M goes back to playing and	

ADULT	CONTEXT	CHILD
	destroys witch)	
		poor little witch/
Oh the poor little witch!/		
		I need more/
You need more?		
		yep/
You're making something big/		
		yep/
Well I'm going to make a Bert head/		
		Bert↑/
Yep/		
	(M plays very energetically; C smiles)	
	(M squishing Ernie)	nah I won't do that/
		what you laughing about?/
I'm just smiling/		
		happy↑/
Yep I'm happy/		
		happy/
	(C puts Bert on windowsill)	
Here's Bert/		
Now he can watch us/		
		Big Bird will watch us when
		I make him/
Cool/		
		I will be really cool when I
		make you Big Bird/

ADULT	CONTEXT	CHILD
	(C picks up Cookie Monster cookie cutter)	
I think I'll make a Cookie Monster/		
		oh you might have a Cookie Monster/
I might/		
		cool dude/
Very cool/		
		anything else you will make↑/
I'm not sure/		
I might make something else/		
	(M pressing Big Bird cookie cutter)	I hope · I hope it happening/
I hope it is happening too/		
Let's see/		
Uh-oh/	(The cookie cutter doesn't work)	
		oh no!/
		you want to do something↑/
	(M pokes broken Big Bird with knife)	
Oh be careful with him Matt/		
		I make him dead/
Yes you did/		
You know what?		
		what?/
Let's clean up and then get		
the race track/		
		what the race track?/
Remember?		
It's the thing you drive on/		

ADULT	CONTEXT	CHILD
	(M cleaning up)	allright/
Grab Bert and Ernie please/		
		okay/
	(play dough falls on floor)	
		that okay↑/
That's okay/		
	(M picking up Bert)	XXX/
		I take this/
Thank you/		
	(M pointing to half-full play dough tub)	how about this?/
		there not enough of that/
There's this too/		
Now there is enough/		
		allright/
	(M finds yellow play dough)	
		yellow!/
Yellow!		
		we not even take out that/
We didn't/		
Oh well/		
Can you get the plastic thing please?		
	(M picking up the plastic bucket	we put toys in here/
	for the play dough)	
We sure do/		
	(C and M pick up play dough)	
	(M tosses play dough and misses container)	

ADULT	CONTEXT	CHILD
		sorry/
That's okay/		
Thank you for picking it up/		
You are a big help/		
	(M starts to leave room but	
	realizes some stuff is left)	
		oh I forgot/
	(M finishes picking up play dough)	
		I will get out the race car/
Good idea/		
	(M bringing in car mat)	this↑/
Yep/		
		this not a race track/
Sure it is/		
	(M rolls out mat)	
		no it not/
Why not?		
		it something to play on/
That too/		
	(M sees gas station)	
		this to play with this↑/
Yep that's to play with too/		
		okay/
		I know that/
	(car mat is stuck on door)	
		that keep breaking/

ADULT	CONTEXT	CHILD
Yep I'll fix it/	(C freeing mat from door)	
	(C and M get out cars and	
	start playing)	
	(M makes car sounds)	
I have two white cars/		
		I have three!/
	(M driving car over picture of	I'm driving in water!/
	water on car mat)	
That's silly/		
	(M drives car over pictures	
	of boats on mat)	
		oh man I run over boats/
You ran over the boats!		
	(C pulls car up to gas station)	
I need gas/		
	(M pretends to pump gas)	
Here's your money/		
		thank you/
	(M crashes cars together)	
Matt we need to be careful/		
		why?/
Because they might break/		
	(M pointing to car)	this one↑/
That one might break/		
		that is metal/
It still might break/		

ADULT	CONTEXT	CHILD
	(M drives car slowly)	
	(M driving into gas station)	I'm driving in/
I am too/		
	(C drives into gas station)	
		you need gas↑/
		right here you not need gas/
Do I get gas here?		
		yeah/
	(M drives his car forward)	
		I never need gas/
Never?		
	(M drives car back to gas station)	
		gas please/
	(M hides his car)	
		not know where me is/
I don't know where your car is/		
		not know where me is/
		oops · there me is/

Glossary

Adjective: A word that describes, identifies, or qualifies a noun, pronoun, or gerund by specifying size, color, number, or other attributes.

Adverb: A word that describes a verb, an adjective, or other adverbs by specifying time, manner, location, degree, number, or quality.

Article: Indefinite *a* or *an,* or definite *the.*

Auxiliary Verb: A verb that has no independent existence in a sentence except to support the main verb (e.g., "He *is* going home"); auxiliary verbs are typically called "helping verbs" because they help the main verb by adding mood, voice, or tense; simple auxiliaries include *be, can, do, have, may, must, shall, will,* and sometimes *get;* the acquisition of the auxiliary *be* is the only auxiliary that is considered one of Brown's (1973) 14 grammatical morphemes. (See pages 111–112 for a list of Brown's 14 grammatical morphemes.)

Catenative Verb: An early semiauxiliary verb form (e.g., *gonna, wanna, hafta)* without an auxiliary that results from a syllabic reduction of the main verb and an infinitive verb form (e.g., *gonna go = going to go);* children tend to be partial toward certain catenatives in the early stages of linguistic production and only later use a full range of semiauxiliaries (e.g., *"I gonna go"* vs. *"I'm gonna go")* (Brown, 1973).

Clause: A group of words that includes a subject and a predicate; **main** or **independent clauses** may stand alone as a sentence; **subordinate** or **dependent clauses** are incomplete and must be used with main clauses to express related ideas.

Complex Sentence: A sentence that contains more than one verb phrase; the additional verb phrase may be a full sentence proposition (compound sentence) or assumed within a clause.

Conjunction: A word used to join words, phrases, clauses, or sentences; **coordinating conjunctions** join words, phrases, or clauses of equivalent value and include *and, but, for, or, nor, either, neither, yet, so,* and *whereas;* **subordinating conjunctions** are used to join two clauses (a main clause and a dependent clause) and include *although, because, since, while, until, whenever, as, as if,* and others that place a condition on a sentence.

Contingent Speech: Speaking turns that are linked to preceding turns by topic (e.g., "I like dogs." [Response] "Me too") and/or other conversational conventions (e.g., "How ya doing?" [Response] "Pretty good. And you?").

Contractible Auxiliary: The contractible form of the verb *be* as an auxiliary (e.g., "She is riding a bike" "She's riding a bike"); keep in mind that this grammatical morpheme deals with the *contractible* auxiliary, not the *contracted* auxiliary, and that the child does not have to contract the auxiliary to count this form.

Contractible Copula: The contractible form of the verb *be* as a main verb (e.g., "She is hungry" → "She's hungry"); keep in mind that this grammatical morpheme deals with the *contractible* copula, not the *contracted* copula, and that the child does not have to contract the copula to count this form.

Copula: A verb typically used as an auxiliary verb that is used as a main verb; the copula is also referred to as a "linking verb" since the copula links the subject of a sentence to the complement (e.g., "She *is* happy" or "He *was* hungry"); in relation to Brown's (1973) stages, only the copular form of the verb *to be* is significant. (See pages 111–112 for a list of Brown's stages.)

Deixis: The process of using the perspective of the speaker as the reference; the use of spatial, temporal, and/or interpersonal features to mark relationships; deictic pronouns include *this, that, me, you;* deictic verbs include *come, go, bring, take.*

Deictic: The adjective form of DEIXIS (see above).

Demonstrative Pronoun: A pronoun that points out the person or object referred to, either as an adjective to the subject of the sentence (e.g., *"That* ball is big") or as the subject of the sentence itself (e.g., *"That* is a big ball"); singular demonstrative pronouns include *this* and *that;* plural forms include *these* and *those;* idiomatic forms include *so* and *such.*

Discourse: A unit of language that is larger than the utterance, encompassing at the very least adjacency pairs (e.g., request-response) and including several speaker changes that are linked by a common topic.

Dummy *DO:* The auxiliary form of the verb *do* used in yes/no and *wh-* questions to permit inversion of the auxiliary and noun phrase (e.g., "I like raisins" becomes "Do you like raisins?"). Children "invent" and use the dummy *do* in question forms with rising intonation (e.g., "You do like raisins?") before they invert it in question forms.

Elicited Speech: Speech that is drawn out either through imitation (by request) (e.g., "This is a doggie. Say *doggie."* [Response] "Doggie") or through fill-in-the-blank (e.g., "This is a _____." [Response] "Doggie").

Ellipsis: A conversational convention that shortens an utterance based on information from a preceding utterance (e.g., "Who likes raisins?" [Response] "I do" [instead of "I like raisins"]).

Embedded Clause: A clause that is subordinated into a full sentence; see SUBORDINATE CLAUSE.

Formal Assessment Procedure: A test, format, or inventory that has been standardized on specific populations of individuals.

Gerund: A verb ending in *-ing* that functions as a noun in a sentence (e.g., *"Jogging* is good for your health"); it can be distinguished from the present participle by the fact that the gerund may be preceded by *the* and followed by *of* (e.g., "The making of the movie *Jaws* was on TV").

Gerund Phrase: A gerund and its modifiers; a gerund phrase can function as the subject of a verb (e.g., *"Counting sheep* puts me to sleep"), the object of a verb (e.g., "I fell asleep *counting sheep"),* or the object of a preposition (e.g., "The monotony of *counting sheep* puts me to sleep").

Grammatical Morpheme: A morpheme that adds to the grammatical structure of a word or phrase, including the 14 free and bound morphemes Brown (1973) studied primarily because of the obligatory context each possesses. (See pages 111–112 for a list of Brown's 14 grammatical morphemes.)

Illocutionary Force: The intended interpretation of an utterance or speech act; the illocutionary force must be combined with a proposition for the speech act to be conveyed.

Imitative speech: Speech that repeats all or part of previous utterances (e.g., "This is a doggie." [Response] "Doggie").

Infinitive: A form of the verb that consists of *to* plus a verb; infinitives typically are used as nouns and thus function as subjects or objects of verbs (e.g., *To know* him is *to love* him); infinitives can also be used as adjectives (e.g., "He ran out of places *to hide")* or adverbs ("She was unable *to go").*

Infinitive Phrase: An infinitive plus its modifiers and subject or object; it may be used as an adjective, an adverb, or a noun (e.g., "I wanted *to eat the biggest cookie"*).

Infinitive Phrase with Subjects Different from That of the Main Sentence: An infinitive form of a verb that has a subject that is not the subject of the main verb (e.g., in the sentence "I wanted the train to go chug-chug," the subject of the sentence is *I,* but the subject of the infinitive is *the train).*

Informal Assessment Procedure: A descriptive analysis procedure based on the techniques used in collecting and interpreting data from research designs.

Irregular Past Tense: The form of an irregular verb indicating that an action has already taken place; there is no consistent device for marking the past tense of irregular verbs (e.g., "She *hit* the ball," "She *ran* to first base," or "She *struck* out").

Irregular Third Person Singular Present Tense: The irregular form of the third person singular form of the present tense of a verb (e.g., "She *has* a cold" or "He *does* the dishes after dinner").

Language Comprehension: The process of understanding language.

Language Production: The process of expressing language.

Mean Length of Utterance (MLU): The average number of morphemes per utterance.

Modal Auxiliary: An auxiliary verb that carries its own meaning and influences the meaning of the main verb; modal auxiliaries include *can, could, may, might, must, ought, shall, should, will,* and *would;* typical meanings are ability *(can),* intent *(will),* obligation *(must),* permission *(may),* and possibility *(might).*

Morpheme: The smallest unit of meaning in a language, typically root words, but also all prefixes and suffixes in a language.

Multiple Embeddings: Sentences that contain more than one type of embedding; may include sentences with relative clauses and infinitives or semiauxiliaries (e.g., "I think *we need to pour some water in it")* and infinitives plus relative clauses (e.g., "We looked all over *to find jellies what's my size").*

Multiterm Utterance: An utterance that contains more than one semantic role or grammatical category (e.g., Agent-Action-Object); there is not a one-to-one relationship between semantic roles or grammatical categories and words in an utterance (e.g., "The boy kicked the ball" has five words and three terms: Agent-Action-Object).

Narrative: A story or description of actual or fictional events; narratives may consist of one of four basic types: recounts, event casts, accounts, or stories.

Negative Sentence: A sentence that contains *no* or *not* within the sentence proposition (e.g., "He is *not* sleeping" or "She wants *no* part of this").

Noncontingent Speech: Speaking turns that are not linked to preceding utterances.

Noun: The name of a person, place, or thing; nouns can be common (e.g., *girl, tree, house, rock)* or proper *(Bridget, Mama, Sara).*

Noun Phrase: A noun, or a phrase functioning as a noun, that fulfills the role of subject or object of a verb in a sentence; the only obligatory component of this sentence constituent is a noun or pronoun.

Object Noun Phrase: A phrase that functions as the object of the verb, or predicate, of a sentence; the form of object noun phrases changes developmentally (e.g., "eat *cookie,"* or "I ate the *chocolate-chip cookie").*

Object Noun Phrase Complement: A part of the predicate, or verb phrase, that serves to complement by stating in a different way the object of the verb or noun phrase (e.g., "She made his room a *mess").*

Obligatory Context: The grammatical obligation of a structure for meaning to be clear; in relation to Brown's (1973) 14 grammatical morphemes, use was judged to be obligatory, rather than optional, so that absence of the morpheme would indicate nonacquisition, not choice. (See pages 111–112 for a list of Brown's 14 grammatical morphemes.)

Perfect Tenses: Pairs of simple tenses (e.g., "I *have written* four letters to the president") and progressive tenses (e.g., "I *have been writing* every week") of verbs indicating that action was, is, or will be completed within a given time.

Phrase: A group of words that functions as a single part of speech but does not have both a subject and a verb; phrases may be used as a noun (*"The red bird* flew away"), a verb (*"I could have eaten* more cookies"), an adjective ("The cat *with brown stripes* ran away"), or an adverb ("The sun came out *in the afternoon").*

Pragmatics: The study of language use independent of language structure; rules and principles that relate the structure of language to its use; a level of linguistic analysis.

Predicate of a Sentence: The verb phrase of the sentence; the explanation of the action, condition, or effect of the subject of a sentence (e.g., The little puppies *wagged their tails).*

Preposition: A word that shows how a noun or pronoun is related to another word in a sentence; most prepositions are simple (i.e., consist of one word: *at, in, over, of, to, under, up, from, with)* and introduce a phrase (e.g., *at the store; in the box*); a preposition may be considered a verb particle; in relation to Brown's (1973) 14 grammatical morphemes, only the prepositions *in* and *on* are considered. (See pages 111–112 for a list of Brown's 14 grammatical morphemes.)

Present Progressive *-ING:* The present tense form of a verb with an *-ing* ending indicating ongoing action; the present tense, progressive aspect of a verb (e.g., *going)* that when used in a sentence requires the use of an auxiliary verb (e.g., "She *is kicking* the ball").

Personal Pronoun: A word that takes the place of a noun, including *I, you, she, them, his,* and *ours,* among others; order of acquisition in production by Brown's (1973) Stages: I = *I, mine;* II = *my, it, me;* III = *you, your, she, them, he, yours, we, her;* IV = *they, us, him, hers, his;* V = *its, our, ours, myself, yourself, their, theirs;* V+ = *herself, himself, itself, ourselves, yourselves, themselves.*

Proposition or Propositional force: The conceptual information contained within an utterance or a speech act; the proposition of a speech act is the speaker's meaning; the proposition must be combined with an intention for the speech act to be conveyed.

Propositional Content: The meaning of a speech act expressed most simply as the noun-verb relationship.

Referent: A word that stands for a concrete thing (e. g., the word *ball* is the referent for a real ball; the word *bounces* stands for the activity of bouncing).

Regular Past Tense: The form of a regular verb indicating that an action has already taken place; the past tense form of a regular verb requires the addition of *-ed* to the verb (e.g., "She *kicked* the ball").

Regular Third Person Singular Present Tense: The regular form of the third person singular form of the present tense of a verb; the regular third person singular present tense requires the addition of *-s* to the verb (e.g., "She *hits* the ball").

Relative Clause: A subordinate clause that is introduced by a relative pronoun (i.e., *who, which, that,* and sometimes the agrammatical *what)* (e.g., "My shoes have these holes *what your toes come out");* see SUBORDINATE CLAUSE.

Semantic Relation: A combination of two or more individual semantic roles and/or residual grammatical categories; typically, semantic relations express meanings in addition to the meanings expressed by individual words (e.g., the semantic relation AGENT-ACTION expresses the relationship between the noun and verb in addition to the meaning expressed by the noun and verb).

Semantics: The study of language content; rules and principles for the expression and understanding of meaning; a level of linguistic analysis.

Semiauxiliary: A word such as *gonna, gotta, wanna,* and *hafta* used with a verb that appears to be the main verb of a sentence (e.g., "He *gonna* go")—including catenatives; the term *semiauxiliary* is really incorrect in that semiauxiliaries are actually semi-infinitives because they are reduced forms of infinitives that appear to function as auxiliaries in sentences (e.g., *gonna* is a reduction of *going to* in relation to a verb).

Semiauxiliary Complement: A noun phrase that is the complement of the infinitive within the semiauxiliary verb phrase (e.g., "I wanna *pour the water").*

Sentence: A subject, or noun phrase (NP), and a predicate, or verb phrase (VP), that together express a complete thought; a sentence can be either simple (i.e., contains only one verb phrase) or complex (i.e., contains more than one verb phrase); in sentence notation, S = sentence and S → NP + VP.

Simple Infinitive: The form of a verb consisting of *to* plus the verb; see INFINITIVE.

Simple Infinitive Clause: The form of a verb consisting of *to* plus the verb used in a sentence without other sentence constituents (e.g., "I wanted *to go").*

Speech Act: A linguistic unit of communication consisting of a proposition (meaning) and illocutionary force (intention); also considered when analyzing speech acts is the listener's interpretation of the speaker's meaning and intention.

Spontaneous Speech: Speech that does not repeat part of preceding utterances.

Subject Noun Phrase: A phrase that functions as the subject of the verb (or predicate) of a sentence; the form of subject noun phrases changes developmentally (e.g., *"boy go"* and *"The little boy* is going to school").

Subject of a Sentence: A person, thing, or idea—expressed as a single noun, pronoun, or noun phrase—being described in a sentence.

Subordinate Clause: A group of words, consisting of at least a noun and a verb, that cannot stand alone because it is introduced by a subordinating conjunction (e.g., *although, because, since, while, until, whenever, as, as if)* or a relative pronoun (e.g., *who, which, that,* and sometimes the agrammatical *what).*

Syntax: The study of language forms; rules and principles for combining grammatical elements and words into utterances and sentences; a level of linguistic analysis.

Topic: An aspect of conversation that holds conversation together; a topic may be viewed as old or new in relation to previous utterances; may be manipulated using a variety of linguistic devices (e.g., a comment, a question, or a repetition).

Type-Token Ratio (TTR): A measure of vocabulary diversity obtained by dividing the number of different words in a sample of 50 utterances by the total number of words.

Uncontractible Auxiliary of the Verb *be*: The uncontractible form of the verb *be* as an auxiliary verb; uncontractible forms are uncontractible because they cannot be pronounced as a contraction without dropping the syllable (e.g., "The mouse *is* sleeping"), cannot be pronounced as a contraction without losing tense or number information (e.g., "They *were* sleeping"), or cannot be reduced further because they are elliptical (e.g., "Who is going to the picnic?" [Response] "I *am");* keep in mind that this grammatical morpheme deals with the *uncontractible* auxiliary, not the *uncontracted* auxiliary, so caution should be used in identifying uncontractible forms.

Uncontractible Copula of the Verb *be*: The uncontractible form of the verb *be* as a main verb; uncontractible forms are uncontractible because they cannot be pronounced as a contraction without dropping a syllable (e.g., "The mouse *is* dead"), cannot be pronounced as a contraction without losing tense or number information (e.g., "She *was* sick"), or cannot be reduced further because they are elliptical (e.g., "Who is hungry?" [Response] "I *am");* keep in mind that this grammatical morpheme deals with the *uncontractible* copula, not the *uncontracted* copula, so caution should be used in identifying uncontractible forms.

Unmarked Infinitive Clause: An infinitive clause in which the *to* is not stated but is implied from the sentence structure (e.g., "Help me [*to*] pick these up"); usually introduced by *let, help, watch, make, need, see, hear,* or *feel.*

Verb: A word that depicts action or state of being; verbs typically function as the predicate of a sentence and explain the action, condition, or effect of the subject of that sentence.

Verb Particle: A relational word (e.g., slow *down,* wake *up,* turn *off*) that is associated with a verb; verb particles can be differentiated from prepositions by transposing the word in question to the right of the object noun and judging grammaticality (e.g., "She *put on* the hat" → "She *put* the hat *on"* = verb particle; "She danced *on* the table" → "She danced the table *on"* = preposition).

Verb Phrase: The verb plus any additional words or phrases that are needed to complete the verb; the only obligatory component of this sentence constituent is a verb; object noun phrases are considered to be part of the verb phrase.

***Wh-* Question:** A question form that requests specific information characterized by one of the following *wh-* words: *who, what, what-doing, where, why, when,* and *how.*

***Wh-* Clause:** A subordinate clause that is introduced by a *wh-* word and provides adjectival information (e.g., "I know *where he is");* typical *wh-* words that introduce *wh-* clauses and not relative clauses include *who, where, when, why, how,* and sometimes *what.*

***Wh-* Infinitive Clause:** An infinitive that is introduced by a *wh-* word, therefore subordinated to the main verb (e.g., "You know *how to make this"* or "Show me *what to do").*

Yes/No Question: A question form that requires a yes or no response (e.g., "More?" or "Do you want a cookie?").

Sources for Glossary

Huddleston, R. (1988). *Introduction to the grammar of English.* New York: Cambridge University Press.

Mosher, J.R. (1968). *English grammar.* Lincoln, NE: Cliff's Notes.

Owens, R.E. (1992). *Language development: An introduction.* Columbus, OH: Merrill.

Quirk, R., Greenbaum, S., Leech, G., and Svartvik, J. (1972). *A grammar of contemporary English.* New York: Seminar Press.

Shertzer, M. (1986). *The elements of grammar.* New York: Macmillan.

REFERENCES

Anderson-Wood, L., and Smith, B. (1997). *Working with pragmatics.* Oxon, UK: Winslow Press.

Barenbaum, E., and Newcomer, P. (1996). *Test of children's language.* Austin, TX: Pro-Ed.

Bates, E. (1976). *Language and context.* New York: Academic Press.

Bedrosian, J.L. (1985). An approach to developing conversational competence. In D.N. Ripich and F.M. Spinelli (Eds.), *School discourse problems* (pp. 231–255). San Diego, CA: College Hill Press.

Beilin, H. (1975). *Studies in the cognitive basis of language development.* New York: Academic Press.

Benedict, H. (1979). Early lexical development: Comprehension and production. *Journal of Child Language, 10,* 321–335.

Berko Gleason, J. (1973). Code switching in children's language. In T.E. Moore (Ed.), *Cognitive development and the acquisition of language* (pp. 159–167). New York: Academic Press.

Beveridge, M., and Conti-Ramsden, G. (1987). *Children with language disabilities.* Milton Keynes, England: Open University Press.

Bishop, D., and Edmundson, A. (1987). Language-impaired 4-year-olds: Distinguishing transient from persistent impairment. *Journal of Speech and Hearing Disorders, 52,* 156–173.

Bloom, L. (1973). *One word at a time: The use of single-word utterances before syntax.* The Hague, The Netherlands: Mouton.

Bloom, L., and Lahey, M. (1978). *Language development and language disorders.* New York: Wiley.

Bloom, L., Lightbown, P., and Hood, L. (1975). Structure and variation in child language. *Monographs of the Society for Research in Child Development, 40*(2, Serial No. 160).

Bloom, L., Rocissano, L., and Hood, L. (1976). Adult-child discourse: Developmental interaction between information processing and linguistic knowledge. *Cognitive Psychology, 8,* 521–552.

Boehm, A. (1986). *Boehm test of basic concepts–Revised.* New York: Psychological Corporation.

Bowers, L., Huisingh, R., Orman, J., and LoGiudice, C. (1998). *The expressive language test.* East Moline, IL: LinguiSystems.

Bray, C., and Wiig, E. (1985). *Let's talk inventory for children.* San Antonio, TX: Psychological Corporation.

Brinton, B. (1990). Peer commentary on "Clinical pragmatics: Expectations and realizations," by Tanya Gallagher. *Journal of Speech-Language Pathology and Audiology, 14*(1), 7–8.

Brinton, B., and Fujuki, M. (1984). Development of topic manipulation skills in discourse. *Journal of Speech and Hearing Research, 27,* 350–358.

Brinton, B., and Fujuki, M. (1989). *Conversational management with language-impaired children: Pragmatic assessment and intervention.* Rockville, MD: Aspen.

Brinton, B., Fujuki, M., Loeb, D., and Winkler, E. (1986). The development of conversational repair strategies in response to requests for clarification. *Journal of Speech and Hearing Research, 29,* 75–81.

Brown, R. (1973). *A first language: The early stages.* Cambridge, MA: Harvard University Press.

Brown, R., and Bellugi, U. (1964). Three processes in the child's acquisition of syntax. *Harvard Educational Review, 34,* 133–151.

Brownell, R. (2000). *Expressive one-word picture vocabulary test 2000.* Novato, CA: Academic Therapy Publications.

Bruner J. (1975). The ontogenesis of speech acts. *Journal of Child Language, 2*(1), 1–19.

Carpenter, L. (1991, November). *Narrative discourse in language minority and language learning disabled children.* Paper presented at the annual convention of the American Speech-Language-Hearing Association, Atlanta, GA.

Carrow-Woolfolk, E. (1974). *Carrow elicited language inventory.* Austin, TX: Pro-Ed

Carrow-Woolfolk, E. (1999). *CASL: Comprehensive assessment of spoken language.* Circle Pines, MN: American Guidance Service.

Carrow-Woolfolk, E. (1999). *Test for auditory comprehension of language–3.* Austin, TX: Pro-Ed.

Cazden, C. (1968). The acquisition of noun and verb inflections. *Child Development, 39,* 433–438.

Chapman, R. (1981). Exploring children's communicative intents. In J. Miller (Ed.), *Assessing language production in children: Experimental procedures* (pp. 111–136). Baltimore: University Park Press.

Chapman, R., Paul, R., and Wanska, S. (1981). *Syntactic structures in simple sentences.* Unpublished raw data.

Coggins, T., and Carpenter, R. (1981). The communicative intention inventory: A system for observing and coding children's early intentional communication. *Applied Psycholinguistics, 2,* 235–251.

Cook-Gumperz, J., and Corsaro, W. (1977). Social-ecological constraints on children's communication strategies. *Sociology, 11,* 411–434.

Craig, H. (1991). Pragmatic characteristics of the child with specific language impairment: An interactionist perspective. In T. Gallagher (Ed.), *Pragmatics of language: Clinical practice issues* (pp. 163–198). San Diego, CA: Singular.

Cross, T. (1984). Habilitating the language-impaired child: Ideas from studies of parent-child interaction. *Topics in Language Disorders, 4(4),* 1–14.

Crystal, D. (1992). *Profiling linguistic disability* (2nd ed.). San Diego, CA: Singular.

Crystal, D., Fletcher, P., and Garman, M. (1976). *The grammatical analysis of language disability: A procedure for assessment and remediation.* London: Edward Arnold.

Crystal, D., Fletcher, P., and Garman, M. (1991). *The grammatical analysis of language disability: A procedure for assessment and remediation* (2nd ed.). San Diego, CA: Singular.

Damico, J. (1991). Clinical discourse analysis: A functional approach to language assessment. In C. Simon (Ed.), *Communication skills and classroom success: Assessment and therapy methodologies for language and learning disabled students* (pp. 165–206). Eau Claire, WI: Thinking Publications.

de Villiers, J., and de Villiers, P. (1973). A cross-sectional study of the acquisition of grammatical morphemes. *Journal of Psycholinguistic Research, 2,* 267–278.

de Villiers, J., and de Villiers, P. (1978). *Language acquisition.* Cambridge, MA: Harvard University Press.

Dore, J. (1974). A pragmatic description of early language development. *Journal of Psycholinguistic Research, 4,* 343–350.

Dore, J. (1978). Variation in preschool children's conversational performances. In K. Nelson (Ed.), *Children's language: Vol. 1* (pp. 397–444). New York: Gardner Press.

Duchan, J.F. (1984). Language assessment: The pragmatics revolution. In R.C. Naremore (Ed.), *Language Science* (pp. 147–180). San Diego: College Hill.

Dunn, T., and Dunn, L. (1997). *Peabody picture vocabulary test–III.* Circle Pines, MN: American Guidance Service.

Ervin-Tripp, S. (1970). Discourse agreement: How children answer questions. In J.R. Hayes (Ed.), *Cognition and the development of language* (pp. 79–107). New York: Wiley.

Ervin-Tripp, S., and Mitchell-Kernan, C. (1977). *Child discourse.* New York: Academic Press.

Fey, M. (1986). *Language intervention with young children.* San Diego, CA: College Hill Press.

Fey, M., and Leonard, L. (1983). Pragmatic skills of children with specific language impairment. In T. Gallagher and C. Prutting (Eds.), *Pragmatic assessment and intervention issues in language* (pp. 65–82). San Diego, CA: College Hill Press.

Gallagher, T. (1983). Pre-assessment: A procedure for accommodating language use variability. In T. Gallagher and C. Prutting (Eds.), *Pragmatic assessment and intervention issues in language* (pp. 1–15). San Diego, CA: College Hill Press.

Gallagher, T. (1991). Language and social skills: Implications for clinical assessment and intervention with school-age children. In T. Gallagher (Ed.), *Pragmatics of language: Clinical practice issues* (pp. 11–41). San Diego, CA: Singular.

Garvey, C. (1975). Requests and responses in child speech. *Journal of Child Language, 2*(1), 41–63.

Gleitman, L., Gleitman, H., and Shipley, E. (1972). The emergence of the child as grammarian. *Cognition, 1,* 137–164.

Golinkoff, R., and Ames, G. (1979). A comparison of fathers' and mothers' speech with their children. *Child Development, 50,* 28–32.

Greenfield, P., and Smith, J. (1976). *The structure of communication in early language development.* New York: Academic Press.

Grice, H.P. (1975). Logic and conversation. In P. Cole and J. Morgan (Eds.), *Syntax and semantics. Volume 3: Speech acts* (pp. 41–58). New York: Academic Press.

Griffith, P.L., Ripich, D.N., and Dastoli, S.L. (1986). Story structure, cohesion and propositions in story recalls by learning-disabled and nondisabled children. *Journal of Psycholinguistic Research, 15*(6), 539–555.

Hall, W., and Cole, M. (1978). On participants' shaping of discourse through their understanding of the task. In K. Nelson (Ed.), *Children's language: Vol. 1* (pp. 445–465). New York: Gardner Press.

Halliday, M. (1977). *Learning how to mean: Explorations in the development of language.* New York: Elsevier.

Hendrick, D., Prather, E., and Tobin, A. (1984). *Sequenced inventory of communication development.* Austin TX: Pro-Ed.

Hodson, B. (1986). *The Assessment of phonological processes–Revised.* Austin, TX: Pro-Ed.

Horgan, D. (1979, May). Nouns: Love 'em or leave 'em. Address to the New York Academy of Sciences. New York.

Hoskins, B. (1987). *Conversations: Language intervention for adolescents.* Allen, TX: DLM Teaching Resources.

Hoskins, B. (1996). *Conversations: A framework for language intervention.* Eau Claire, WI: Thinking Publications.

Hresko, W., Reid, D., and Hammill, D. (1999). *Test of early language development–3.* Austin, TX: Pro-Ed.

Hughes, D., McGillivray, L., and Schmidek, M. (1997). *Guide to narrative language: Procedures for assessment.* Eau Claire, WI: Thinking Publications.

Huisingh, R., Barrett, M., Zachman, L., Blagden, C., and Orman, J. (1990). *The WORD test–Elementary.* East Moline, IL: LinguiSystems.

Huttenlocher, J. (1974). The origins of language comprehension. In R.L. Solso (Ed.), *Theories in cognitive psychology* (pp. 331–368). New York: Halsted.

Ingram, D. (1972). The development of phrase structure rules. *Language Learning, 22,* 65–77.

Ingram, D. (1981). *Assessing communication behavior: Procedures for the phonological analysis of children's language (Vol. 2).* Baltimore: University Park Press.

Keenan, E., and Schieffelin, B. (1976). Topic as a discourse notion: A study of topic in the conversation of children and adults. In C.L. (Ed.), *Subject and topic* (pp. 337–383). New York: Academic Press.

Klima, E., and Bellugi, U. (1966). Syntactic regularities in the speech of children. In J. Lyons and R. Wales (Eds.), *Psycholinguistic papers* (pp. 183–208). Edinburgh, England: Edinburgh University Press.

Kramer, C., James, S., and Saxman, J. (1979). A comparison of language samples elicited at home and in the clinic. *Journal of Speech and Hearing Disorders, 44,* 321–330.

Larson, V. Lord, and McKinley, N. (1998). Characteristics of adolescents' conversations: A longitudinal study. *Clinical Linguistics and Phonetics, 12*(3), 183–203.

Lee, L. (1966). Developmental sentence types: A method for comparing normal and deviant syntactic development. *Journal of Speech and Hearing Disorders, 31,* 311–330.

Lee, L. (1974). *Developmental sentence analysis.* Evanston, IL: Northwestern University Press.

Leinonen, E., and Smith, B. (1994). Appropriacy judgements and pragmatic performance. *European Journal of Disorders of Communication, 29*(1), 77–84.

Leonard, L. (1976). *Meaning in child language.* New York: Greene and Stratton.

Leonard, L., and Fey, M. (1991). Facilitating grammatical development: The contribution of pragmatics. In T. Gallagher (Ed.), *Pragmatics of language: Clinical practice issues* (pp. 333–355). San Diego, CA: Singular.

Liles, B. (1985a). Cohesion in the narratives of normal and language-disordered children. *Journal of Speech and Hearing Research, 28,* 123–133.

Liles, B. (1985b). Production and comprehension of narrative discourse in normal and language-disordered children. *Journal of Communication Disorders, 18,* 409–427.

Liles, B. (1987). Episode organization and cohesion conjunctions in narratives of children with and without language disorder. *Journal of Speech and Hearing Research, 30,* 185–196.

Limber, J. (1973). The genesis of complex sentences. In T. Moore (Ed.), *Cognitive development and the acquisition of language* (pp. 169–185). New York: Academic Press.

Long, S.H., Fey, M.E., and Channel, R.W. (2000). Computerized Profiling (CP) (Version 9.26) [Computer software, Windows only]. Cleveland, OH: Case Western Reserve University. (Available as a free download at *http://www.cwru.edu/artsci/cosi/cp.htm)*

Longhurst, T., and File, J. (1977). A comparison of developmental sentence scores from head start children collected in four conditions. *Language, Speech, and Hearing Services in Schools, 8,* 54–64.

MacDonald, J. (1978). *Environmental language inventory.* Columbus, Ohio: Merrill.

Martlew, M. (1980). Mothers' control strategies in dyadic mother/child conversations. *Journal of Psycholinguistic Research, 9*(4), 327–346.

Martlew, M., Connolly, K., and McCleod, C. (1978). Language use, role, and context in a five-year-old. *Journal of Child Language, 5,* 81–99.

Mayer, M. (1973). *Froggie on his own.* New York: Dial Books.

McLean, J., and Snyder-McLean, L. (1978). *Transactional approach to early language training.* Columbus, Ohio: Merrill.

McNeill, D. (1970). *The acquisition of language: The study of developmental psycholinguistics.* New York: Harper and Row.

McTear, M. (1985). *Children's conversation.* Oxford, England: Blackwell.

McTear, M., and Conti-Ramsden, G. (1991). *Pragmatic disability in children.* San Diego, CA: Singular.

Merritt, D.D., and Liles, B.Z. (1987). Story grammar ability in children with and without language disorder: Story generation, story retelling, and story comprehension. *Journal of Speech and Hearing Research, 30,* 539–552.

Miller, J. (1981). *Assessing language production in children: Experimental procedures.* Baltimore: University Park Press.

Miller, J. (1991). Quantifying productive language disorder. In J. Miller (Ed.), *Research on child language disorders: A decade of progress* (pp. 211–220). Austin, TX: Pro-Ed.

Miller, J.F., and Chapman, R.S. (1981). The relation between age and mean length of utterance in morphemes. *Journal of Speech and Hearing Research, 24,* 154–161.

Miller, J.F., and Chapman, R.S. (2000). SALT: A computer program for the systematic analysis of language transcripts [Computer software]. Madison, WI: Language Analysis Laboratory, Waisman Center, University of Wisconsin.

Miller, J., and Yoder, D. (1984). *Miller-Yoder language comprehension test.* Baltimore: University Park Press.

Moore, M.E. (2000). *Transcript Builder.* [CD-ROM] Eau Claire, WI: Thinking Publications.

Mordecai, D., Palin, M., and Palmer, C. (1982). Lingquest 1: Language Sample Analysis [Computer software]. Napa, CA: Lingquist Software.

Nelson, K. (1973). Structure and strategy in learning to talk. *Monographs of the Society for Research in Child Development, 38*(1–2, Serial No. 149).

Newcomer, P., and Hammill, D. (1997). *Test of language development–Primary.* Austin, TX: Pro-Ed.

Nisswandt, B. (1983). *The effects of situational variability on the grammatical speech forms of three-year-olds.* Unpublished master's thesis, University of Wisconsin, Eau Claire.

Norris, J., and Damico, J. (1990). Whole language in theory and practice: Implications for language intervention. *Language, Speech, and Hearing Services in Schools, 21,* 212–220.

Olswang, L., and Carpenter, R. (1978). Elicitor effects on the language obtained from young language-impaired children. *Journal of Speech and Hearing Disorders, 43,* 76–88.

Owens, R. (1991). *Language disorders: A functional approach to assessment and intervention.* New York: Macmillan.

Owens, R. (1992). *Language development: An introduction.* Columbus, OH: Merrill.

Paul, R. (1981). Analyzing complex sentence development. In J. Miller (Ed.), *Assessing language production in children.* Baltimore: University Park Press.

Penn, C. (1988). The profiling of syntax and pragmatics in aphasia. *Clinical Linguistics and Phonetics, 2,* 179–207.

Phelps-Terasaki, D., and Phelps-Gunn, T. (1992). *Test of pragmatic language.* Austin, TX: Pro-Ed.

Phillips, J. (1973). Syntax and vocabulary of mother's speech to young children: Age and sex comparisons. *Child Development, 44,* 182–185.

Prutting, C., and Kirchner, D. (1983). Applied pragmatics. In T. Gallagher and C. Prutting (Eds.), *Pragmatic assessment and intervention issues in language* (pp. 29–64). San Diego, CA: College Hill Press.

Prutting, C., and Kirchner, D. (1987). A clinical appraisal of pragmatic aspects of language. *Journal of Speech and Hearing Disorders, 52,* 105–119.

Pye, C. (1987). Pye Analysis of Language (PAL) [Computer software]. Lawrence, KS: University of Kansas, Linguistics Department.

Renfrew, C. (1969). *The bus story: A test of continuous speech.* (Available from the author at North Place, Old Headington, Oxford, England)

Retherford, K., Schwartz, B., and Chapman, R. (1977, September). *The changing relationship between semantic relations in mother and child speech.* Paper presented at the Second Annual Boston University Conference on Language Acquisition, Boston.

Retherford, K., Schwartz, B., and Chapman, R. (1981). Semantic roles in mother and child speech: Who tunes into whom? *Journal of Child Language, 8,* 583–608.

Retherford, K. (1980). *[Appropriateness judgments.]* Unpublished class materials, University of Wisconsin, Eau Claire.

Retherford, K.S. (1987). *Guide to analysis of language transcripts.* Eau Claire, WI: Thinking Publications.

Rice, M., Sell, M., and Hadley, P. (1990). The Social Interactive Coding System (SICS): An on-line, clinically relevant descriptive tool. *Language, Speech, and Hearing Services in Schools, 21,* 2–14.

Rizzo, J., and Stephens, M. (1981). Performance of children with normal and impaired oral language production on a set of auditory comprehension tests. *Journal of Speech and Hearing Disorders, 46,* 150–159.

Roth, F.P. (1986). Oral narrative abilities of learning-disabled students. *Topics in Language Disorders, 7*(1), 21–30.

Roth, F., and Spekman, N. (1984). Assessing the pragmatic abilities of children: Part I. Organizational framework and assessment parameters. *Journal of Speech and Hearing Disorders, 49,* 2–11.

Sachs, J., and Devin, J. (1976). Young children's use of age-appropriate speech styles in social interaction and role playing. *Journal of Child Language, 3,* 81–98.

Schlesinger, I. (1971). Learning grammar: From pivot to realization rule. In R. Huxley and E. Ingram (Eds.), *Language acquisition: Models and methods* (pp. 79–89). New York: Academic Press.

Schwartz, A. (1985). Microcomputer-assisted assessment of linguistic and phonological processes. *Topics in Language Disorders, 6*(1), 26–40.

Scott, C., and Taylor, A. (1978). A comparison of home and clinic gathered language samples. *Journal of Speech and Hearing Disorders, 43,* 482–495.

Searle, J. (1969). *Speech acts.* Cambridge, MA: Cambridge University Press.

Shatz, M., and Gelman, R. (1973). The development of communication skills: Modifications in the speech of young children as a function of listener. *Monographs of the Society for Research in Child Development, 38*(1–2, Serial No. 149).

Shriberg, L., and Kwiatkowski, J. (1980). *Natural process analysis (NPA): A procedure for phonological analysis of continuous speech samples.* New York: Wiley.

Shulman, B. (1985). *Test of pragmatic skills.* Tucson, AZ: Communication Skill Builders.

Smedley, M. (1989). Semantic-pragmatic language disorder: A description with some practical suggestions for teachers. *Child Language Teaching and Therapy, 5,* 174–190.

Smith, B., and Leinonen, E. (1992). *Clinical pragmatics: Unravelling the complexities of communicative failure.* London: Chapman and Hall.

Smith, P., and Daglish, L. (1977). Sex differences in parent and infant behavior in the home. *Child Development, 48*(4), 1250–1254.

Stalnaker, L., and Craighead, N. (1982). An examination of language samples obtained under three experimental conditions. *Language, Speech, and Hearing Services in Schools, 13,* 121–128.

Stein, N., and Glenn, C. (1979). An analysis of story comprehension in elementary school children. In R. Freedle (Ed.), *New directions in discourse processing* (Vol. 2, pp. 53–120). Norwood, NJ: Ablex.

Strong, C. (1998). *The Strong narrative assessment procedure.* Eau Claire, WI: Thinking Publications.

Templin, M. (1957). *Certain language skills in children: Their development and interrelationships* (Institute of Child Welfare Monograph Series No. 26). Minneapolis, MN: University of Minnesota Press.

Tomasello, M. (1992). The social bases of language acquisition. *Social Development, 1*(1), 67–87.

Tyack, D., and Gottsleben, R. (1974). *Language sampling, analysis, and training: A handbook for teachers and clinicians.* Palo Alto, CA: Consulting Psychological Press.

Tyack, D., and Ingram, D. (1977). Children's production and comprehension of questions. *Journal of Child Language, 4*(2), 211–224.

Tyack, D., and Venable, G. (1998). *Language sampling, analysis, and training: A handbook* (3rd ed.) (LSAT–3). Austin, TX: Pro-Ed.

Wallace, G., and Hammill, D. (1994). *Comprehensive receptive and expressive vocabulary test.* Austin, TX: Pro-Ed.

Weiner, F. (1984). Computerized Language Sample Analysis (CLSA) [Computer software]. State College, PA: Parrot Software.

Weiner, F. (1988). Parrot Easy Language Sample Analysis (PELSA) [Computer software]. State College, PA: Parrot Software.

Wells, G. (1981). *Learning through interaction: The study of language development.* Cambridge, MA: Cambridge University Press.

Wetherby, A., and Prizant, B. (1992). Profiling young children's communicative competence. In S. Warren and J. Reichle (Eds.), *Causes and effects in communication and language intervention* (pp. 217–253). Baltimore: Brookes.

Wiig, E. (1982). *Let's talk inventory for adolescents.* Columbus, OH: Merrill.

Wilkinson, L., Hiebert, E., and Rembold, K. (1981). Parents' and peers' communication to toddlers. *Journal of Speech and Hearing Research, 24,* 383–388.

Zimmerman, I., Steiner, V., and Pond, R. (1992). *Preschool language scale–3.* New York: Psychological Corporation.

Using the Guide Practice CD-ROM

System Requirements

Windows

- Windows 95/98/NT/ME/2000/XP
- Pentium processor (166 MHz+ recommended)
- 32 MB of RAM (64 MB+ recommended)

Macintosh

- Macintosh System 7.5 to 9 (Not compatible with OS X or higher)
- Power PC chip (100 MHz+ recommended)
- 16 MB of available RAM (32 MB+ recommended)

Running Guide Practice from the CD-ROM

Guide Practice was designed to be run from the CD-ROM; you do not need to install anything on your computer. To run Guide Practice from the CD-ROM:

Windows

1. Insert the CD-ROM into the CD-ROM drive.

   Note to Windows XP Users: When you insert the CD-ROM, you may get a dialog box with the following message: "Windows can perform the same action each time you insert a disk or connect a device with this kind of file:" along with a list of a number of actions that you can take. If you get this dialog box, click **Take No Action** from the list that is displayed and then click **OK.**
2. Double-click the **My Computer** icon.
3. Double-click the **Guide Practice** CD-ROM icon.
4. Double-click the **Guide Practice.exe** program file.

Macintosh

1. Insert the CD-ROM into the CD-ROM drive. A window displaying the contents of the CD-ROM should be displayed automatically. (If the window does not display, double-click on the **Guide Practice** CD-ROM icon.)
2. Double-click the **Guide Practice** program file.

Contents of Guide Practice

Analysis practice is provided on the Guide Practice CD-ROM for the following eight analysis types.

Chapter 2: Semantic Analysis

1. Semantic Roles Analysis
2. Parts of Speech Analysis
3. Type-Token Ratio Analysis

Chapter 3: Syntactic Analysis

4. Morpheme Analysis
5. Grammatical Morphemes Analysis
6. Structural Analysis

Chapter 4: Pragmatic Analysis

7. Primitive and Conversational Speech Acts Analysis
8. Conversational Moves/Appropriateness Judgments Analysis

Each analysis type has 5–12 worksheets for practice of the analysis procedure. The worksheets present language transcripts from a variety of language stages. The rules for each analysis procedure, the directions for each worksheet, and the answers are provided.

Important Notes Before You Begin

- When you launchGuide Practice, it will ask you where you want to save your log file. You may save your log to your desktop, to your hard drive, or to a floppy disk (which you must supply). Be sure to note the file path so you can access your log in the future. If you have saved your log to a floppy disk, copy the log from the disk to the hard drive. Then at the Guide Practice login screen, select the log on the hard drive to continue adding to it (rather than creating a new log). When finished, copy the new log back to your disk.

- The actual size of the Guide Practice screen is 640 x 480 pixels, so if your monitor is set to 640 x 480, parts of the Guide Practice screen may not be visible. A simple solution is to change your settings to a higher resolution, if available. Otherwise, you will need to move the Guide Practice screen up by clicking on the title bar and dragging it upward until the buttons on the bottom become fully visible.

- The screen for Guide Practice is designed to cover your entire monitor, so there is no minimize feature. If you wish to open another application while working in Guide Practice, you must first quit Guide Practice. If you wish to access another already open application without quitting Guide Practice, use the toggle feature on your keyboard (typically **Alt** + **Tab** for PCs and through your Finder for Macs) to switch applications. NOTE: The other programs must be open *before* launching Guide Practice to use the toggle feature.

- Only single-click on items in Guide Practice. At no point is double-clicking needed and, in some cases, it can cause the program to lockup or to display an error message.

Once in the Program

- To open a worksheet, click on the **Analysis Type** button. Next, click on a type of worksheet. Finally, select a worksheet.

- When you first enter one of the eight analysis types and select a worksheet, click on the **Directions** button. Then sequentially roll over the numbers for a "guided tour" of how to complete the worksheet.

- If you have selected an incorrect answer for an utterance, you are allowed two more tries before the answer is provided. Before you can move on to another utterance, you will need to either select a correct answer or have the answer provided for you.

- Note that the **Check Answer** button is occasionally available as soon as you click an utterance (e.g., if you are not supposed to count any morphemes because the utterance should not be analyzed).

- Each worksheet has a **Why?** Button that is only available when lit. The **Why?** Button is lit when particular answers may be debatable. Clicking the **Why?** Button supplies the rationale for the authors' answer.

- You may start a worksheet over at any time. From the Options pull-down menu, select **Start Worksheet Over** and the worksheet will reset. Your work log will record that you started the worksheet over.

- You may start an analysis type over at any time. From the Options pull-down menu, select **Start Analysis Type Over** and the analysis type will reset. Your work log will reflect that you started the analysis type over.

- The two analysis types with calculations (i.e., Type-Token Ration and Morpheme Analysis) must have all utterances analyzed before the cursor becomes available for entering numeric information. A calculator is provided for calculating and can be opened by clicking on its icon. The calculator may need to be moved if it covers data (e.g., the extended list that appears after a down arrow is clicked). You can use your computer keyboard, your computer numeric keypad, or the calculator to enter the numbers. The calculator can be cleared using **Esc** for PCs or **Clear** for Macs.

- After you are done working on a worksheet, and wish to print it, go to the File menu and choose **Close Worksheet.** Click on the **Back** button. Click on the **Work Logs** button. From the File menu, choose **Print Log.** Select a Print Option, and **Print** the worksheet.

Troubleshooting

- If you receive an error message while in the program, one of the following steps may help:

1. Click the **Clear Utterance** button.
2. From the *File* menu, select **Close Worksheet.** Then open the worksheet again.
3. From the *Options* menu, select **Start Worksheet Over.**
4. Force the program to quit (**Ctl** + **Alt** + **Del** then click **End Task** for PCs or **Option** + **Apple** + **Esc** then click Force Quit for Macs).

ATTENTION:

Before using the Guide Practice CD-ROM, please read pages 334–336.

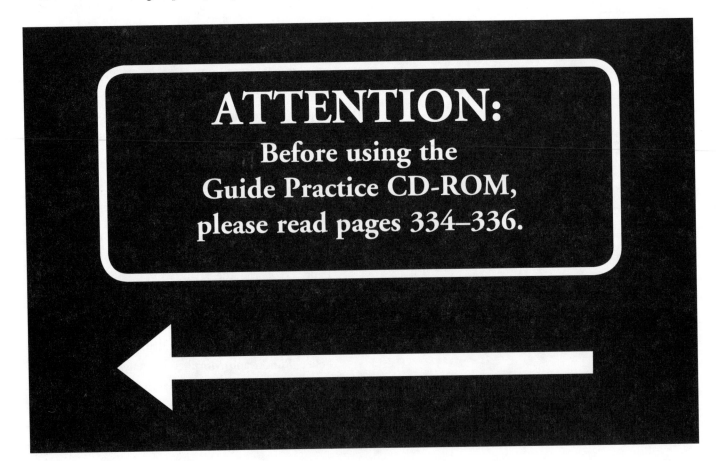

Notes

Notes

Notes

Notes